PEARSON Chemistry

Reading
and
Study Workbook

PEARSON
Prentice
Hall

Boston, Massachusetts
Upper Saddle River, New Jersey

ISBN-13: 978-0-13-252588-6

ISBN-10:   0-13-252588-7

12 13 V031 16 15

CONTENTS

1 Introduction to Chemistry

 CHEMISTRY AS THE CENTRAL SCIENCE

1.1 The Scope of Chemistry

Essential Understanding A knowledge of chemistry helps to understand how almost all processes in nature work.

Lesson Summary

What Is Chemistry? Chemistry is the study of the composition of matter and the changes that matter undergoes.
- ▶ All living and nonliving things are made of matter.
- ▶ Anything that occupies space and has mass is matter.

Areas of Study There are five main areas of study in chemistry.
- ▶ Traditional areas of study include organic chemistry, inorganic chemistry, biochemistry, analytical chemistry, and physical chemistry.
- ▶ Each area of study focuses on a particular type of chemistry.

Big Ideas in Chemistry Most topics in chemistry are connected by organizing principles, or "big ideas."
- ▶ Big ideas narrow the study of chemistry and make it more understandable.
- ▶ Each big idea builds on and interacts with the others.

After reading Lesson 1.1, answer the following questions.

What Is Chemistry?

1. What is matter?

_____

_____

2. What is chemistry?

_____

_____

Areas of Study

3. Is the following sentence true or false? The boundaries between the five areas of chemistry are not firm. _____

4. Read each goal and complete the table by filling in one of the five main areas of chemistry.

	Investigating ways to slow down the rusting of steel
	Developing a better insulin-delivery system for diabetics
	Determining the amount of mercury present in a soil sample
	Comparing the hardness of copper and silver
	Developing a new carbon-based fiber for clothing

Big Ideas in Chemistry

5. Another name for a "big idea" is _____.

6. What are the eight "big ideas" listed in the lesson?

a. _____   e. _____

b. _____   f. _____

c. _____   g. _____

d. _____   h. _____

1.2 Chemistry and You

(Essential Understanding) The study of chemistry is useful in many areas of life.

Reading Strategy

Table A table helps you organize lesson information. Write "Chemistry and Me" above the table on the following page. In the *Section* column, write the section titles that appear in red in your book. In the *Take Aways* column, summarize in your own words the information that is in each section. In the *Details* column, add details to help you understand how chemistry connects with your life. An example has been provided.

As you read Lesson 1.2, fill in the table on the next page to help you understand how chemistry is all around you.

_____

Section	Take Aways	Details
Why Study Chemistry?	3 reasons: • explain natural world • •	• Chemical reactions are everywhere (eggs frying, apples spoiling) • •

Lesson Summary

Why Study Chemistry?
Chemistry helps people understand the world around them.

▶ Chemistry explains things in the natural world.

▶ Many careers use chemistry.

▶ Informed citizens need a knowledge of chemistry.

Chemistry, Technology, and Society
Research in chemistry brings about advances in many areas.

▶ Chemists use technology to develop new materials that are better for the environment.

▶ Scientists who understand chemistry develop new energy sources and medical breakthroughs.

▶ Chemists study matter from objects in space to expand our knowledge of the universe.

Role of Chemistry in Technology and Society		
	Chemistry and technology	Examples
Materials and the environment	Make new, improved materials while conserving resources and protecting the environment	Plastics
Energy	Produce and conserve energy	Hybrid cars; solar energy technology
Medicine and biotechnology	Supply medicines, materials, and technology that doctors use to treat their patients; work to understand chemical changes in the body	Prescription and OTC (over-the-counter) medications; artificial hips and knees
The universe	Study data from space and use earth-based chemistry to understand objects in outer space	Analysis of moon rocks and soil from Mars

After reading Lesson 1.2, answer the following questions.

Why Study Chemistry?

1. What will knowledge of chemistry enable you to do?

   a. _____

   b. _____

   c. _____

2. List three careers that require some knowledge of chemistry.

   _____

   _____

Chemistry, Technology, and Society

3. What is technology?

   _____

   _____

4. What are some problems that chemists must consider when developing new technologies?

   _____

   _____

5. List two ways that chemists can help to meet the demand for energy.

   a. _____

   b. _____

6. What is the role of chemistry in the development of medicines?

   _____

   _____

7. List three new materials chemists have developed that have medical applications.

   a. _____

   b. _____

   c. _____

8. The field that applies science to the production of biological products is _____.

9. Scientists can learn about the chemical composition of stars by analyzing the _____ they transmit to Earth.

10. Why won't the method used to discover the chemical composition of stars work for the moon and planets?

    _____

    _____

11. What did chemists learn about the moon's surface by analyzing moon rocks?

    _____

    _____

1.3 Thinking Like a Scientist

Essential Understanding The scientific method is important in modern science.

Lesson Summary

An Experimental Approach to Science Modern science is based on experiments that include careful observation and measurement.

▶ Lavoisier transformed experiments by making careful measurements.

The Scientific Method Scientific problems are solved through the use of the scientific method.

▶ The scientific method includes making observations, testing hypotheses, and developing theories.

▶ Experiments that test hypotheses involve variables that can be changed.

▶ Successfully repeated experiments may become a theory or be summarized by a scientific law.

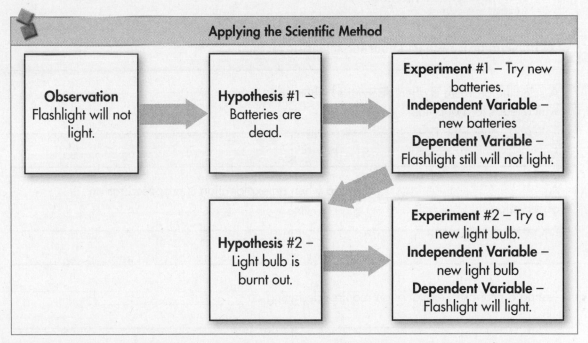

Applying the Scientific Method

Observation Flashlight will not light.

Hypothesis #1 – Batteries are dead.

Experiment #1 – Try new batteries.
Independent Variable – new batteries
Dependent Variable – Flashlight still will not light.

Hypothesis #2 – Light bulb is burnt out.

Experiment #2 – Try a new light bulb.
Independent Variable – new light bulb
Dependent Variable – Flashlight will light.

Collaboration and Communication It is important for scientists to work together and check each other's work.

▶ Successful collaboration brings together the knowledge and skills of different scientists.

▶ Scientists communicate in different ways including publishing their results in scientific journals and communicating through e-mail, on the phone, and in person.

After reading Lesson 1.3, answer the following questions.

An Experimental Approach to Science

1. Practical alchemy focused on _____
_____ .

2. Alchemists developed processes for separating _____ and purifying _____ .

3. How did Lavoisier help to transform chemistry?

_____

4. Circle the letter of the word that completes the sentence. Lavoisier demonstrated that
_____ is necessary for materials to burn.

    a. phlogiston   **c.** oxygen

    b. nitrogen   **d.** metals

The Scientific Method

5. What is the scientific method?

_____

6. Complete the flowchart about the scientific method.

A scientific problem is often discovered when an _____ is made, which leads to a question.

↓

A _____ is formed when an explanation is proposed for an observation.

↓

Testing a proposed explanation requires designing an _____.

↓

For the results of the experiment to be accepted, the experiment must produce the same results _____.

↓

An explanation may become a _____ if the same results are found after many tests.

7. Circle the letter of the activity that involves using the senses to gather information directly.

   a. forming a hypothesis

   b. making an observation

   c. planning an experiment

   d. analyzing data

8. What do scientists do if the results of an experiment do not support the hypothesis?

   _____

   _____

9. The _____ variable is changed during an experiment.

   The _____ variable is observed during an experiment.

10. Is the following sentence true or false? Once a theory has been accepted, no experiment will ever disprove it. _____

11. What is a scientific law?

    _____

    _____

12. Circle the letter of each statement that expresses a scientific law.

    a. As the temperature of a balloon increases, the balloon expands.

    b. Increasing the temperature of a balloon might cause it to burst.

    c. If all other variables are kept constant, the volume of a gas increases as the temperature increases.

    d. Sometimes increasing the temperature of a gas causes the gas to expand.

Collaboration and Communication

13. Several scientists working together to solve a problem is _____.

14. Is the following statement true or false? Scientists from different disciplines may need to work together on a problem because the problem is too complex for one person to solve.

    _____

15. Exchanging ideas about science is called _____.

16. How are journals helpful to scientists?

    _____

17. Is the following statement true or false? Experts in an author's field review articles before they are published in a journal. _____

1.4 Problem Solving in Chemistry

Essential Understanding For any type of scientific problem, effective problem solving always involves planning and implementing a series of steps.

Lesson Summary

Skills Used in Solving Problems It is helpful to make and follow a plan when trying to solve a problem.

▶ Sometimes there is a set of visual data to consider.

▶ Similar skills are used to solve life problems and word problems in chemistry.

Solving Numeric Problems Following a three-step plan is an effective way to solve chemistry problems that require math.

▶ The three-step plan for solving a numeric problem is analyze, calculate, and evaluate.

Solving Nonnumeric Problems A nonnumeric problem can be solved by identifying what is known and making a plan to find the unknown.

▶ The two steps for solving a nonnumeric problem are analyze and solve.

Solving Numeric Problems	
Analyze	Determine what is known and what you want to know. Then decide on a method you can use to find what you want to know.
Calculate	Apply the method you have decided on to the problem. This may involve solving an equation, making a graph, or some other math skill.
Evaluate	Check your answer to see if it makes sense and if it has correct units and significant figures.
Solving Nonnumeric Problems	
Analyze	Identify the relevant factors and concepts.
Solve	Apply factors and concepts to a given situation.

 BUILD Math Skills

Estimating and Rounding When you estimate, you are looking for an approximate answer, rather than an exact answer. Rounding is a kind of estimating. The first step in rounding is finding the rounding digit, or the digit that is in the place value you're rounding to. Then look at the digit to the right of it. If it's 5 or greater, add 1 to the rounding digit. If it's less than 5, leave the rounding digit alone.

If you're rounding a decimal number, drop all of the digits following the rounding digit.

If you're rounding a whole number, all the digits to the right of the rounding digit become 0.

Sample Problem Round 16,745.258361 to the nearest thousandth.

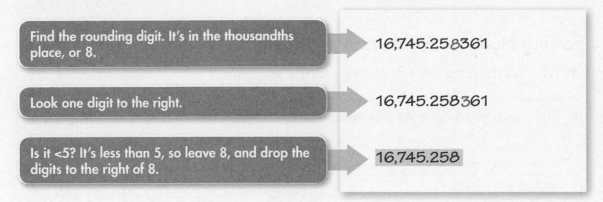

Find the rounding digit. It's in the thousandths place, or 8.

16,745.25**8**361

Look one digit to the right.

16,745.258**3**61

Is it <5? It's less than 5, so leave 8, and drop the digits to the right of 8.

16,745.258

Sample Problem Round 19,764.230 to the nearest hundred.

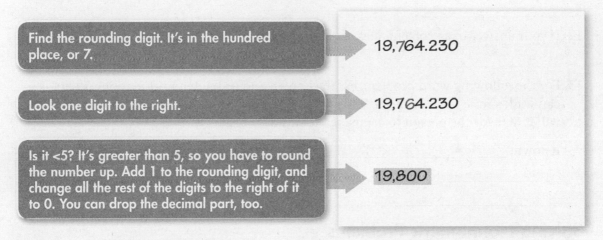

Find the rounding digit. It's in the hundred place, or 7.

19,**7**64.230

Look one digit to the right.

19,7**6**4.230

Is it <5? It's greater than 5, so you have to round the number up. Add 1 to the rounding digit, and change all the rest of the digits to the right of it to 0. You can drop the decimal part, too.

19,800

Now it's your turn to practice rounding.

1. Round to the nearest hundred dollars: $5,918 _____

2. Round to the nearest thousand: 13,513.323 _____

3. Round to the place of the underlined digit: 30.62355 _____

4. Round to the nearest hundred: 956 _____

5. You are figuring the gas mileage on your parents' car. They filled up the tank with 18.376 gallons of fuel. What figure would be the most efficient to use in your calculations? _____

6. At a restaurant your bill is $12.37. You want to leave a 20 percent tip. You estimate 20 percent by moving the decimal point over one place, rounding to the nearest tenth, and then doubling that amount. How much tip should you leave? _____

After reading Lesson 1.4, answer the following questions.

Skills Used in Solving Problems

7. Name an everyday situation that requires problem-solving skills.

_____

8. What is involved in effective problem solving?

_____

Solving Numeric Problems

9. What are the three steps for solving numeric problems?

a. _____ b. _____ c. _____

10. What must you determine first when solving a word problem?

_____

_____

11. What are two skills that you may need to use as you calculate an answer to a problem?

_____

_____

12. If your answer to a problem does not seem reasonable, list two things you can do.

_____

13. For the following word problem, list the known and unknown information: A person can walk a mile in 20 minutes. The person is going for a 10-mile walk. How many hours will it take for the person to complete the walk?

Known: _____   **Unknown:** _____

_____

_____

Solving Nonnumeric Problems

14. What are the steps for solving nonnumeric problems? _____

Apply the Big idea

Read the activity in the left column. Then, in the right column, describe a situation in which chemistry might affect you personally.

Activity	Situation
Understand the natural world	Figure out why a cake failed to rise, recognize the cause of an unpleasant odor, determine what fertilizer to use to make vegetables grow faster.
Prepare for a career	
Act as an informed citizen	
Use technology	

1 Self-Check Activity

For Questions 1–11, complete each statement by writing the correct word or words. If you need help, you can go online.

1.1 The Scope of Chemistry

1. _____ affects all aspects of life because all living and nonliving things are made of matter.

2. Five traditional areas of chemistry are organic, _____, biochemistry, _____, and _____.

3. Some of chemistry's big ideas are: chemistry as the _____, _____ and the structure of atoms, and matter and _____.

1.2 Chemistry and You

4. Chemistry can be useful in explaining _____, preparing people for career opportunities, and producing _____.

5. Research in chemistry can lead to _____ that benefit the environment, improve human life, and expand knowledge of the universe.

1.3 Thinking Like a Scientist

6. _____ helped transform chemistry into a science of measurement.

7. Steps in the scientific method include making _____, testing _____, and developing _____.

8. Scientists _____ and _____ with one another to increase the likelihood of a successful outcome.

1.4 Problem Solving in Chemistry

9. Effective problem solving always involves _____ a plan and then _____ that plan.

10. The steps for solving a numeric word problem are _____, calculate, and _____.

11. The steps for solving a nonnumeric problem are analyze and _____.

If You Have Trouble With...										
Question	1	2	3	4	5	6	7	8	9	10	11
See Page	2	3	4	6	8	15	15	18	22	23	25

Review Key Facts

Describe the steps you would take to solve a numeric and a non-numeric problem.

Numeric		Non-Numeric
1.		1.
2.	Problem	2.
3.		

EXTENSION Show the steps needed to solve the following problem.

The school day begins at 8:00 A.M. and ends at 3:30 P.M. 30 minutes of the day are taken up by lunch. There are 7 class periods in the day. If each class period is 50 minutes long, what is the total time spent in getting from one class or lunch period to another?

Review Key Vocabulary

Read the description and find the vocabulary term that matches it.

Description

1. _____ study of processes that take place in living organisms
2. _____ systematic approach to solving a scientific problem
3. _____ variable that you change during an experiment
4. _____ the study of matter and how it reacts
5. _____ deals with mechanism, rate, and energy transfer
6. _____ proposed explanation for an observation
7. _____ well-tested explanation for a broad set of observations.
8. _____ concise statement summarizing results of many experiments
9. _____ variable that is observed during an experiment

Vocabulary Term

a. theory

b. chemistry

c. scientific law

d. dependent or responding variable

e. scientific method

f. biochemistry

g. physical chemistry

h. independent or manipulated variable

i. hypothesis

2 Matter and Change

 Big idea CHEMISTRY AS THE CENTRAL SCIENCE

2.1 Properties of Matter

Essential Understanding   All matter has certain characteristics, or properties, that can be used to classify and identify it.

Lesson Summary

Describing Matter All properties used to identify matter are either extensive or intensive properties.

▶ Extensive properties, such as mass and volume, depend on the amount of matter in a sample.

▶ An intensive property, such as density, depends not on the amount of matter in a sample, but on the type of matter.

▶ A substance is a type of matter that has a definite composition and can be identified by its unique set of properties.

▶ A physical property can be observed without changing a substance's composition.

States of Matter The three most common states of matter on Earth are solid, liquid, and gas.

▶ A solid has a definite shape and a definite volume.

▶ A liquid has a definite volume, but it takes the shape of its container.

▶ A gas takes both the shape and the volume of its container.

▶ A vapor is the gaseous state of a substance that is usually a solid or a liquid at room temperature.

Physical Changes The identity of a material does not change during a physical change.

▶ Some physical changes, such as melting or boiling, are reversible.

▶ Some physical changes, such as breaking or cutting, are irreversible.

BUILD Math Skills

Negative Numbers Negative numbers are numbers that are less than zero and are indicated with a minus sign in front of the number. Negative numbers lie to the left of zero on a number line.

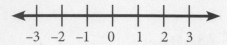

On a number line, the number to the left is less than the number to the right. Since −3 is to the left of −2, −3 is less than −2.

▶ When adding numbers of the same sign, you add the absolute value of the numbers and give the result the same sign as the numbers.

▶ If you are adding numbers of different signs, you treat the negative sign as a minus sign and subtract the negative number from the positive number.

▶ When subtracting a number, you can think of it as adding its opposite. For instance, if you have −2 − (−3), you would take the opposite of −3, which is 3, and add it to −2, so: −2 − (−3) = −2 + 3 = 1.

▶ If you multiply a positive number by a negative number, the result will be negative. If you multiply a negative number by a negative number, the result will be positive.

▶ The same rules that apply to multiplication also apply to division.

Sample Problem What is the answer to −6 − (−3)?

First, determine the opposite of −3 to follow the subtraction rule. → The opposite of −3 is 3.

Hint: Remember, as you go farther left of zero, the numbers have less and less value, but their absolute values increase.

Apply the rule of "add the opposite" to find the answer. → −6 + 3 = −3

Now it's your turn to practice dealing with negative numbers. Remember the guidelines stated above when dealing with mathematical properties.

1. Which number is larger, −234 or −250? _____

2. What is the result of −7 + −10 − (−3)? _____

3. What is the result of −8 ÷ −2? _____

4. What is the result of −4 × 4? _____

After reading Lesson 2.1, answer the following questions.

Describing Matter

5. The _____ of an object is a measure of the amount of matter the object contains.

6. How does an extensive property differ from an intensive property?

_____

_____

7. Matter that has a uniform and definite composition is called a _____.

8. Is the following sentence true or false? All samples of a substance have different physical properties. _____

9. A physical property is a quality or condition of a substance that can be _____ or _____ without changing the substance's composition.

10. Circle the letter of the term that is NOT a physical property.

   a. hardness

   b. color

   c. boiling point

   d. melting

11. Look at Table 2.1. What is the melting point of bromine? _____

12. Look at Table 2.1. Circle the letter of the substance that is a yellow solid and melts at 115°C.

   a. sulfur

   b. chlorine

   c. gold

   d. copper

13. Is the following sentence true or false? Physical properties can help a chemist identify a substance. _____

States of Matter

14. Circle the letter of the term that is NOT a physical state of matter.

   a. water

   b. gas

   c. liquid

   d. solid

15. Complete the table about the properties of the three states of matter. Use these terms: *definite*, *indefinite*, *easily*, and *not easily*.

Properties of the States of Matter			
Property	**Solid**	**Liquid**	**Gas or Vapor**
Shape		indefinite	
Volume	definite		indefinite
Can be compressed		not easily	

16. Match each arrangement of the particles in matter with a physical state.

Physical State

_____ gas

_____ liquid

_____ solid

Arrangement

a. packed tightly together

b. close, but free to flow

c. spaced relatively far apart

17. Is the following sentence true or false? The words *gas* and *vapor* describe the same thing.
_____

18. The term *gas* is limited to those substances that exist in the gaseous state at
_____.

19. What does *vapor* describe?
_____

_____

Physical Changes

20. A physical change alters a given material without changing its chemical
_____.

21. What are some words that describe physical changes?
_____

_____

22. What is true about all physical changes that involve a change of state?
_____

_____

2.2 Mixtures

Essential Understanding A mixture is a physical blend of two or more components that can be separated by physical means.

Lesson Summary

Classifying Mixtures Mixtures can be classified according to how their components are distributed.

▶ In a heterogeneous mixture, the components are not evenly distributed.

▶ In a homogeneous mixture, or solution, the components are evenly distributed.

▶ A heterogeneous mixture consists of at least two phases, but a homogeneous mixture contains exactly one phase.

Separating Mixtures The physical properties of the components of a mixture can be used to separate the mixture.

▶ A solid and a liquid can be separated by filtration because of the difference in the physical properties of the two components.

▶ A liquid solution might be separated by distillation, during which the component with the lowest boiling point is boiled off, and the resulting vapors are then condensed.

After reading Lesson 2.2, answer the following questions.

Classifying Mixtures

1. Is the following sentence true or false? Most samples of matter are mixtures.
   _____

2. What is a mixture?

   _____

   _____

3. Is the following sentence true or false? A heterogeneous mixture is one that has a completely uniform composition. _____

4. What is another name for a homogeneous mixture? _____

5. Circle the letter of the term that describes a part of a sample having uniform composition and properties.

   a. solution

   b. mixture

   c. state

   d. phase

6. How many phases exist in these types of mixtures?

   a. Homogeneous _____

   b. Heterogeneous _____

Separating Mixtures

7. In general, what is used to separate mixtures?

_____

_____

8. The process that separates a solid from a liquid in a heterogeneous mixture is called

_____.

9. What happens during distillation?

_____

_____

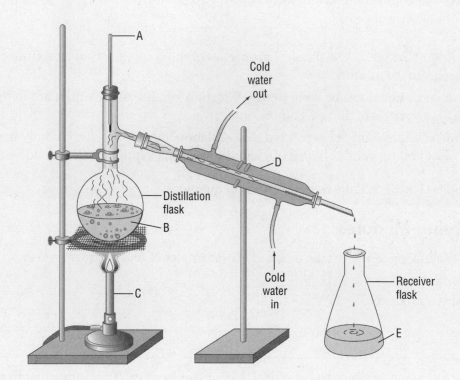

Match each term with its location in the diagram.

_____ **10.** condenser

_____ **11.** heat source

_____ **12.** thermometer

_____ **13.** tap water

_____ **14.** distilled water

2.3 Elements and Compounds

| Essential Understanding | Elements and compounds are both types of substances because both types of materials have definite and uniform composition.

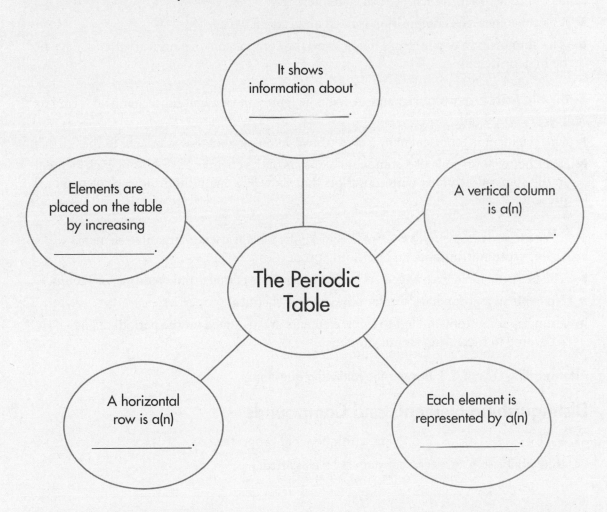

Reading Strategy

Cluster Diagram Cluster diagrams help you show how concepts are related. To create a cluster diagram, write the main idea or topic in the center circle. Draw lines branching off the main idea, connected to circles that contain concepts related to the main concept. Continue adding facts and details to the branches.

As you read Lesson 2.3, use the cluster diagram below. Complete the cluster diagram to show how the main idea of the periodic table relates to details about the periodic table.

EXTENSION Add details to the cluster diagram showing how groups and periods are identified.

Lesson Summary

Distinguishing Elements and Compounds
While both elements and compounds are substances, they have distinct differences.

▶ An element is the simplest form of matter that has its own unique set of properties.

▶ A compound is made up of two or more elements chemically combined in a definite proportion.

▶ A compound can be broken down into its component elements by a chemical change.

▶ A chemical change produces a new kind of matter that has a composition different from the original matter.

▶ Usually, the properties of a compound are quite different from the properties of the elements the compound contains.

Distinguishing Substances and Mixtures
Substances and mixtures can appear the same, but they differ in their general characteristics.

▶ In a substance, the composition is fixed and cannot vary.

▶ The composition of a mixture might vary; the components in a mixture do not have to be in definite ratios.

Symbols and Formulas
Chemical symbols represent elements, and chemical formulas represent compounds.

▶ Each element is represented by a one- or two-letter symbol that is unique to that element.

▶ The chemical formula of a compound consists of the chemical symbols of each element in the compound, along with subscripts that show how many atoms of each element are present.

The Periodic Table—A Preview
The periodic table is used to organize elements according to atomic number and repeating properties.

▶ The periodic table is arranged according to rows, or *periods*, and columns, or *groups*.

▶ Elements in a group have similar physical and chemical properties.

▶ From top to bottom and left to right, elements are arranged on the periodic table according to increasing atomic number.

After reading Lesson 2.3, answer the following questions.

Distinguishing Elements and Compounds

1. Each _____ has a unique set of properties.

2. Into what two groups can substances be classified?

_____

_____

3. Is the following sentence true or false? Elements can be easily separated into simpler substances. _____

4. Compounds are substances that can be separated into simpler substances only by _____ means.

5. Is the following sentence true or false? The properties of compounds are different from those of their component elements. _____

6. Complete this sentence.

Sodium chloride (table salt) is a _____ of sodium, which is a soft _____, and chlorine, which is a pale yellow _____.

Distinguishing Substances and Mixtures

7. Describe one way to decide whether a sample of matter is a substance or a mixture.

_____

_____

_____

8. Complete the labels in the diagram below.

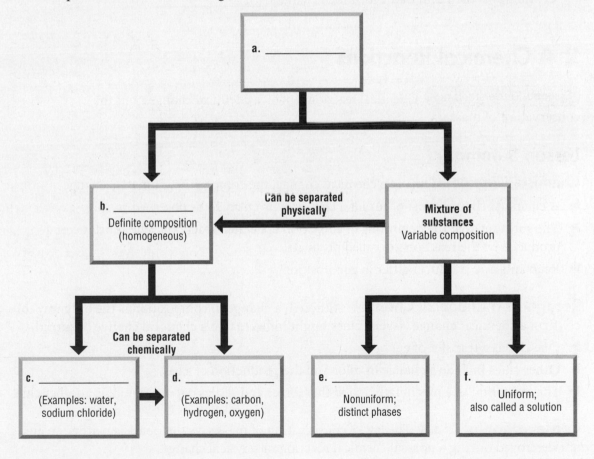

Symbols and Formulas

9. What is used to represent an element?

_____

_____

10. What are chemical symbols used for?

_____

_____

11. Subscripts in chemical formulas are used to indicate the relative proportions of the elements in a _____.

12. Is the following sentence true or false? The elements that make up a compound are always present in the same proportions. _____

13. Use Table 2.2 to answer the following questions.

    a. Pb is the symbol for what element? _____

    b. What is the symbol for gold? _____

    c. Stibium is the Latin name for which element? _____

2.4 Chemical Reactions

Essential Understanding   Chemical reactions involve chemical changes and the conservation of mass.

Lesson Summary

Chemical Changes During a chemical change, the composition of matter changes.

▶ A chemical change must occur for a chemical property to be observed.

▶ The substances at the beginning of a reaction are called reactants. The substances produced by the reaction are called products.

▶ Reactants and products differ in composition.

Recognizing Chemical Changes Although a change in composition is the only way to confirm a chemical change, several clues might indicate that a chemical change occurred.

▶ One clue is a transfer of energy.

▶ Other clues include a change in color and the production of a gas.

▶ The formation of a precipitate, a solid that forms and settles out of a liquid, is another clue.

Conservation of Mass The law of conservation of mass says that mass is neither created nor destroyed during a normal chemical reaction or physical change.

▶ During chemical reactions, the total mass of the reactants equals the total mass of the products.

▶ Mass is also conserved during physical changes, such as a change of state.

After reading Lesson 2.4, answer the following questions.

Chemical Changes

1. What is a chemical property?

_____

_____

2. Is the following sentence true or false? Chemical properties are observed only when a substance undergoes a chemical change. _____

3. What happens during a chemical reaction?

_____

4. In chemical reactions, the substances present at the start of the reaction are called _____, and the substances produced are called _____.

5. Circle the letter of the term that best completes the sentence. A change in the composition of matter _____ occurs during a chemical reaction.

   a. sometimes

   b. rarely

   c. always

   d. never

6. Which representation of a chemical reaction is correct?

   a. products → reactants

   b. reactants → products

Recognizing Chemical Changes

7. List four possible clues to a chemical change.

_____

_____

_____

8. Is the following statement true or false? If you observe a clue for chemical change, you can be certain that a chemical change has taken place. _____

9. Define a precipitate.

_____

_____

Conservation of Mass

10. During a chemical reaction, the mass of the products is always equal to the mass of the _____ .

11. The law of conservation of mass states that in any physical change or chemical reaction, mass is neither _____ nor _____ .

12. Look at Figure 2.16. How do you know that mass was conserved?

_____

_____

Apply the Big idea

A camper burned a piece of paper to start a campfire. Answer these questions about burning the paper.

a. Is burning paper a physical change or a chemical change? How do you know?

_____

_____

b. If you said the change was chemical, what are the reactants? What are the products?

_____

_____

c. The ash produced by the burning paper has much less mass than the mass of the original paper. Was mass conserved during this change? Explain your answer.

_____

_____

_____

_____

_____

2 Self-Check Activity

For Questions 1–12, complete each statement by writing the correct word or words. If you need help, you can go online.

2.1 Properties of Matter

1. For a specific substance, every sample has the same _____ properties.

2. Solid, _____, and gas are all states of matter.

3. A change of state is an example of a(n) _____ physical change.

2.2 Mixtures

4. Depending on the distribution of components, mixtures are either heterogeneous or _____.

5. Mixtures can be separated by differences in the _____ of their components.

2.3 Elements and Compounds

6. _____ can be broken down into simpler substances by chemical means.

7. If the composition of a material is not fixed, the material is a(n) _____.

8. _____ represent compounds, and _____ represent elements.

9. The _____ can be used to easily compare properties of different elements.

2.4 Chemical Reactions

10. When a _____ change occurs, the composition of matter changes.

11. A chemical change might have occurred if energy transfers, color changes, a gas forms, or a(n) _____ forms.

12. In a chemical reaction, the mass of the reactants _____ the mass of the products.

If You Have Trouble With...											
Question	1	2	3	4	5	6	7	8	9	10	11	12
See Page	34	36	37	39	40	42	44	45	46	48	49	50

Review Vocabulary

Complete this puzzle using the vocabulary terms and the clues below.

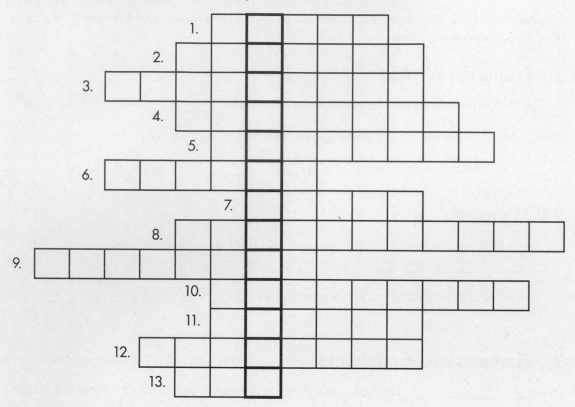

Clues

1. any part of a sample with uniform composition and properties
2. the simplest type of substance
3. matter that has a uniform and definite composition
4. the type of change that results in a change in identity
5. the results of a chemical reaction
6. a row across the periodic table
7. a column down the periodic table
8. a solid formed by a chemical reaction between two liquids
9. a substance that can be broken down into simpler substances by chemical means
10. the substances present before a chemical reaction occurs
11. the amount of space something takes up
12. another name for a homogeneous mixture
13. the state of matter that has no definite shape or volume

Terms

volume

substance

gas

solution

phase

element

compound

chemical

period

group

products

precipitate

reactants

Write and define the term found in the outlined boxes.

_____

3 Scientific Measurement

QUANTIFYING MATTER

3.1 Using and Expressing Measurements

Essential Understanding In science, measurements must be accurate, precise, and written to the correct number of significant figures.

 ## Reading Strategy

Venn Diagram A Venn diagram is a useful tool in visually organizing related information. A Venn diagram shows which characteristics the concepts share and which characteristics are unique to each concept.

As you read Lesson 3.1, use the Venn diagram to compare *accuracy* and *precision*.

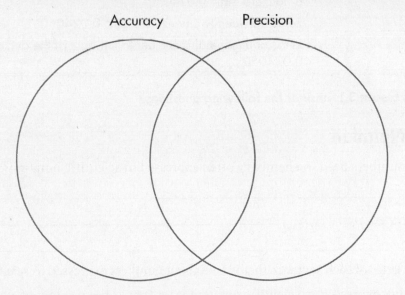

EXTENSION Add the term *error* in the correct location in your Venn diagram. Then explain why you placed this term where you did.

Lesson Summary

Scientific Notation Scientific notation is a kind of shorthand to write very large or very small numbers.

▶ Scientific notation always takes the form (a number ≥ 1 and < 10) $\times 10^x$.

Accuracy, Precision, and Error Accuracy, precision, and error help determine the reliability of measurements.

▶ The accuracy of a measurement is determined by how close the measured value is to the actual value.

▶ The precision of a measurement is determined by how close repeated measurements are to one another.

▶ Error is the difference between the measured value and the accepted value.

Significant Figures Significant figures include all known digits plus one estimated digit.

▶ The number of significant figures reflects the precision of reported data.

▶ In calculations, the number of significant figures in the least precise measurement is the number of significant figures in the answer.

Significant Figures	
Sample number: 0.024050 (5 significant figures)	
Not significant	leftmost zeros in front of nonzero digits: **0.0**24050
Significant	a nonzero digit: 0.0**24**050
	zeros between two nonzero digits: 0.024**0**50
	zeros at the end of a number to the right of the decimal point: 0.02405**0**

After reading Lesson 3.1, answer the following questions.

Scientific Notation

1. Why are numbers used in chemistry often expressed in scientific notation?

_____

_____

_____

2. Circle the letter of each sentence that is true about numbers expressed in scientific notation.

   a. A number expressed in scientific notation is written as the product of a coefficient and 10 raised to a power.

   b. The power of 10 is called the exponent.

   c. The coefficient is always a number greater than or equal to one and less than ten.

   d. For numbers less than one, the exponent is positive.

3. Circle the letter of the answer in which 503,000,000 is written correctly in scientific notation.

    a. 5.03×10^{-7}

    b. 503×10^{6}

    c. 5.03×10^{8}

    d. 503 million

Accuracy, Precision, and Error

4. Is the following sentence true or false? To decide whether a measurement has good precision or poor precision, the measurement must be made more than once.

_____

Label each of the three following sentences that describes accuracy with an *A*. Label each sentence that describes precision with a *P*.

_____ **5.** Four of five repetitions of a measurement were numerically identical, and the fifth varied from the others in value by less than 1%.

_____ **6.** Eight measurements were spread over a wide range.

_____ **7.** A single measurement is within 1% of the correct value.

8. On a dartboard, darts that are closest to the bull's-eye have been thrown with the greatest accuracy. On the second target, draw three darts to represent three tosses of lower precision, but higher accuracy than the darts on the first target.

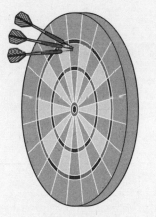

        First target   Second target

9. What is the meaning of "accepted value" with respect to an experimental measurement?

_____

10. Complete the following sentence. For an experimental measurement, the experimental value minus the accepted value is called the _____.

11. Is the following sentence true or false? The value of an error must be positive.

_____

12. Relative error is also called _____.

13. The accepted value of a length measurement is 200 cm, and the experimental value is 198 cm. Circle the letter of the value that shows the percent error of this measurement.

    a. 2%

    b. −2%

    c. 1%

    d. −1%

Significant Figures

14. If a thermometer is calibrated to the nearest degree, to what part of a degree can you estimate the temperature it measures? _____

15. Circle the letter of the correct digit. In the measurement 43.52 cm, which digit is the most uncertain?

    a. 4

    b. 3

    c. 5

    d. 2

16. Circle the letter of the correct number of significant figures in the measurement 6.80 m.

    a. 2

    b. 3

    c. 4

    d. 5

17. List two situations in which measurements have an unlimited number of significant figures.

    a. _____

    _____

    b. _____

    _____

18. Circle the letter of each sentence that is true about significant figures.

    a. Every nonzero digit in a reported measurement is assumed to be significant.

    b. Zeros appearing between nonzero digits are never significant.

    c. Leftmost zeros acting as placeholders in front of nonzero digits in numbers less than one are not significant.

    d. All rightmost zeros to the right of the decimal point are always significant.

    e. Zeros to the left of the decimal point that act as placeholders for the first nonzero digit to the left of the decimal point are not significant.

19. Is the following sentence true or false? An answer is as precise as the most precise measurement from which it was calculated. _____

Round the following measurements as indicated.

20. Round 65.145 meters to 4 significant figures. _____

21. Round 100.1°C to 1 significant figure. _____

22. Round 155 cm to two significant figures. _____

23. Round 0.000718 kilograms to two significant figures. _____

24. Round 65.145 meters to three significant figures. _____

3.2 Units of Measurement

Essential Understanding Measurements are fundamental to the experimental sciences.

Lesson Summary

Using SI Units Scientists use an internationally recognized system of units to communicate their findings.

▶ The SI units are based on multiples of 10.

▶ There are seven SI base units: second, meter, kilogram, Kelvin, mole, ampere, and candela.

▶ Prefixes are added to the SI units because they extend the range of possible measurements.

Temperature Scales Temperature is a quantitative measure of the average kinetic energy of particles in an object.

▶ Scientists most commonly use the Celsius and Kelvin scales.

▶ The zero point on the Kelvin scale is called absolute zero.

▶ Kelvin-Celsius Conversion Equation is K = °C + 273.

▶ One degree on the Celsius scale is the same as one kelvin on the Kelvin scale.

Density Density is a ratio that compares the amount of mass per unit volume.

▶ The formula for density is density $= \dfrac{\text{mass}}{\text{volume}}$.

▶ Density depends on the kind of material but not on the size of the sample.

▶ The density of a substance changes with temperature.

BUILD Math Skills

Converting Among Temperatures The Fahrenheit scale is based on the melting point of ice (32 degrees above 0) and the boiling point of water (212 degrees above 0). However, since most of the rest of the world uses degrees Celsius, it is important to be able to convert from units of degrees Fahrenheit to degrees Celsius.

   The SI base unit for temperature is Kelvin, or K. A temperature of 0 K refers to the lowest possible temperature that can be reached.

To convert degrees Celsius into kelvins:
▶ add 273 to the °C.

To convert kelvins into degrees Celsius:
▶ subtract 273 from the K.

Sample Problem Mercury melts at −39°C. What temperature is that in K?

| Add 273 to the °C. | ➡ | −39°C + 273 = 234K |

To convert Celsius temperatures into Fahrenheit:
▶ multiply the Celsius temperature by 9.
▶ divide the answer by 5.
▶ add 32.

Sample Problem Convert 40°C to °F.

| Multiply the Celsius temperature by 9. | ➡ | 40 × 9 = 360 |

Hint: You can also use the equation $T_F = \dfrac{9}{5} T_C + 32$.

| Divide the answer by 5. | ➡ | 360 ÷ 5 = 72 |

| Add 32. | ➡ | 72 + 32 = 104°F |

To convert Fahrenheit temperatures into Celsius:

▶ subtract 32 from the Fahrenheit temperature.

▶ multiply the answer by 5.

▶ divide that answer by 9.

Sample Problem Convert 77°F to °C.

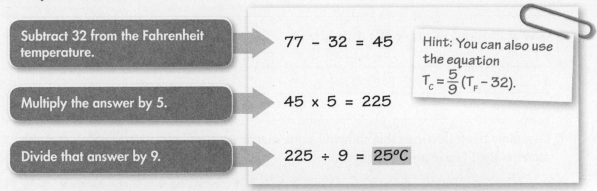

Subtract 32 from the Fahrenheit temperature.	77 − 32 = 45
Multiply the answer by 5.	45 × 5 = 225
Divide that answer by 9.	225 ÷ 9 = 25°C

Hint: You can also use the equation
$T_c = \frac{5}{9}(T_F - 32)$.

Now it's your turn to practice converting temperatures.

1. Fill in the table below with the correct degrees.

Common Temperatures			
	Fahrenheit (°F)	Celsius (°C)	Kelvin (K)
Water boils		100	
Human body	98.6		
Average room			293
Water freezes	32		

After reading Lesson 3.2, answer the following questions.

Using SI Units

2. Complete the table showing selected SI base units of measurement.

Units of Measurement		
Quantity	SI Base Unit	Symbol
Length		
Mass		
Temperature		
Time		

3. All metric units of length are based on multiples of _____.

4. The International System of Units (SI) is a revised version of the _____.

5. Explain what is meant by a "derived unit."

_____

_____

_____

6. Give at least one example of a derived unit.

_____

_____

_____

7. Complete the following table showing some metric units of length. Remember that the meter is the SI base unit for length.

Metric Units of Length		
Unit	**Symbol**	**Factor Multiplying Base Unit**
Meter	m	1
Kilometer		
Centimeter		
Millimeter		
Nanometer		

Match each metric unit with the best estimate of its length or distance.

_____ **8.** Height of a stove top above the floor   **a.** 1 km

_____ **9.** Thickness of about 10 sheets of paper   **b.** 1 m

_____ **10.** Distance along a road spanning about   **c.** 1 cm
10 telephone poles

                                           d. 1 mm

_____ **11.** Width of a key on a computer keyboard

12. The space occupied by any sample of matter is called its _____.

13. Circle the letter of each sentence that is true about units of volume.

  a. The SI unit for volume is derived from the meter, the SI unit for length.

  b. The liter (L) is a unit of volume.

  c. The liter is an SI unit.

  d. There are 1000 cm^3 in 1 L, and there are also 1000 mL in 1 L, so 1 cm^3 is equal to 1 mL.

Match each of the three descriptions of a volume to the appropriate metric unit of volume.

Example   **Unit of Volume**

_____ **14.** Interior of an oven   **a.** 1 L

_____ **15.** A box of cookies   **b.** 1 m^3

_____ **16.** One-quarter teaspoon   **c.** 1 mL

17. A volume of 1 L is also equal to

    a. 1000 mL

    b. 1 dm^3

    c. 1000 cm

18. The volume of any solid, liquid, or gas will change with _____.

19. A kilogram was originally defined as the mass of _____.

20. Circle the letter of the unit of mass commonly used in chemistry that equals 1/1000 kilogram.

    a. gram

    b. milligram

    c. milliliter

Match each unit of mass with the object whose mass would be closest to that unit.

Mass   **Unit of Mass**

_____ **21.** A few grains of sand   **a.** 1 kg

_____ **22.** A liter bottle of soda   **b.** 1 g

_____ **23.** Five aspirin tablets   **c.** 1 mg

24. Is the following sentence true or false? The mass of an object changes with location. _____

25. When brought to the surface of the moon, will a mass have more or less weight than it did on the surface of Earth, or will it be the same weight? Explain.

_____

_____

_____

Temperature Scales

26. Draw an arrow below the diagram, showing the direction of heat transfer between two objects.

lower temperature	higher temperature

27. What properties explain the behavior of liquid-filled thermometers?

_____

_____

_____

_____

28. What are the two reference temperatures on the Celsius scale?

_____

_____

29. What is the zero point, 0 K, on the Kelvin scale called? _____

30. A change of temperature equal to one kelvin is equal to a change of temperature of how many degrees Celsius? _____

31. Complete the diagram to show the reference temperatures in the Celsius and Kelvin scales.

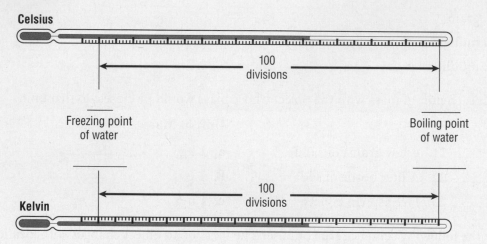

Celsius

100 divisions

Freezing point of water

Boiling point of water

100 divisions

Kelvin

Density

32. Is the mass of one pound of lead greater than, less than, or equal to the mass of one pound of feathers? _____

33. Which material has a greater density, lead or feathers? _____

34. How is density defined?

_____

35. The mass of a sample is measured in grams, and its volume is measured in cubic centimeters. In what units would its density be reported?

_____

36. Look at Table 3.6. Circle the letter of the material that will sink in liquid water at 4°C.

    a. aluminum   **c.** ice

    b. corn oil   **d.** gasoline

37. The density of a substance generally decreases as its temperature increases. Are there any exceptions to this statement? Explain.

_____

_____

_____

3.3 Solving Conversion Problems

Essential Understanding The numerical value of a measurement generally changes when you convert from one system to another, but the actual amount of the quantity measured does not change.

Lesson Summary

Conversion Factors Conversion factors are used to change a given measurement to some other unit of measure.

▶ A conversion factor is a ratio of equivalent measurements. It equals 1.

▶ Conversion factors have an unlimited number of significant figures. They are not considered when rounding the answer.

Dimensional Analysis Dimensional analysis is a way to solve problems using the units, or dimensions, of measurements.

▶ Dimensional analysis problems can be done in one step or they can require several steps.

▶ When using dimensional analysis, a measurement with one unit is changed to an equivalent measurement with another unit.

Multi-Step Dimensional Analysis
Change meters/second to kilometers/hour.
Multiply by a conversion factor to change meters to kilometers: $\text{m/s} \times \dfrac{1 \text{ km}}{1000 \text{ m}}$
Multiply by a conversion factor to change seconds to hours: $\text{m/s} \times \dfrac{1 \text{ km}}{1000 \text{ m}} \times \dfrac{3600 \text{ s}}{1 \text{ h}}$ or $\times \dfrac{60 \text{ s}}{1 \text{ min}} \times \dfrac{60 \text{ min}}{1 \text{ h}}$
Notice that there usually is some choice in what conversion factors are used.

After reading Lesson 3.3, answer the following questions.

Conversion Factors

1. How are the two parts of a conversion factor related?

_____

2. Look at Figure 3.12. In a conversion factor, the smaller number is part of the quantity that has the _____ unit. The larger number is part of the quantity that has the _____ unit.

3. Is the following sentence true or false? The actual size of a measurement multiplied by a conversion factor remains the same, because the measurement being converted is multiplied by unity. _____

4. Write two conversion factors based on the relationship between hours and minutes.

_____   _____

5. The average lead for a mechanical pencil is 6.0 cm long when it is new. Circle the letter of the conversion factor you would use to find its length in inches.

   a. $\dfrac{2.54 \text{ cm}}{1 \text{ in.}}$

   b. $\dfrac{1 \text{ in.}}{2.54 \text{ cm}}$

   c. $\dfrac{1 \text{ in.}}{6.0 \text{ cm}}$

   d. $\dfrac{6.0 \text{ cm}}{1 \text{ in.}}$

6. A student is asked to calculate the volume, in milliliters, of 2 cups of oil. There are 225 mL per cup. The student calculates the volume as follows:

$$\text{Volume} = 2 \text{ cups} \times \frac{1 \text{ cup}}{25 \text{ mL}} = 0.08 \text{ cup}$$

List three errors the student made.

_____

_____

_____

Dimensional Analysis

7. What is dimensional analysis?

_____

_____

_____

8. A container can hold 65 g of water. Circle the conversion factor needed to find the mass of water that 5 identical containers can hold.

a. $\dfrac{5 \text{ containers}}{65 \text{ g water}}$

b. $\dfrac{1 \text{ container}}{65 \text{ g water}}$

c. $\dfrac{65 \text{ g water}}{1 \text{ container}}$

d. $\dfrac{65 \text{ g water}}{5 \text{ containers}}$

9. Converting between units is easily done using _____.

10. Circle the letter of the conversion factor that you would use to convert tablespoons to milliliters.

a. $\dfrac{4 \text{ fluid ounces}}{1 \text{ tablespoon}}$

b. $\dfrac{1 \text{ tablespoon}}{4 \text{ fluid ounces}}$

c. $\dfrac{1 \text{ tablespoon}}{15 \text{ mL}}$

d. $\dfrac{15 \text{ mL}}{1 \text{ tablespoon}}$

11. Show the calculation you would use to convert the following:

a. 0.25 m to centimeters _____

b. 9.8 g to kilograms _____

c. 35 ms to seconds _____

d. 4.2 dL to liters _____

12. Complex conversions between units may require using _____ conversion factor.

13. How many conversion factors would you need to use to find the number of liters in a cubic decimeter? What are they?

_____

_____

14. How would you calculate the number of nanometers in 8.1 cm?

_____

15. What is the equivalent of 0.35 lb in grams?

_____

16. A scientist has 0.46 mL of a solution. How would she convert this volume to microliters?

_____

17. Describe the steps you would use to solve this problem. In a scale drawing of a dining room floor plan, 10 mm equals 2 meters. If the homeowners wanted to purchase flooring that costs $10.89 per square yard, how much would they spend on flooring for the dining room? The dimensions of the dining room on the floor plan are 40 mm × 32 mm.

_____

_____

_____

18. Name three common measurements that are expressed as a ratio of two units.

_____

19. What technique can be used to convert complex units?

_____

20. A normal concentration of glucose, or sugar, in the blood is 95 mg/dL. How many grams of sugar would be present per liter of blood? Show the conversion factors you use.

_____

21. A man can run a mile in 4 minutes. Calculate his average speed in kilometers per hour. Show your work. (1 mile = 1.61 km)

_____

_____

22. A baseball player's batting average is .254 (254 hits per 1000 at bats). If she is at bat an average of 3 times per game, how many hits will she make in 52 games? Show your work.

_____

_____

Guided Practice Problems

Answer the following questions about Practice Problem 6a.

Round 87.073 meters to three significant figures. Write your answer in scientific notation.

Analyze

a. To round to three significant figures, round to the nearest tenth.

_____

Calculate

b. Write the number in scientific notation. Change to a coefficient between 1 and 10×10 with an integer exponent.

_____ meters

Answer the following questions about Practice Problem 21.

A student finds a shiny piece of metal that she thinks is aluminum. In the lab, she determines that the metal has a volume of 245 cm^3 and a mass of 612 g. Calculate the density. Is the metal aluminum?

Analyze

a. List the known values.

Volume = 245 cm^3

Mass = 612 g

b. List the unknown.

_____

Calculate

c. Use the following relationship to find the density. Remember to round your answer to three significant figures.

$$\text{Density} = \frac{\text{mass}}{\text{volume}} = \frac{612 \text{ g}}{\boxed{} \text{ cm}^3} = \boxed{} \text{ g/cm}^3$$

d. To determine whether the piece of metal is aluminum, compare the density of the metal to the density of aluminum given in Table 3.6. Is the metal aluminum?

_____

Evaluate

e. Underline the correct word(s) that complete(s) this statement. Because the mass of the metal is about two and one-half times the volume, a density of about 2.5 g/cm^3 is reasonable. Because a density of 2.50 g/cm^3 is nearly 10% less than 2.7 g/cm^3, the density of aluminum, the metal (is, is not) aluminum.

Answer the following questions about Practice Problem 45.

The radius of a potassium atom is 0.227 nm. Express this radius in centimeters.
Complete the following steps to solve the problem.

Analyze

a. Use the conversion factors for nanometers and centimeters.

$$0.227 \text{ nm} \times \frac{\boxed{}}{1 \times 10^9 \text{nm}} \times \frac{\boxed{}}{1 \text{ m}}$$

Calculate

b. Simplify.

$$= 0.227 \times \frac{10^2}{10^9} \boxed{}$$

c. Divide.

$$= \boxed{} \text{ cm}$$

Apply the Big idea

A student places a cube of ironwood in water and it sinks. To find out why this wood sinks, he wants to find its density. He found that a large sample of ironwood has a mass of 1.8 kg and a volume of 1.5 L.

a. What is the density of ironwood in g/cm³? Show your work.

_____

_____

_____

b. Why did the ironwood sink in water?

_____

_____

_____

3 Self-Check Activity

For Questions 1–9, complete each statement by writing the correct word or words. If you need help, you can go online.

3.1 Using and Expressing Measurements

1. In writing numbers in scientific notation, the _____ is always a number greater than or equal to one and less than ten.

2. _____ is a measure of how close a measurement comes to the actual or true value of whatever is measured.

3. _____ is a measure of how close measurements in a series are to one another, irrespective of the actual value.

4. Measurements must always be reported to the correct number of _____.

3.2 Units of Measurement

5. Metric units are easy to convert because they are based on _____.

6. Scientists commonly use two equivalent units of temperature, the degree _____ and the kelvin.

7. The ratio of the mass of an object to its volume is _____.

3.3 Solving Conversion Problems

8. The two measurements used in a conversion factor are _____, which means that they equal the same thing.

9. _____ is a way to analyze and solve problems using the units of the measurements.

If You Have Trouble With...								
Question	1	2	3	4	5	6	7	8	9
See Page	62	64	64	66	74	78	80	84	86

Review Key Equations

For each problem below, write the equation used to solve it.

1. Miguel found the density of a piece of iron. The accepted value of the density of iron is 7.87 g/cm³.

    a. The piece of iron that Miguel measured had a mass of 51.1 g and a volume of 6.63 cm³. What did Miguel calculate to be the density of iron?

    _____

    b. What was the error?

    _____

    c. What was the percent error?

    _____

2. Isabella measured the temperature of a gas as 24.3°C. To use this value in a calculation, she needed to convert the temperature to kelvins. What is this temperature in kelvins?

    _____

EXTENSION Solve each equation above.

   1. a. _____

       b. _____

       c. _____

   2. _____

Review Vocabulary

Place the letter of each of the terms in the vocabulary box by each location in the equation where it is used.

a. conversion factor	d. gram	g. significant figure
b. density	e. kilogram	
c. dimensional analysis	f. liter	

A box had a mass of 4.5 kg and a volume of 6.4 L. Calculate the density of the box to two decimal places in g/cm³.

$$\text{_____} = \frac{4.5 \text{ kg}}{6.4 \text{ L}} \times \frac{1000 \text{ g}}{1 \text{ kg}} \times \frac{1 \text{L}}{1000 \text{ mL}} \times \frac{1 \text{ mL}}{1 \text{ cm}^3} = \frac{0.70 \text{ g}}{\text{cm}^3}\text{\_\_\_}$$

4 Atomic Structure

 ELECTRONS AND THE STRUCTURE OF ATOMS

4.1 Defining the Atom

Essential Understanding Atoms are the fundamental building blocks of matter.

Lesson Summary

Early Models of the Atom The scientific study of the atom began with John Dalton in the early 1800s.

▶ The ancient Greek Democritus first proposed that matter is made up of small, indivisible particles that he called atoms.

▶ John Dalton made the first accepted theory on atoms almost 2000 years after the work of Democritus.

▶ Dalton's atomic theory included that all atoms of an element are alike, the atoms of different elements are different, and atoms can combine to form compounds.

Sizing up the Atom Atoms are extremely small, but technology enables scientists to view atoms.

▶ An atom is the smallest part of an element that has the properties of that element.

▶ Individual atoms can be seen and even moved around using instruments such as scanning electron microscopes.

After reading Lesson 4.1, answer the following questions.

Early Models of the Atom

1. Democritus, who lived in Greece during the fourth century B.C., suggested that matter is made up of tiny particles that cannot be divided. He called these particles

   _____.

2. List two reasons why the ideas of Democritus were not useful in a scientific sense.

   _____

   _____

3. The modern process of discovery about atoms began with the theories of an English schoolteacher named _____.

4. Circle the letter of each sentence that is true about Dalton's atomic theory.

   a. All elements are composed of tiny, indivisible particles called atoms.

   b. An element is composed of several types of atoms.

   c. Atoms of different elements can physically mix together, or can chemically combine in simple, whole-number ratios to form compounds.

   d. Chemical reactions occur when atoms are separated, joined, or rearranged; however, atoms of one element are never changed into atoms of another element by a chemical reaction.

5. In the diagram, use the labels *mixture* and *compound* to identify the mixture of elements A and B and the compound that forms when the atoms of elements A and B combine chemically.

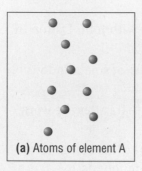 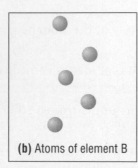  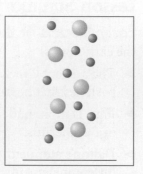

(a) Atoms of element A   (b) Atoms of element B   _____   _____

Sizing up the Atom

6. Suppose you could grind a sample of the element copper into smaller and smaller particles. The smallest particle that could no longer be divided, yet still has the chemical properties of copper, is _____.

7. About how many atoms of copper when placed side by side would form a line 1 cm long?
_____

4.2 Structure of the Nuclear Atom

Essential Understanding An atom is made up of a nucleus that contains protons and neutrons. Electrons move around the nucleus.

 ## Reading Strategy

Combination Notes Combination notes help you to convey ideas in words and pictures at the same time. Write "Atomic Structure" at the top of the T on the following page. In the left column, write notes about the subatomic particles. In the right column, draw pictures that help you visualize subatomic particles.

As you read Lesson 4.2, use the T-Chart Graphic Organizer below to summarize in words and pictures what you know about protons, neutrons, and electrons.

Parts of an atom	How I visualize it
Electrons:	
Protons:	
Neutrons:	

EXTENSION Write linking sentences that show the relationship between protons, neutrons, and electrons.

Lesson Summary

Subatomic Particles
Subatomic particles are made up of protons, neutrons, and electrons.

▶ Electrons are negatively charged subatomic particles discovered by J. J. Thomson in the late 1800s.

▶ At about the same time, Eugen Goldstein discovered the proton, which is a positively charged subatomic particle.

▶ In the 1900s, James Chadwick discovered the neutron, which is a subatomic particle with no charge.

The Atomic Nucleus
Modern atomic theory states that the protons and neutrons exist at the center of an atom in a small nucleus, and electrons move around this nucleus.

▶ Thomson proposed an atomic model in which electrons were stuck in a sphere of positive charge.

▶ The atom is mostly empty space containing a small, dense, positively charged core called the nucleus.

▶ According to Rutherford's nuclear atom theory, electrons are distributed around the nucleus and occupy most of the space in an atom.

After reading Lesson 4.2, answer the following questions.

Subatomic Particles

1. How is the atomic theory that is accepted today different from Dalton's atomic theory?

_____

_____

2. Which subatomic particles carry a negative charge? _____

Match each term from the experiments of J. J. Thomson with the correct description.

_____ 3. anode   **a.** an electrode with a negative charge

_____ 4. cathode   **b.** a glowing beam traveling between charged electrodes

_____ 5. cathode ray   **c.** an electrode with a positive charge

_____ 6. electron   **d.** a negatively charged particle

7. The diagram shows electrons moving from left to right in a cathode-ray tube. Draw an arrow showing how the path of the electrons will be affected by the placement of the negatively and positively charged plates.

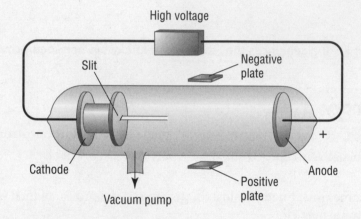

8. Thomson observed that the production of cathode rays did not depend on the kind of gas in the tube or the type of metal used for the electrodes. What conclusion did he draw from these observations?

_____

9. What two properties of an electron did Robert Millikan determine from his experiments?

_____

10. Circle the letter of each sentence that is true about atoms, matter, and electric charge.

    a. All atoms have an electric charge.

    b. Electric charges are carried by particles of matter.

    c. Electric charges always exist in whole-number multiples of a single basic unit.

    d. When a given number of positively charged particles combines with an equal number of negatively charged particles, an electrically neutral particle is formed.

11. Circle the letter next to the number of units of positive charge that remain if a hydrogen atom loses an electron.

    a. 0   **b.** 1   **c.** 2   **d.** 3

12. The positively charged subatomic particle that remains when a hydrogen atom loses an electron is called a(n) _____.

13. What charge does a neutron carry? _____

14. Complete the table about the properties of subatomic particles.

Properties of Subatomic Particles				
Particle	Symbol	Relative electrical charge	Relative mass (mass of proton = 1)	Actual mass (g)
Electron	e^-			9.11×10^{-28}
Proton	p^+			1.67×10^{-24}
Neutron	n^0			1.67×10^{-24}

The Atomic Nucleus

15. Is the following sentence true or false? An alpha particle has a double positive charge because it is a helium atom that has lost two electrons. _____

16. Explain why in 1911 Rutherford and his coworkers were surprised when they shot a narrow beam of alpha particles through a thin sheet of gold foil.

_____

_____

_____

_____

17. Circle the letter of each sentence that is true about the nuclear theory of atoms suggested by Rutherford's experimental results.

   a. An atom is mostly empty space.

   b. All the positive charge of an atom is concentrated in a small central region called the nucleus.

   c. The nucleus is composed of protons.

   d. The nucleus is large compared with the atom as a whole.

   e. Nearly all the mass of an atom is in its nucleus.

4.3 Distinguishing Among Atoms

Essential Understanding The mass number and number of protons define the type of atom.

Lesson Summary

Atomic Number and Mass Number Atomic number and mass number can be used to determine the number of protons and neutrons in an atom.

▶ Each element has a unique atomic number, which is the number of protons the atom contains.

▶ Mass number is the total number of protons and neutrons in an atom.

▶ The number of neutrons in an atom can be found by subtracting the atomic number from the mass number.

Isotopes Most elements contain several different isotopes that differ in the number of neutrons they contain.

▶ Isotopes are atoms of the same element that have different numbers of neutrons.

▶ Isotopes are chemically alike because they contain the same number of protons and electrons.

Atomic Mass The atomic mass of an atom is its actual mass, based on the actual number of each type of subatomic particle it contains.

▶ The atomic mass of an element is a weighted average of the mass of the isotopes of the element.

▶ Atomic mass is measured in atomic mass units (amu), which is based on the mass of a carbon-12 atom.

▶ The atomic mass of an element usually is close to the mass of its most abundant isotope.

BUILD Math Skills

Percents A percent is a ratio that compares a number to 100. It's a shorthand way of expressing a fraction whose denominator is 100. For example, 75% is equivalent to 0.75 or $\frac{75}{100}$.

One way to calculate percent is to multiply the ratio of the part to the whole by 100%.

$$\text{percent} = \frac{\text{part}}{\text{whole}} \times 100\%$$

Because a percent represents a relationship between two quantities, it can be used as a conversion factor. If you know the percent and one variable, you can use dimensional analysis to find the unknown.

Sample Problem Margarete has a monthly salary of $1200. She spends $240 per month on food. What percent of her monthly salary does she spend on food?

List the knowns and unknown.

KNOWNS	UNKNOWN
$240 is the part	percent of monthly salary
$1200 is the whole	

Solve for the unknown.

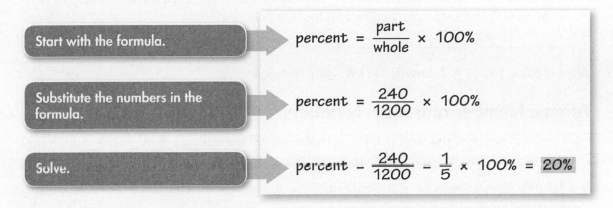

Start with the formula.	$percent = \dfrac{part}{whole} \times 100\%$
Substitute the numbers in the formula.	$percent = \dfrac{240}{1200} \times 100\%$
Solve.	$percent = \dfrac{240}{1200} = \dfrac{1}{5} \times 100\% = \boxed{20\%}$

Sample Problem A friend tells you that he got a score of 85% on a test that had 40 questions. How many questions did he answer correctly?

List the knowns and unknown.

KNOWNS	UNKNOWN
85% correct for every 100 questions	number of correct answers
40 questions total	

Solve for the unknown.

Set up the conversion factor.	$40 \text{ questions} \times \dfrac{(85 \text{ correct})}{100 \text{ questions}} = \text{total correct answers}$
Solve.	$\dfrac{40 \times 85}{100} = \dfrac{3400}{100} = \boxed{34 \text{ total correct answers}}$

Now it's your turn to practice using percents. Answer the following questions.

1. A store discounted a leather jacket by 25%. If the original price was $250, what is the new price of the jacket?

   _____

2. A nighttime cold medicine is 22% alcohol (by volume). How many mL of alcohol are in a 250 mL bottle of this cold medicine?

   _____

3. Hydrogen peroxide is sold as a 3.0% (by mass) solution. The rest of the solution is water. How many grams of hydrogen peroxide are in 250 g of this solution?

   _____

4. A compound is broken down into 34.5 g of element A, 18.2 g of element B, and 2.6 g of element C. What is the percent (by mass) of each element?

   _____

After reading Lesson 4.3, answer the following questions.

Atomic Number and Mass Number

5. Circle the letter of the term that correctly completes the sentence. Elements are different because their atoms contain different numbers of _____.

   a. electrons   **c.** neutrons

   b. protons   **d.** nuclei

6. Complete the table showing the number of protons and electrons in atoms of six elements.

Atoms of Six Elements				
Name	Symbol	Atomic number	Number of protons	Number of electrons
Hydrogen	H	1		
Helium	He		2	
Lithium	Li	3		
Boron	B	5		
Carbon	C	6		
Oxygen	O			8

7. The total number of protons and neutrons in an atom is its _____.

8. What is the mass number of a helium atom that has two protons and two neutrons? _____

9. How many neutrons does a beryllium atom with four protons and a mass number of nine have? _____

10. Place the labels *chemical symbol*, *atomic number*, and *mass number* in the shorthand notation below.

11. Designate the atom shown in Question 10 in the form "name of element"-"mass number." _____

12. How many protons, neutrons, and electrons are in the atom discussed in Questions 10 and 11? Protons: [   ]   Neutrons: [   ]   Electrons: [   ]

Isotopes

13. How do atoms of neon-20 and neon-22 differ?

_____

_____

14. Neon-20 and neon-22 are called _____.

15. Is the following sentence true or false? Isotopes are chemically alike because they have identical numbers of protons and electrons. _____

Match the designation of each hydrogen isotope with its commonly used name.

_____ 16. hydrogen-1   a. tritium

_____ 17. hydrogen-2   b. hydrogen

_____ 18. hydrogen-3   c. deuterium

Atomic Mass

19. Why is the atomic mass unit (amu), rather than the gram, usually used to express atomic mass?

_____

_____

20. What isotope of carbon has been chosen as the reference isotope for atomic mass units? What is the defined atomic mass in amu of this isotope?

_____

21. Is the following sentence true or false? The atomic mass of an element is always a whole number of atomic mass units. _____

22. Circle the letter of each statement that is true about the average atomic mass of an element and the relative abundance of its isotopes.

a. In nature, most elements occur as a mixture of two or more isotopes.

b. Isotopes of an element do not have a specific natural percent abundance.

c. The average atomic mass of an element is usually closest to that of the isotope with the highest natural abundance.

d. Because hydrogen has three isotopes with atomic masses of about 1 amu, 2 amu, and 3 amu, respectively, the average atomic mass of natural hydrogen is 2 amu.

23. Circle the letter of the correct answer. When chlorine occurs in nature, there are three atoms of chlorine-35 for every one atom of chlorine-37. Which atomic mass number is closer to the average atomic mass of chlorine?

a. 35 amu

b. 37 amu

Guided Practice Problems

Answer the following questions about Practice Problem 19.

Use Table 4.2 to express the compositions of carbon-12, fluorine-19, and beryllium-9 in shorthand form.

Carbon-12

Analyze

Step 1. The number of protons in an atom is called its _____ number. The number of protons in an atom of carbon-12 is _____.

Calculate

Step 2. The number of protons plus the number of neutrons in an atom is called its _____ number. For carbon-12, this number is _____.

Step 3. The shorthand notation for carbon-12 is:

mass number ⟶ ☐

atomic number ⟶ ☐ **C**

Evaluate

Step 4. Except for hydrogen-1, the mass number of an isotope is always greater than its atomic number. Is the mass number reasonable? _____

Fluorine-19

Step 1. The atomic number of fluorine-19 is _____.
Step 2. Its mass number is _____.
Step 3. The shorthand notation for fluorine-19 is:

☐
☐ **F**

Step 4. Is your answer reasonable? Why?

_____

_____

Beryllium-9

Step 1. The atomic number of beryllium-9 is _____.

Step 2. Its mass number is _____.

Step 3. The shorthand notation for beryllium-9 is:

☐
☐ **Be**

Step 4. Is your answer reasonable? Why?

_____

_____

 Apply the Big idea ▸

A student knows the atomic number and the atomic mass for several different elements. He organized this information in the following table. For these elements, the mass number of the most common isotope is closest to the atomic mass of the element.

a. How do you determine the number of electrons, protons, and neutrons in one atom of the most common isotope from this information?

_____

_____

_____

b. Complete the table for a sample of each element.

Element	Atomic Number	Most Common Isotopes	Atomic Mass	Mass Number (of most common isotope)	Number of (in one atom of the most common isotope):		
					Electrons	Protons	Neutrons
Titanium	22	^{46}Ti, ^{47}Ti, ^{48}Ti, ^{49}Ti,	47.9				
Calcium	20	^{40}Ca, ^{42}Ca, ^{44}Ca	40.1				
Tantalum	73	^{180}Ta, ^{181}Ta	180.9				

4 Self-Check Activity

For Questions 1–9, complete each statement by writing the correct word or words. If you need help, you can go online.

4.1 Defining the Atom

1. _____ first proposed that atoms are small, indestructible particles that make up all matter.

2. _____ used experimental methods to propose an atomic theory based on earlier ideas.

3. Although atoms are extremely small, scientists can observe them using instruments such as the _____.

4.2 Structure of the Nuclear Atom

4. The particles that make up atoms—protons, neutrons, and electrons—are known as _____ particles.

5. There is a small core known as a(n) _____ in the center of an atom which contains the protons and neutrons.

6. Most of the volume of an atom is occupied by _____.

4.3 Distinguishing Among Atoms

7. The identity of an element is determined by the number of _____ it contains.

8. Each of an element's _____ has a different number of neutrons and a different mass number.

9. The _____ of an element is the weighted average of all the isotopes of the element.

If You Have Trouble With...								
Question	1	2	3	4	5	6	7	8	9
See Page	102	102	104	105	108	109	112	114	117

Review Key Equations

For each problem, write the key equation you would use to solve it. Then solve the problem.

1. How many neutrons are in an atom with atomic number of 53 and mass number of 127?

   _____

   _____

2. In a sample of silver, 51.84% of the atoms have a mass of 106.905 amu and 48.16% have a mass of 108.905 amu. What is the atomic mass of silver?

   _____

   _____

   _____

   _____

   _____

EXTENSION **Explain how you would estimate the answer to Problem 2.**

_____

_____

_____

_____

_____

Review Vocabulary

Complete each sentence with a vocabulary term.

The center of a certain atom contains 5 positively charged particles. It also contains 11 other particles.

1. The center of this atom is called the _____.

2. The atom contains 5 _____ and 5 _____.

3. The atom contains 6 _____.

4. The _____ of the atom is 5.

5. The _____ of the atom is 16.

6. The _____ of a sample of the element is 10.81 _____.

   This number is not a whole number because the sample contains different _____ of the element.

5 Electrons in Atoms

 ELECTRONS AND THE STRUCTURE OF ATOMS

5.1 Revising the Atomic Model

Essential Understanding An electron's energy depends on its location around the nucleus of an atom.

 Reading Strategy

Frayer Model The Frayer Model is a vocabulary development tool. The center of the diagram shows the concept being defined, while the quadrants around the concept are used for providing the details. Use this model when you want to understand a vocabulary term in more detail.

As you read Lesson 5.1, use the Frayer Model below. Place the term *quantum mechanical model* in the center of the model. Use the details you place in the appropriate quadrant to help you understand the vocabulary term.

Definition in your own words	Facts/characteristics
Examples	Nonexamples

EXTENSION Read through the details you wrote in the Frayer Model. If the details do not include all the vocabulary terms from this lesson, add details that show how the other vocabulary terms in the lesson relate to the quantum mechanical model.

Lesson Summary

Energy Levels in Atoms
Electrons in atoms are found in fixed energy levels.

▶ Niels Bohr proposed that electrons move in specific orbits around the nucleus.

▶ In these orbits, each electron has a fixed energy called an energy level.

▶ A quantum of energy is the amount of energy needed to move an electron from one energy level to another.

The Quantum Mechanical Model
The quantum mechanical model determines how likely it is to find an electron in various locations around the atom.

▶ The quantum mechanical model is based on mathematics, not on experimental evidence.

▶ This model does not specify an exact path an electron takes around the nucleus, but gives the probability of finding an electron within a certain volume of space around the nucleus.

▶ This volume of space is described as an electron cloud, which has no boundary. The electron cloud is denser where the probability of finding the electron is high.

Atomic Orbitals
An atomic orbital describes where an electron is likely to be found.

▶ Numbered outward from the nucleus, each energy level is assigned a principal quantum number, n, which is also the number of sublevels.

▶ Each energy sublevel differs in shape and orientation and contains orbitals, each of which can contain up to two electrons.

▶ Each energy level contains a maximum of $2n^2$ electrons.

After reading Lesson 5.1, answer the following questions.

Energy Levels in Atoms

1. Complete the table about atomic models and the scientists who developed them. Refer to Chapter 4 if you need to.

Scientist	Model of Atom
Dalton	
Thomson	
Rutherford	
Bohr	

2. Is the following sentence true or false? The electrons in an atom can exist between energy levels. _____

3. What are the fixed energies of electrons called?

_____

4. Circle the letter of the term that completes the sentence correctly. A quantum of energy is the amount of energy required to

a. place an electron in an energy level.

b. maintain an electron in its present energy level.

c. move an electron from its present energy level to a higher one.

5. In general, the higher the electron is on the energy ladder, the _____ it is from the nucleus.

The Quantum Mechanical Model

6. What is the difference between the previous models of the atom and the modern quantum mechanical model?

_____

_____

_____

7. Is the following sentence true or false? The quantum mechanical model of the atom estimates the probability of finding an electron in a certain position.

_____

Atomic Orbitals

8. A(n) _____ is often thought of as a region of space in which there is a high probability of finding an electron.

9. Circle the letter of the term that is used to label the energy levels of electrons.

a. atomic orbitals   **c.** quantum

b. quantum mechanical numbers   **d.** principal quantum numbers (n)

10. The letter _____ is used to denote a spherical orbital.

11. Label each diagram below p_x, p_y, or p_z.

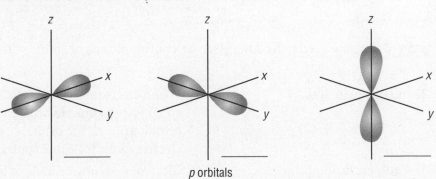

p orbitals

12. Use the diagram above. Describe how the p_x, p_y, and p_z orbitals are similar.

_____

13. Describe how the p_x, p_y, and p_z orbitals are different.

_____

_____

14. Circle the letter of the formula for the maximum number of electrons that can occupy a principal energy level. Use n for the principal quantum number.

a. $2n^2$ **b.** n^2 **c.** $2n$ **d.** n

5.2 Electron Arrangement in Atoms

Essential Understanding Three rules determine the electron arrangement in an atom: the aufbau principle, the Pauli exclusion principle, and Hund's rule.

Lesson Summary

Electron Configurations An electron configuration describes the arrangement of electrons in an atom.

▶ The aufbau principle says that electrons occupy the orbitals of lowest energy first.

▶ According to the Pauli exclusion principle, each orbital can contain at most two electrons. The two electrons must have opposite spin.

▶ Hund's rule states that single electrons occupy orbitals in a specific sublevel until each orbital contains an electron. Then electrons pair with these single electrons.

▶ Some electron configurations are exceptions to these rules because of the relative stability of half-full sublevels.

After reading Lesson 5.2, answer the following questions.

Electron Configurations

1. The ways in which electrons are arranged into orbitals around the nuclei of atoms are called _____.

Match the name of the rule used to find the electron configurations of atoms with the rule itself.

_____ **2.** aufbau principle

_____ **3.** Pauli exclusion principle

_____ **4.** Hund's rule

a. When electrons occupy orbitals of equal energy, one electron enters each orbital until all the orbitals contain one electron with the same spin direction.

b. Electrons occupy orbitals of lowest energy first.

c. An atomic orbital may describe at most two electrons.

5. Look at the aufbau diagram, Figure 5.5. Which atomic orbital is of higher energy, a 4*f* or a 5*p* orbital? _____

6. Fill in the electron configurations for the elements given in the table.

Use the orbital filling diagrams to complete the table.

Electron Configurations for Some Selected Elements							
	Orbital filling						**Electron configuration**
Element	**1s**	**2s**	**2p$_x$**	**2p$_y$**	**2p$_z$**	**3s**	
☐	↑	☐	☐	☐	☐	☐	1s^1
He	↑↓	☐	☐	☐	☐	☐	☐
☐	↑↓	↑	☐	☐	☐	☐	1s^{2}2s^1
C	↑↓	↑↓	↑	↑	☐	☐	☐
☐	↑↓	↑↓	↑	↑	↑	☐	1s^{2}2s^{2}2p^3
O	↑↓	↑↓	↑↓	↑	↑	☐	☐
☐	↑↓	↑↓	↑↓	↑↓	↑	☐	1s^{2}2s^{2}2p^5
Ne	↑↓	↑↓	↑↓	↑↓	↑↓	☐	☐
☐	↑↓	↑↓	↑↓	↑↓	↑↓	↑	1s^{2}2s^{2}2p^{6}3s^1

7. In an electron configuration, what does a superscript stand for?

_____

_____

8. In an electron configuration, what does the sum of the superscripts equal?

_____

_____

9. Is the following sentence true or false? Every element in the periodic table follows the aufbau principle. _____

10. Filled energy sublevels are more _____ than partially filled sublevels.

11. Half-filled levels are not as stable as _____ levels, but are more stable than other configurations.

5.3 Atomic Emission Spectra and the Quantum Mechanical Model

Essential Understanding The electromagnetic radiation emitted by excited electrons returning to a lower energy level is unique for that particular element and is based on differences in energy among energy levels in the atom.

Lesson Summary

Light and Atomic Emission Spectra When electrons lose energy, they emit light of specific wavelengths when they return to lower energy levels.

▶ Each electromagnetic wave has a wavelength (λ) and a frequency (ν) related by the equation $c = \lambda\nu$, where c is the speed of light.

▶ When atoms absorb energy, their electrons move to a higher energy level.

▶ When excited electrons lose energy, they emit a unique set of light waves, known as the atomic emission spectrum, for that element.

The Quantum Concept and Photons Photons are units of light that behave like particles.

▶ Max Planck proposed that the energy of a body changes only in quanta, which are small, discrete units.

▶ Planck's theory helped explain the photoelectric effect, which happens when electrons are ejected from matter under certain wavelengths of light.

▶ Quantum theory implies that light behaves both as a wave and as a particle.

An Explanation of Atomic Spectra The lines in an element's atomic spectrum result from electrons moving from a higher to a lower energy level.

▶ The lowest energy level an electron occupies is its ground state.

▶ The frequency of the light emitted when an electron drops from a higher energy level to a lower one is proportional to the energy change of the electron.

Quantum Mechanics Quantum mechanics describes the motions of extremely small particles, such as electrons, as waves.

▶ Experiments confirm that light behaves both as waves and particles.

▶ All moving particles act as waves, but larger objects have wavelengths too small to observe.

▶ The Heisenberg uncertainty principle states that it is impossible to know both the velocity and the location of a particle at the same time.

BUILD Math Skills

Algebraic Equations An algebraic equation shows the relationship between two or more variables. Often, an equation must be solved for the unknown variable before substituting the known values into the equation and doing the arithmetic.

Most equations can be solved if you remember that you can perform any mathematical operation without destroying equality as long as you do it to both sides of the equals sign.

Sample Problem What is the volume of 622 g of lead if the density of lead is 11.3 g/cm³?

List the knowns and the unknown.

You know that *g* is a measure of mass, so 622 g is the mass of lead.

KNOWNS	UNKNOWN
Mass (*m*) = 622 g	(*v*) Volume
Density (*d*) = 11.3 g/cm³	

Solve for the unknown.

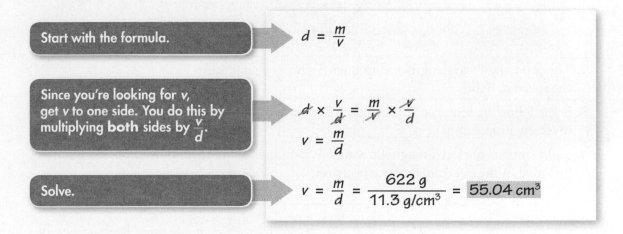

Start with the formula.

$$d = \frac{m}{v}$$

Since you're looking for *v*, get *v* to one side. You do this by multiplying **both** sides by $\frac{v}{d}$.

$$d \times \frac{v}{d} = \frac{m}{v} \times \frac{v}{d}$$

$$v = \frac{m}{d}$$

Solve.

$$v = \frac{m}{d} = \frac{622\ g}{11.3\ g/cm^3} = 55.04\ cm^3$$

Now it's your turn to practice solving algebraic equations. Answer the following questions.

1. A football field that is 60 m wide and 110 m long is being paved over to make a parking lot. The builder ordered 660,000,000 cm³ of cement. How thick must the cement be to cover the field using 660,000,000 cm³ of cement? (Use the formula $V = l \times w \times h$.)

_____

2. X-rays are used to diagnose diseases of internal body organs. What is the frequency of an X-ray with a wavelength of 1.15×10^{-10} m?

_____

3. What is the speed of an electromagnetic wave with a frequency of 1.33×10^{17} Hz and a wavelength of 2.25 nm?

_____

After reading Lesson 5.3, answer the following questions.

Light and Atomic Emission Spectra

4. Match each term describing waves to its definition.

_____ amplitude

_____ wavelength

_____ frequency

a. the distance between two crests

b. the wave's height from zero to the crest

c. the number of wave cycles to pass a given point per unit of time

5. The units of frequency are usually cycles per second. The SI unit of cycles per second is called a(n) _____.

6. Label the parts of a wave in this drawing. Label the wavelength, the amplitude, and the crest.

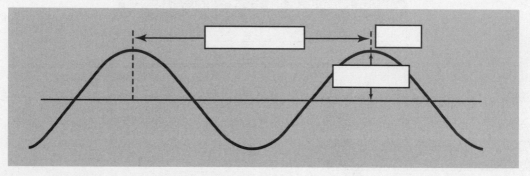

7. The product of wavelength and frequency always equals a(n) _____, the speed of light.

8. Is the following sentence true or false? The wavelength and frequency of light are inversely proportional. _____

9. Light consists of electromagnetic waves. What kinds of visible and invisible radiation are included in the electromagnetic spectrum?

_____

_____

10. When sunlight passes through a prism, the different wavelengths separate into a(n) _____ of colors.

11. Put the visible colors in order of increasing frequency.

_____ orange

_____ green

_____ violet

_____ yellow

_____ blue

_____ red

12. Look at Figure 5.8. The electromagnetic spectrum consists of radiation over a broad band of wavelengths. What type of radiation has the lowest frequency? The highest frequency?

_____

13. What happens when an electric current is passed through the gas or vapor of an element?

_____

14. Passing the light emitted by an element through a prism gives the _____ of the element.

15. Is the following sentence true or false? The emission spectrum of an element can be the same as the emission spectrum of another element. _____

16. Only electrons moving from _____ to _____ energy levels lose energy and emit light.

The Quantum Concept and Photons

17. What did Albert Einstein call the quanta of light energy? _____

An Explanation of Atomic Spectra

18. What is the lowest possible energy of an electron called? _____

Quantum Mechanics

19. What does de Broglie's equation predict about the behavior of particles?

_____

20. Is the following sentence true or false? Quantum mechanics describes the motions of subatomic particles and atoms as waves. _____

21. According to the Heisenberg uncertainty principle, it is impossible to know exactly both the _____ and the _____ of a particle at the same time.

22. Does the Heisenberg uncertainty principle apply to cars and airplanes?

_____

Guided Practice Problem

Answer the following questions about Practice Problem 15.

What is the wavelength of radiation with a frequency of 1.50×10^{13} Hz? Does this radiation have a longer or shorter wavelength than red light?

Analyze

Step 1. What is the equation for the relationship between frequency and wavelength?

_____

Step 2. What does c represent, and what is its value?

_____

Step 3. What is the wavelength of red light in m?

_____

Calculate

Step 4. Solve the equation for the unknown. $\lambda =$ _____

Step 5. Substitute the known quantities into the equation and solve.

$$\frac{2.998 \times 10^8 \text{ m/s}}{\boxed{}} = \boxed{}$$

Step 6. Compare the answer with the wavelength of red light. Does the given radiation have a wavelength longer or shorter than that of red light?

_____

_____

Evaluate

Step 7. Explain why you think your result makes sense.

_____

_____

Step 8. Are the units in your answer correct? How do you know?

_____

 Apply the **Big** idea

Explain how each of these rules was used to write this electron configuration.

	1s	2s	2p	2p	2p	3s	3p	3p	3p	3d	3d	3d	3d	3d	4s
Co	↑↓	↑↓	↑↓	↑↓	↑↓	↑↓	↑↓	↑↓	↑↓	↑↓	↑↓	↑	↑	↑	↑↓

a. aufbau principle

_____

_____

b. Pauli exclusion principle

_____

_____

b. Hund's rule

_____

_____

5 Self-Check Activity

For Questions 1–9, complete each statement by writing the correct word or words.
If you need help, you can go online.

5.1 Revising the Atomic Model

1. Bohr proposed that an electron is found only in specific circular paths, or _____, around the nucleus.

2. The _____ model describes the energy an electron can have and the probability of finding the electron in various locations around the nucleus of an atom.

3. Orbitals, which are found in _____, have different shapes, depending on the energy of the electrons they contain.

5.2 Electron Arrangement in Atoms

4. Electron configurations can be written by using the _____, the Pauli exclusion principle, and Hund's rule.

5.3 Atomic Emission Spectra and the Quantum Mechanical Model

5. When atoms absorb energy, their electrons move to higher _____.

6. Describing light as _____ of energy that behave as particles helps to explain the photoelectric effect.

7. When an electron drops to a lower energy level, it emits light that has a _____ directly proportional to the energy change of the electron.

8. _____ describes the motion of large bodies.

9. _____ describes the motion of very small particles, such as subatomic particles.

If You Have Trouble With...								
Question	1	2	3	4	5	6	7	8	9
See Page	129	130	131	134	140	143	145	147	147

Review Key Equations

Define each term in the following equations. If a term is a constant, include its value.

1. $c = \lambda v$

_____

_____

2. $E = hv$

_____

_____

3. If you know the value of E but do not know the value of v, how can you find λ?

_____

_____

_____

Review Vocabulary

In each of these sets of terms, circle the one term that does not belong. Then explain your reasoning.

1. electron configuration, Planck's constant, aufbau principle

_____

_____

2. spectrum, amplitude, wavelength

_____

_____

3. hertz, quantum, photon

_____

_____

4. Hund's rule, Pauli exclusion principle, Heisenberg uncertainty principle

_____

_____

5. atomic orbital, frequency, energy level

_____

_____

6 The Periodic Table

 ELECTRONS AND THE STRUCTURE OF ATOMS

6.1 Organizing the Elements

Essential Understanding Although Dmitri Mendeleev is often credited as the father of the periodic table, the work of many scientists contributed to its present form.

Reading Strategy

Compare and Contrast Organizing information in a table helps you compare and contrast several topics at one time. For example, you might compare and contrast different groups of elements. As you read, ask yourself, "How are they similar? How are they different?"

As you read Lesson 6.1, use the compare and contrast table below. Fill in the table with _increases or decreases_ to show the patterns of the listed periodic trends.

	Across a period	Down a group
Metallic		
Nonmetallic		
Atomic number		

EXTENSION On a blank periodic table, use arrows and labels to illustrate the results in your compare and contrast table.

Lesson Summary

Searching for an Organizing Principle As more and more elements were discovered, scientists needed a way to classify them.

▶ Elements were first classified according to their properties.

Mendeleev's Periodic Table Mendeleev developed the first periodic table, arranging elements according to a set of repeating, or periodic, properties.

▶ Elements were also placed in order, according to increasing atomic mass.

▶ Mendeleev used his table to predict the properties of yet undiscovered elements.

Today's Periodic Table Today's periodic table is a modification of Mendeleev's periodic table.

▶ The modern periodic table arranges elements by increasing atomic number.

▶ Periodic law states that when elements are ordered by increasing atomic number, their chemical and physical properties repeat in a pattern.

Metals, Nonmetals, and Metalloids Within the periodic table, elements are classified into three large groups based on their properties.

▶ Metals are good conductors and many are ductile and malleable.

▶ Nonmetals are mostly gases whose properties are opposite to those of metals.

▶ Metalloids can behave like metals or nonmetals, depending on the conditions.

After reading Lesson 6.1, answer the following questions.

Searching for an Organizing Principle

1. How many elements had been identified by the year 1700? _____

2. What caused the rate of discovery to increase after 1700?

_____

3. What did chemists use to sort elements into groups?

_____

_____

Mendeleev's Periodic Table

4. Who was Dmitri Mendeleev?

_____

5. What property did Mendeleev use to organize the elements into a periodic table?

_____

6. Is the following sentence true or false? Mendeleev used his periodic table to predict the properties of undiscovered elements. _____

Today's Periodic Table

7. How are the elements arranged in the modern periodic table?

_____

8. Is the following statement true or false? The periodic law states that when elements are arranged in order of increasing atomic number, there is a periodic repetition of physical and chemical properties. _____

Metals, Nonmetals, and Metalloids

9. Explain the color coding of the squares in the periodic table in Figure 6.4.

_____

_____

10. Which property below is NOT a general property of metals?

    a. ductile   **c.** malleable

    b. poor conductor of heat   **d.** high luster

11. Is the following statement true or false? The variation in properties among metals is greater than the variation in properties among nonmetals. _____

12. Under some conditions, a metalloid may behave like a _____. Under other conditions, a metalloid may behave like a _____.

6.2 Classifying the Elements

Essential Understanding   A periodic table shows much information about an element in an element's square, and arranges elements by their electron configuration.

Lesson Summary

Reading the Periodic Table An element's square has the element's symbol and name, atomic number and mass, and electron configuration.

▶ The elements are grouped into alkali metals, alkaline earth metals, and halogens.

Electron Configurations in Groups The properties of elements are largely determined by the arrangement of electrons, or electron configuration, in each atom.

▶ Based on their electron configurations, elements are classified as noble gases, representative elements, transition metals, or inner transition metals.

After reading Lesson 6.2, answer the following questions.

Reading the Periodic Table

1. Label the sample square from the periodic table below. Use the labels *element name*, *element symbol*, *atomic number*, and *average atomic mass*.

2. List three things, other than the name, symbol, atomic number, and average atomic mass, you can discover about an element using the periodic table in Figure 6.9.

a. _____

b. _____

c. _____

Electron Configurations in Groups

3. Is the following sentence true or false? The subatomic particles that play the key role in determining the properties of an element are electrons. _____

4. Why are Group A elements called representative elements?

_____

5. Classify each of the following elements as a(n) *alkali metal, alkaline earth metal, halogen,* or *noble gas.*

   a. sodium _____

   b. chlorine _____

   c. calcium _____

   d. fluorine _____

   e. xenon _____

   f. potassium _____

6. For elements in each of the following groups, how many electrons are in the highest occupied energy level?

   a. Group 3A _____

   b. Group 1A _____

   c. Group 8A _____

7. Complete the table about classifying elements according to the electron configuration of their highest occupied energy level.

Category	Description of Electron Configuration
Noble gases	
Representative elements	
	s sublevel and nearby *d* sublevel contain electrons
	s sublevel and nearby *f* sublevel contain electrons

8. Circle the letter of the elements found in the *p* block.

   a. Groups 1A and 2A and helium

   b. Groups 3A, 4A, 5A, 6A, 7A, and 8A except for helium

   c. transition metals

   d. inner transition metals

Match the category of elements with an element from that category.

_____ 9. noble gases

_____ 10. representative elements

_____ 11. transition metals

_____ 12. inner transition metals

   a. gallium

   b. nobelium

   c. argon

   d. vanadium

13. Use Figure 6.9. Write the electron configurations for the following elements.

   a. magnesium _____

   b. cobalt _____

   c. sulfur _____

6.3 Periodic Trends

Essential Understanding An element's properties are related to its position on the periodic table, and these properties follow trends on the table.

Lesson Summary

Trends in Atomic Size Atomic size is an atom's atomic radius, or one-half the distance between two like atoms when they are joined together.

► Atomic size generally increases from top to bottom within a group because the number of energy levels increases.

► Atomic size decreases from left to right across a period because electrons are added to the same energy level and are pulled closer to the nucleus by increasing numbers of protons.

Ions Ions form when atoms gain or lose electrons.

► A positively charged cation forms when an atom loses one or more electrons.

► A negatively charged anion forms when an atom gains one or more electrons.

Trends in Ionization Energy Ionization energy is a measure of how much energy is required to remove an electron from an atom.

► First ionization energy is the amount of energy required to remove one electron from a neutral atom.

► Ionization energy tends to decrease from top to bottom within a group and increase from left to right across a period.

Trends in Ionic Size Trends in ionic size are based on the fact that metals tend to lose electrons, and nonmetals tend to gain electrons.

► A cation is smaller than the atom that formed it; an anion is larger than the atom that formed it.

► Ionic size generally increases from top to bottom within a group and decreases from left to right across a period.

Trends in Electronegativity Electronegativity is a measure of an atom's ability to attract an electron when the atom is bonded to another atom.

► The trends in electronegativity are similar to the trends in ionization energy.

► Electronegativity tends to decrease from top to bottom within a group and to increase from left to right across a period.

📌 BUILD Math Skills

Reading a Graph A graph is a visual way to interpret or understand data. A graph shows relationships that exist among the data.

The title of the graph tells you what information the graph shows. The *x*-axis is the horizontal axis and the *y*-axis is the vertical axis. Examine each axis to find what each one represents and what units are used.

The two main types of graphs are bar graphs and line graphs.

Turn the page to learn more about reading a graph.

A bar graph has bars that run horizontally or vertically. To obtain data for a horizontal bar graph, you will need to match the end of the bar to the information on the horizontal axis at the bottom. The title of the vertical axis tells what the bar represents. To obtain data for a vertical bar graph, compare the end of the bar to the information on the vertical axis to the side. The title of the vertical axis tells what the bar represents.

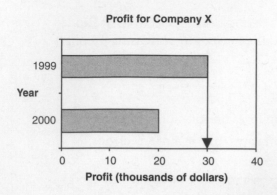

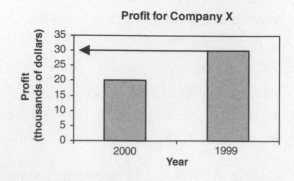

The graphs above provide the same information, but in two different ways. Look at the horizontal bar graph for the year 1999. Follow the end of the bar to the bottom axis and you will see that Company X made a profit of $30,000. The same data can be found on the vertical bar graph by following the end of the bar for year 1999 to the vertical axis.

A line graph shows points connected by a line. Each point has a corresponding value for both the horizontal and vertical axes. If you are given a value on the horizontal axis, you can find the point corresponding to that value on the vertical axis.

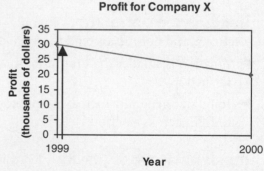

To find out how much profit Company X made in 1999, you would first locate year 1999 on the horizontal axis. Next, you would find the corresponding point on the vertical axis. The value that point represents on the vertical axis is the profit for 1999. In this example, the profit is $30,000.

Sample Problem Use the bar graph to determine how many students earned a B in the class.

Follow the end of the bar representing the letter grade B to the vertical axis.

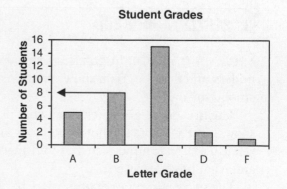

The value on the vertical axis is 8, which means that 8 students received a B in that class.

Sample Problem Determine how much profit Company Y made in March of 1999.

Locate the point associated with March and determine the value on the vertical axis.

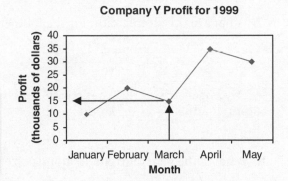

Company Y Profit for 1999

The value on the vertical axis is 15, which means that Company Y made $15,000 in profit.

Now it's your turn to practice interpreting graphs. Remember to examine the title and the units and labels of each axis to understand what the graph is representing.

Use the bar graph below to answer the following questions.

1. How many students received an A?

_____

2. How many students passed the class with a D or higher?

_____

3. What grade did the highest number of students receive?

_____

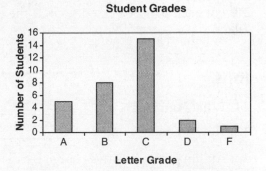

Student Grades

For the line graph below, answer the following questions.

4. How much did Company Y make for the month of May?

_____

5. In what month did Company Y make the most profit?

_____

6. How much did Company Y make for all 5 months?

_____

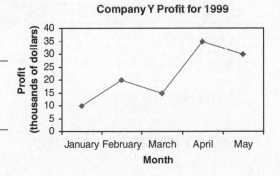

Company Y Profit for 1999

After reading Lesson 6.3, answer the following questions.

Trends in Atomic Size

7. What are the atomic radii for the following molecules?

Hydrogen
atomic radius =
_____

Oxygen
atomic radius =
_____

Nitrogen
atomic radius =
_____

Chlorine
atomic radius =
_____

8. What is the general trend in atomic size within a group? Across a period?

_____

_____

9. What are the two variables that affect atomic size within a group?

a. _____ **b.** _____

10. For each pair of elements, circle the element with the larger atom.

   a. helium and argon   **b.** potassium and argon

Ions

11. What is an ion? _____

12. How are ions formed? _____

13. An ion with a positive charge is called a(n) _____; an ion with a negative charge is called a(n) _____.

14. Complete the table about anions and cations.

	Anions	Cations
Charge		
Metal/Nonmetal		
Minus sign/Plus sign		

Trends in Ionization Energy

15. _____ is the energy required to overcome the attraction of protons in the nucleus and remove an electron from a gaseous atom.

16. Why does ionization energy tend to decrease from top to bottom within a group?

_____

_____

_____

17. Why does ionization energy tend to increase as you move across a period?

_____

_____

_____

18. There is a large increase in ionization energy between the second and the third ionization energies of a metal. What kind of ion is the metal likely to form? Include the charge in your answer. _____

Trends in Ionic Size

19. Metallic elements tend to _____ electrons and form _____ ions. Nonmetallic elements tend to _____ electrons and form _____ ions.

20. Circle the letter of the statement that is true about ion size.

  a. Cations are always smaller than the neutral atoms from which they form.

  b. Anions are always smaller than the neutral atoms from which they form.

  c. Within a period, a cation with a greater charge has a larger ionic radius.

  d. Within a group, a cation with a higher atomic number has a smaller ionic radius.

21. Which ion has the larger ionic radius: Ca^{2+} or Cl^- ? _____

Trends in Electronegativity

22. Use Table 6.2. What trend do you see in the relative electronegativity values of elements within a group? Within a period?

_____

_____

23. Circle the letter of each statement that is true about electronegativity values

  a. The electronegativity values of the transition elements are all zero.

  b. The element with the highest electronegativity value is sodium.

  c. Nonmetals have higher electronegativity values than metals.

  d. Electronegativity values can help predict the types of bonds atoms form.

24. Use Figure 6.24. Circle the letter of each property for which aluminum has a higher value than silicon.

  a. first ionization energy   **c.** electronegativity

  b. atomic radius   **d.** ionic radius

Guided Practice Problems

Answer the following questions about Practice Problem 9.

Use Figure 6.9 and Figure 6.13 to write the electron configurations of the following elements:

  a. carbon   **b.** strontium   **c.** vanadium

Analyze

a. What is the number of electrons for each element?

C _____   Sr _____   V _____

b. What is the highest occupied energy sublevel for each element, according to its position on the periodic table? Remember that the energy level for the *d* block is always one less than the period.

C _____   Sr _____   V _____

c. According to its position on the periodic table, how many electrons does each element have in the sublevel listed above?

C _____   Sr _____   V _____

Solve

d. Begin filling in electron sublevels. Start from the top left and move right across each period in Figure 6.13 until you reach the highest occupied sublevel for each element. Make sure the *d* block is in the correct energy level.

C _____

Sr _____

V _____

e. Add all the superscripts in the electron configurations to check your answers. This sum should equal the atomic number for that element.

C _____

Sr _____

V _____

Apply the Big idea

Make a seating chart for students in your class. Seat students according to their birth months and first names.

a. Survey your class and write down the first name and birth month of each student.

b. Make a seating chart with six columns. Label each column with the name of two consecutive months, starting with January/February and ending with November/December.

c. Place student names in the appropriate column in alphabetical order from top to bottom.

1. Suppose a new student named Maria joins the class. Her birthday is in August. Where would she sit?

_____

2. What other categories might you use to seat students?

_____

6 Self-Check Activity

For Questions 1–11, complete each statement by writing the correct word or words. If you need help, you can go online.

6.1 Organizing the Elements

1. Early scientists first sorted elements into groups according to their _____.

2. In Mendeleev's periodic table, elements were arranged by increasing _____.

3. Currently, elements are arranged on the periodic table according to increasing _____.

4. Each element is either a metal, a(n) _____, or a metalloid.

6.2 Classifying the Elements

5. The periodic table contains much information about the elements, including their _____, names, and information about the structure of their atoms.

6. Elements can be sorted into groups with similar properties based on their _____.

6.3 Periodic Trends

7. Atomic size increases from top to bottom within a(n) _____ and from left to right across a(n) _____ of the periodic table.

8. _____ with a positive or negative charge forms when electrons are transferred from one atom to another.

9. The first ionization energy of atoms tends to _____ from top to bottom within a group and _____ from left to right across a period.

10. When an atom loses one or more electrons to form an ion, the ion is _____ than the original atom; when an atom gains one or more electrons to form an ion, the ion is _____ than the original atom.

11. Trends in electronegativity follow the same pattern as trends in _____.

If You Have Trouble With...										
Question	1	2	3	4	5	6	7	8	9	10	11
See Page	160	161	162	164	167	170	174	176	177	179	181

Review Vocabulary

Match each of the following with its location on the periodic table, using letters a–i. Use each choice only once.

_____ **1.** alkali metals

_____ **2.** alkaline earth metals

_____ **3.** halogens

_____ **4.** inner transition metals

_____ **5.** metalloids

_____ **6.** metals

_____ **7.** noble gases

_____ **8.** nonmetals

_____ **9.** transition metals

Use the letters j–m to show periodic trends in the following properties. The arrows point in the direction the properties increase. Two letters should be in each blank.

_____ **10.** atomic radius

_____ **11.** electronegativity

_____ **12.** ionization energy

_____ **13.** size of anion

_____ **14.** size of cation

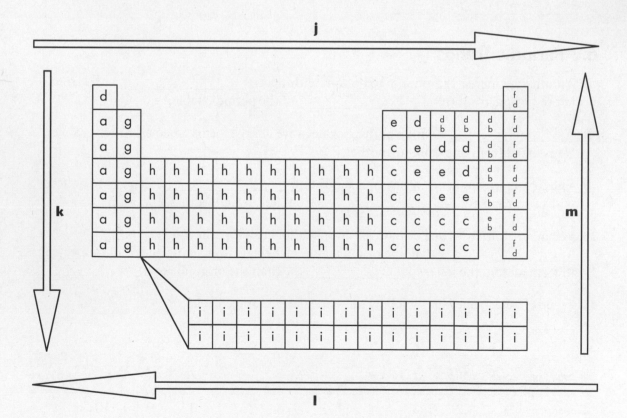

7 Ionic and Metallic Bonding

 BONDING AND INTERACTIONS

7.1 Ions

Essential Understanding Ions form when atoms gain or lose valence electrons, becoming electrically charged.

Lesson Summary

Valence Electrons Valence electrons are the electrons in the outermost occupied energy level and are involved in ion formation.

▶ For a representative element, the group number equals the number of valence electrons the atom contains.

▶ An electron dot structure shows the symbol of the element and its valence electrons.

▶ Atoms tend to gain or lose the number of electrons that will provide the atom with a noble gas electron configuration.

Formation of Cations Cations are positively charged ions formed when an atom loses one or more valence electrons.

▶ Atoms and the cations formed from them have different properties.

▶ Elements in Group 1A form cations with a charge of 1+, and those in Group 2A form cations with a charge of 2+.

▶ Many transition metals form more than one cation.

Formation of Anions Anions are negatively charged ions formed when an atom gains one or more valence electrons.

▶ Commonly, the name of an anion ends in -ide.

▶ Anions form from nonmetallic elements.

▶ The anions formed from halogens are known as halides.

After reading Lesson 7.1, answer the following questions.

Valence Electrons

1. What are valence electrons?

_____

_____

2. The valence electrons largely determine the _____ of an element and are usually the only electrons used in _____.

3. Is the following sentence true or false? The group number of a representative element in the periodic table is related to the number of valence electrons it has. _____

4. What is an electron dot structure?

_____

_____

5. Draw the electron dot structure for each of the following atoms.

   a. argon _____

   b. calcium _____

   c. iodine _____

6. What is the octet rule?

_____

_____

_____

7. Metallic atoms tend to _____ valence electrons to produce a positively charged ion. Most nonmetallic atoms achieve a complete octet by gaining or _____ electrons.

Formation of Cations

8. Write the electron configurations for these metals, and circle the electrons lost when each metal forms a cation.

   a. Mg _____

   b. Al _____

   c. K _____

Match the noble gas with its electron configuration.

_____ **9.** argon	**a.** $1s^2$
_____ **10.** helium	**b.** $1s^2 2s^2 2p^6$
_____ **11.** neon	**c.** $1s^2 2s^2 2p^6 3s^2 3p^6$
_____ **12.** krypton	**d.** $1s^2 2s^2 2p^6 3s^2 3p^6 3d^{10} 4s^2 4p^6$

13. What is the electron configuration called that has 18 electrons in the outer energy level and all of the orbitals filled?

_____

14. Write the electron configuration for zinc.

_____

15. Fill in the electron configuration diagram for the copper(I) ion.

Copper atom
Cu

Copper(I) ion
Cu⁺

Formation of Anions

16. Atoms of most nonmetallic elements achieve noble-gas electron configurations by gaining electrons to become _____ , or negatively charged ions.

17. What property of nonmetallic elements makes them more likely to gain electrons than lose electrons?

_____

18. Is the following sentence true or false? Elements of the halogen family lose one electron to become halide ions. _____

19. How many electrons will each element gain in forming an ion?

    a. nitrogen _____

    b. oxygen _____

    c. sulfur _____

    d. bromine _____

20. Write the symbol and electron configuration for each ion from Question 19, and name the noble gas with the same configuration.

    a. nitride _____

    b. oxide _____

    c. sulfide _____

    d. bromide _____

7.2 Ionic Bonds and Ionic Compounds

Essential Understanding Ionic compounds are the result of ionic bonds forming between oppositely charged ions.

Lesson Summary

Formation of Ionic Compounds An ionic compound is made up of anions and cations and has an overall charge of 0.

▶ The electrostatic attraction between an anion and a cation is an ionic bond.

▶ The representative unit of an ionic compound is its formula unit.

▶ A formula unit of an ionic compound shows the ions in the compound in their lowest, whole-number ratio.

Properties of Ionic Compounds Ionic compounds have characteristic properties that distinguish them from other substances.

▶ Most ionic compounds are crystalline solids at room temperature.

▶ In general, ionic compounds have high melting points because the ions have a strong attraction for one another.

▶ Ionic compounds conduct an electric current when melted or in an aqueous solution because the ions are then free to move.

After reading Lesson 7.2, answer the following questions.

Formation of Ionic Compounds

1. What is an ionic bond?

_____

_____

2. In an ionic compound, the charges of the _____ and _____ must balance to produce an electrically _____ substance.

3. Complete the electron dot structures below to show how beryllium fluoride (BeF_2) is formed. Use the diagram on page 203 as a model.

$$
\begin{array}{ccc}
& F & & & F \\
Be\ + & & \longrightarrow & Be \\
& F & & & F
\end{array}
$$

4. Why do beryllium and fluorine combine in a 1:2 ratio?

_____

_____

_____

5. A chemical formula shows the types and _____ of atoms in the smallest representative unit of a substance.

6. List the numbers and types of atoms represented by these chemical formulas.

a. Fe_2O_3 _____

b. $KMnO_4$ _____

c. CH_3 _____

d. NH_4NO_3 _____

7. What is a formula unit?

_____

8. Explain why the ratio of magnesium ions to chloride ions in $MgCl_2$ is 1:2.

_____

_____

9. Describe the structure of ionic compounds.

_____

_____

Properties of Ionic Compounds

10. Most ionic compounds are _____ at room temperature.

11. Is the following sentence true or false? Ionic compounds generally have low melting points. _____

12. What does a coordination number tell you?

_____

_____

13. What is the coordination number of the ions in a crystal of NaCl? _____

14. Circle the letter of each statement that is true about ionic compounds.

a. When dissolved in water, ionic compounds can conduct electricity.

b. When melted, ionic compounds do not conduct electricity.

c. Ionic compounds have very unstable structures.

d. Ionic compounds are electrically neutral.

7.3 Bonding in Metals

(Essential Understanding) The characteristic properties of metals depend on the mobility of valence electrons among metal atoms.

 Reading Strategy

Cause and Effect A cause and effect chart is a useful tool when you want to describe how, when, or why one event causes another. A cause is the reason something happens. The effect is what happens.

As you read Lesson 7.3, use the cause and effect chart below. Complete the chart to show how the mobility of electrons in a metal causes the properties of metals.

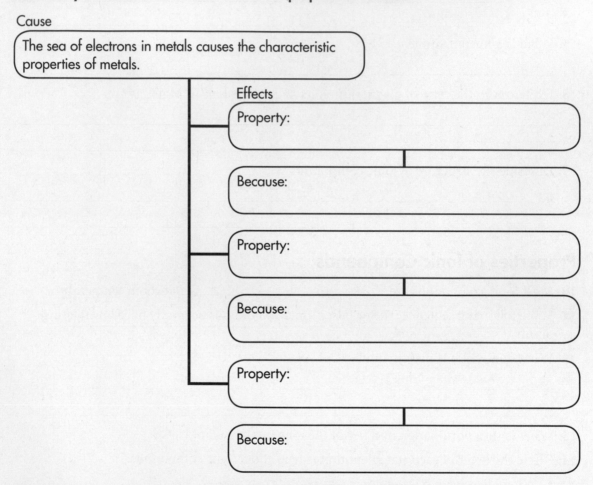

Cause

The sea of electrons in metals causes the characteristic properties of metals.

Effects

Property:

Because:

Property:

Because:

Property:

Because:

EXTENSION Draw a diagram that illustrates each effect in the chart.

Lesson Summary

Metallic Bonds and Metallic Properties The properties of metals are based on the attraction between stationary metal cations and the valence electrons that surround them.

▶ The valence electrons in metals surround metallic cations in what is called a sea of electrons.

▶ Properties of metals, such as conductivity, ductility, and malleability, are the result of these electrons being free to move from one part of the metal to another.

▶ Metal atoms are packed together tightly in crystalline structures.

Alloys Alloys are mixtures of elements, at least one of which is a metal.

▶ The composition of alloys can be varied to result in an alloy with desired properties.

▶ A widely used alloy is steel, which contains iron, carbon, and other metals.

▶ Alloys are either substitutional or interstitial, depending on how they form.

After reading Lesson 7.3, answer the following questions.

Metallic Bonds and Metallic Properties

1. Is the following sentence true or false? Metals are made up of cations and valence electrons, not neutral atoms. _____

2. What are metallic bonds?

   _____

   _____

   _____

3. Name three properties of metals that can be explained by metallic bonding.

   a. _____

   b. _____

   c. _____

4. What happens to an ionic crystal when a force is applied to it?

   _____

   _____

5. Metal atoms in crystals are arranged into very _____ and orderly patterns.

6. Label each of the following arrangements of atoms with the correct name.

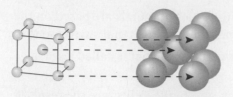

_____

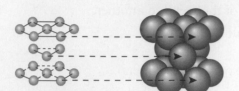

_____

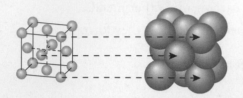

_____

7. Circle the letter of each metal whose atoms form a face-centered cubic pattern.

a. magnesium   **c.** sodium

b. copper   **d.** aluminum

Match the arrangement with the number of neighbors belonging to each atom in the arrangement.

_____ **8.** body-centered cubic   **a.** 12

_____ **9.** face-centered cubic   **b.** 8

_____ **10.** hexagonal close-packed

Alloys

11. A mixture of two or more elements, at least one of which is a metal, is called a(n) _____.

12. Is the following sentence true or false? Pure metals are usually harder and more durable than alloys. _____

13. The most common use of nonferrous alloys is in _____.

14. What four properties make steel an important alloy?

a. _____

b. _____

c. _____

d. _____

15. What are the component elements for the following alloys?

a. sterling silver _____

b. brass _____

c. stainless steel _____

d. cast iron _____

16. _____ alloys have smaller atoms that fit into the spaces between larger atoms. _____ alloys have component atoms that are roughly equal in size.

Guided Practice Problems

Answer the following questions about Practice Problem 10.

Use electron dot structures to determine formulas of the ionic compounds formed when

    a. potassium reacts with iodine.

    b. aluminum reacts with oxygen.

Potassium Reacts with Iodine

Analyze

Step 1. Is one of the elements a metal? If so, which one? _____

Step 2. Metal atoms _____ their valence electrons when forming ionic compounds. Nonmetal atoms _____ electrons when forming ionic compounds.

Solve

Step 3. Draw the electron dot structures for potassium and iodine.

potassium _____   iodine _____

Step 4. The metal atom, _____, must lose _____ electron(s) in order to achieve an octet in the next-lowest energy level. The nonmetal atom, _____, must gain _____ electron(s) in order to achieve a complete octet.

Step 5. Using electron dot structures, write an equation that shows the formation of the ionic compound from the two elements. Make sure that the electrons lost equals the electrons gained.

Step 6. The chemical formula for the ionic compound formed is _____.

Aluminum Reacts with Oxygen

Analyze

Step 1. Is one of the elements a metal? If so, which one? _____

Step 2. Metal atoms _____ valence electrons when forming ionic compounds. Nonmetal atoms _____ electrons when forming ionic compounds.

Solve

Step 3. Draw the electron dot structures for aluminum and oxygen.

aluminum _____   oxygen _____

Step 4. The metal atom, _____, must lose _____ electron(s) in order to achieve an octet in the next-lowest energy level. The nonmetal atom, _____, must gain _____ electron(s) in order to achieve a complete octet.

Step 5. Using electron dot structures, write an equation that shows the formation of the ionic compound from the two elements. Make sure that the electrons lost equals the electrons gained.

Step 6. The chemical formula for the ionic compound formed is _____.

Apply the Big idea

Sodium is a very reactive element. It can make compounds with elements from Groups 5A, 6A, and 7A. Draw electron dot diagrams of compounds made with sodium as the cation and elements from Groups 5A, 6A, and 7A as the anions. How do they differ?

_____

Name _____ Class _____ Date _____

7 Self-Check Activity

For Questions 1–9, complete each statement by writing the correct word or words. If you need help, you can go online.

7.1 Ions

1. The _____ of a representative element is also the number of valence electrons it has.

2. When an atom loses one or more valence electrons, it becomes a _____ charged ion, also known as a(n) _____.

3. When an atom gains one or more valence electrons, it becomes a _____ charged ion, also known as a(n) _____.

7.2 Ionic Bonds and Ionic Compounds

4. Ionic compounds are composed of positive and negative ions, but the compounds themselves are electrically _____.

5. At room temperature, most ionic compounds are _____.

6. In general, ionic compounds have _____ melting points.

7. Ionic compounds exhibit the property of electrical _____ when they are melted or in an aqueous solution.

7.3 Bonding in Metals

8. In a pure metal, the _____ can be modeled as a sea of electrons.

9. The properties of alloys are often _____ to the properties of the elements they contain.

If You Have Trouble With...								
Question	1	2	3	4	5	6	7	8	9
See Page	194	195	198	201	204	204	206	209	211

Review Vocabulary

Write the meaning of each vocabulary term below. Then invent a method that will help you remember the meaning of the terms. One has been done for you.

Vocabulary	Meaning	How I'm going to remember the meaning
formula unit	shows what anions and cations are in an ionic compound and the simplest ratio of these ions	formula unit - "for" showing ions and ratio simply, e.g., NaCl
ionic bond		
ionic compound		
metallic bond		
valence electron		
chemical formula		
electron dot formula		
halide ion		
coordination number		
alloy		
octet rule		

8 Covalent Bonding

BONDING, INTERACTIONS, AND NAMING COMPOUNDS

8.1 Molecular Compounds

Essential Understanding Ionic and molecular compounds can both be represented by formulas, but contain different types of bonding and representative units.

Reading Strategy

Frayer Model The Frayer Model is a vocabulary development tool. The center of the diagram shows the concept being defined, while the quadrants around the concept are used for providing the details. Use this model when you want to understand a vocabulary term in more detail.

As you read Lesson 8.1, use the Frayer Model below to better understand the word *molecule*.

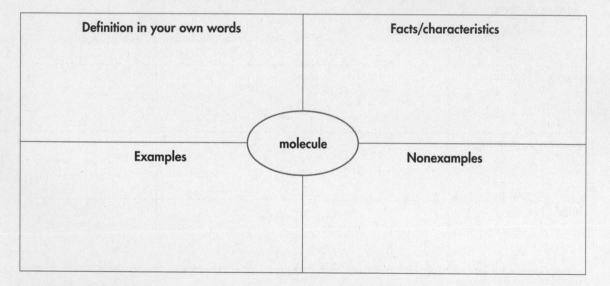

EXTENSION Create a Frayer Model for each of the terms *covalent bond, diatomic molecule, molecular compound*, and *molecular formula*.

Lesson Summary

Molecules and Molecular Compounds The electrons in a molecular compound are shared.

▶ The atoms in a molecular compound are held together by covalent bonds.

▶ Molecular compounds can be represented by molecular formulas, which tell how many of each type of atom are in the compound.

Types of Molecular Compounds	
Diatomic	**More than one element**
H_2, O_2, N_2, Cl_2	H_2O, NH_3, C_2H_6O

Comparing Molecular and Ionic Compounds Unlike ionic compounds, molecular compounds have no charge and are held together by covalent bonds.

▶ The formula for a molecular compound describes the combination of atoms that make up one molecule.

▶ The formula for an ionic compound describes a ratio of ions in the compound.

After reading lesson 8.1, answer the following questions.

Molecules and Molecular Compounds

1. What is a covalent bond?

_____

2. Many elements found in nature exist as _____.

3. What is a molecule?

_____

_____

4. Compounds that are formed when two or more atoms combine to form molecules are called _____.

5. Circle the letter of the substances that do NOT exist as molecules in nature.

    a. oxygen   **d.** ozone

    b. water   **e.** helium

    c. neon

6. List two general properties of molecular compounds.

    a. _____

    b. _____

7. What is a molecular formula?

_____

_____

Match each compound with its molecular formula.

_____ 8. carbon dioxide   **a.** C_2H_6O

_____ 9. ethanol   **b.** NH_3

_____ 10. ammonia   **c.** CO_2

11. Is the following sentence true or false? A molecular formula shows the arrangement of the atoms in a molecule. _____

In the diagram, match the type of model or formula with its representation.

    a. ball-and-stick drawing   **d.** space-filling molecular model

    b. molecular formula   **e.** structural formula

    c. perspective drawing

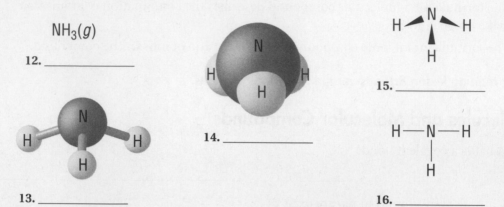

NH$_3$(g)

12. _____

13. _____

14. _____

15. _____

16. _____

17. What term describes the arrangement of atoms within a molecule?

_____

Comparing Molecular and Ionic Compounds

18. How do the formulas differ for molecular and ionic compounds?

_____

_____

_____

8.2 The Nature of Covalent Bonding

Essential Understanding Covalent bonds form when atoms share electrons.

Reading Strategy

Cluster Diagram Cluster diagrams help you know how concepts are related. Write the main idea or topic on a sheet of paper. Circle it. Draw lines branching off the main idea, connected to circles that contain concepts related to the main concept. Continue adding facts and details to the branches.

As you read Lesson 8.2, use the cluster diagram below to show how each section of the lesson relates to covalent bonding. Add circles if necessary.

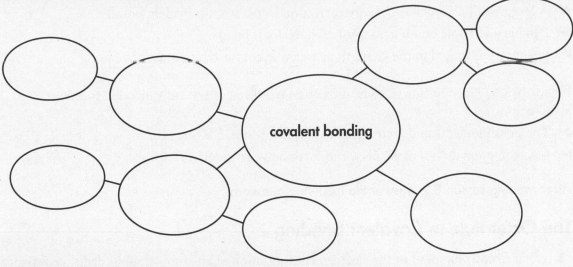

EXTENSION Draw a cluster diagram for each type of bond.

Lesson Summary

The Octet Rule in Covalent Bonding Covalent compounds are most stable when each atom has eight electrons.

► Single, double, and triple covalent bonds depend on the number of pairs of electrons shared between two atoms.

► Atoms form double or triple covalent bonds if they can attain a noble gas structure by doing so.

Type of Covalent Bond	Attributes
Single	**One** shared electron pair with **one** electron from each atom
Double	**Two** shared electron pairs with **two** electrons from each atom
Triple	**Three** shared electron pairs with **three** electrons from each atom

Coordinate Covalent Bonds In a coordinate covalent bond, one atom contributes both electrons in the bonding pair.

► One atom may contribute a pair of unshared electrons to a bond to give both atoms an inert gas configuration.

► Coordinate covalent bonds can also occur in polyatomic ions, such as NH_4^+.

Exceptions to the Octet Rule Some molecules have fewer, or more, than a complete octet of valence electrons.

► Molecules that have an odd number of total valence electrons cannot satisfy the octet rule.

► Some molecules that have an even number of valence electrons may also fail to follow the octet rule.

Bond Dissociation Energies The energy needed to break a covalent bond depends on the strength of the bond.

▶ A large bond dissociation energy corresponds to a strong covalent bond.

▶ Double and triple bonds are stronger than single bonds.

▶ Reactivity is linked to the strength or weakness of the covalent bonds.

Resonance The bonding in some molecules is a blend of several valid electron dot structures.

▶ The possible electron dot structures are called resonance forms.

▶ Electron pairs do not move back and forth between resonance forms.

After reading Lesson 8.2, answer the following questions.

The Octet Rule in Covalent Bonding

1. What usually happens to the electron configuration of an atom when it forms a covalent bond?

_____

2. Is the following sentence true or false? In a structural formula a shared pair of electrons is represented by two dashes. _____

3. Structural formulas show the arrangement of _____ in molecules.

4. Use the electron dot structure below. Circle each unshared pair of electrons in a water molecule.

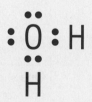

5. Complete the electron dot structure for each molecule. Each molecule contains only single covalent bonds.

H   H   H

N H   O O   H C H

H   H   H

a. NH₃   **b.** H₂O₂   **c.** CH₄

6. A chemical bond formed when atoms share two pairs of electrons is called a(n)

_____ .

7. How many covalent bonds are in a nitrogen molecule?

_____

8. Is the following sentence true or false? All diatomic molecules contain double bonds.

_____

Coordinate Covalent Bonds

9. What is a coordinate covalent bond?

_____

_____

10. Look at Table 8.2. Which nitrogen compounds contain coordinate covalent bonds?

_____

11. Complete the electron dot structure for the chlorate ion (ClO_3^-) by filling in the bonds and unpaired electrons.

$$
\left[\quad O \quad Cl-\ddot{\underset{\cdot\cdot}{O}}: \quad \right]^-
$$
$$
\qquad\qquad O
$$

Exceptions to the Octet Rule

12. Why does the NO_2 molecule not follow the octet rule?

_____

_____

Bond Dissociation Energies

13. What is bond dissociation energy?

_____

_____

14. Is the following sentence true or false? Molecules with high bond dissociation energies are relatively unreactive. _____

15. What is the bond dissociation energy for a typical C — C covalent bond?

_____

Resonance

16. The actual bonding in ozone is a _____ of the extremes represented by its _____.

17. When can resonance structures be written for a molecule?

_____

_____

8.3 Bonding Theories

Essential Understanding Scientists use a variety of theories and models to explain how and why covalent bonds form.

Lesson Summary

Molecular Orbitals One model of molecular bonding pictures a molecular orbital that is a combination of individual atomic orbitals.

▶ A bonding orbital can be occupied by a pair of electrons.

▶ In a sigma (σ) bond, the molecular orbital is symmetrical around the axis connecting two atomic nuclei.

▶ In a pi (π) bond, the orbitals are sausage-shaped regions above and below the bond axis.

VSEPR Theory The VSEPR theory explains the shape of molecules in three-dimensional space.

▶ The acronym VSEPR stands for valence-shell electron-pair repulsion theory.

▶ This model assumes that electron pairs repel each other as far as possible.

▶ Unshared pairs of electrons also affect the shape of the molecules.

Hybrid Orbitals Orbital hybridization describes how orbitals from different energy levels combine to make equivalent hybrid orbitals.

▶ Information about the kind and shape of the bonds is explained by hybridization.

▶ Hybrid orbitals can form with single, double, or triple covalent bonds.

After reading Lesson 8.3, answer the following questions.

Molecular Orbitals

1. What is a molecular orbital?

_____

_____

2. Is the following sentence true or false? Electrons first fill the antibonding molecular orbital to produce a stable covalent bond. _____

3. When two *s* atomic orbitals combine and form a molecular orbital, the bond that forms is called a(n) _____ bond.

4. Circle the letter of each type of covalent bond that can be formed when *p* atomic orbitals overlap.

    a. pi   **b.** beta   **c.** sigma   **d.** alpha

VSEPR Theory

5. What is VSEPR theory?

_____

_____

_____

6. When the central atom of a molecule has unshared electrons, the bond angles will be _____ than when all the central atom's electrons are shared.

7. What is the bond angle in carbon dioxide? Why?

_____

_____

8. What are the names of these common molecular shapes?

_____   _____   _____

   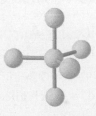

_____   _____   _____

Hybrid Orbitals

9. Is the following sentence true or false? Orbital hybridization theory can describe both the shape and bonding of molecules. _____

10. What is orbital hybridization?

_____

_____

Match the hybrid orbitals formed by carbon with the carbon compound in which they are found.

_____ **11.** sp^3 **a.** ethyne

_____ **12.** sp^2 **b.** ethene

_____ **13.** sp **c.** methane

8.4 Polar Bonds and Molecules

Essential Understanding A chemical bond's character is related to each atom's attraction for the electrons in the bond.

Lesson Summary

Bond Polarity In a polar covalent bond, the electrons are shared unequally.

▶ A difference in electronegativity causes a molecule to have a slightly positive and a slightly negative end.

Attractions Between Molecules Several different forces cause attraction between molecules.

▶ If polar bonds within a molecule cancel out, the molecule itself is nonpolar.

▶ Dipole interactions occur between polar molecules.

▶ Moving electrons cause weak attractions called dispersion forces.

▶ A hydrogen bond is a strong dipole interaction in which a hydrogen that is covalently bonded to a very electronegative atom is also weakly bonded to an unshared electron pair of another electronegative atom.

Intermolecular Attractions and Molecular Properties Varying intermolecular attractions cause a diversity of physical properties in covalent compounds.

▶ Molecular compounds have lower melting and boiling points than ionic compounds.

▶ A solid in which all atoms are covalently bonded is a very stable substance called a network solid.

BUILD Math Skills

Absolute Value The absolute value of an integer is its numerical value without regard to whether the sign is negative or positive.

The symbol for absolute value is to enclose the number between vertical bars such as $|-3| = 3$, and is read *"the absolute value of negative 3 is 3."*

On a number line the absolute value is the distance between the number and zero.

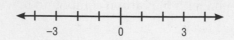

Both 3 and −3 are a *distance* of 3 units from 0. $|3| = |-3| = 3$. Distance, in mathematics, is never negative. This is why absolute value is never negative; absolute value only asks *how far?* not *in which direction?* This means not only that $|3| = 3$, because 3 is three units to the right of zero, but also that $|-3| = 3$, because −3 is three units to the left of zero.

Sample Problem Simplify $-|-3|$.

First, simplify $|-3|$.

$$-|-3| = -|3|$$

Hint: Remember that the absolute-value notation is bars, not parentheses or brackets. Use the proper notation; the other notations do *not* mean the same thing.

Now remove the absolute value bars.

$$-|-3| = -3$$

Sample Problem Simplify $|2 + 3(-4)|$.

Follow the order of operations. First, multiply 3×-4.

$$|2 + 3(-4)| = |2 - 12|$$

Now subtract.

$$|2 + 3(-4)| = |2 - 12| = |-10|$$

Finally, remove the absolute value bars.

$$|2 + 3(-4)| = |2 - 12| = |-10| = 10$$

Now it's your turn to practice simplifying absolute values. Remember to do the order of operations in the correct sequence.

1. Simplify $1 - |-1|$.

_____

2. Simplify $|0 - 6|$.

_____

3. Simplify $|8| + |-4|$.

_____

4. Simplify $-|(-2)^2|$.

_____

5. Simplify $\dfrac{-4}{|-4|}$.

_____

6. Simplify $-8 + |-7|$.

_____

After reading Lesson 8.4, answer the following questions.

Bond Polarity

7. Describe how electrons are shared in each type of bond. Write *equally* or *unequally*.

a. Nonpolar bond _____   **b.** Polar bond _____

8. Why does the chlorine atom in hydrogen chloride acquire a slightly negative charge?

_____

_____

9. What symbols are used to represent the charges on atoms in a polar covalent bond? The polarity of the bond? _____

Match the electronegativity difference range with the type of bond that will form.

_____ **10.** 0.0–0.4   **a.** ionic

_____ **11.** 0.4–1.0   **b.** nonpolar covalent

_____ **12.** 1.0–2.0   **c.** very polar covalent

_____ **13.** > 2.0   **d.** moderately polar covalent

14. Circle the letter of each sentence that is true about polar molecules.

a. Some regions of a polar molecule are slightly negative and some are slightly positive.

b. A molecule containing a polar bond is always polar.

c. A molecule that has two poles is called a dipolar molecule.

d. When polar molecules are placed in an electric field, they all line up with the same orientation in relation to the charged plates.

15. Are the following molecules polar or nonpolar?

a. H_2O _____

c. NH_3 _____

b. CO_2 _____

d. HCl _____

Attraction Between Molecules

16. What causes dispersion forces?

_____

17. Is the following sentence true or false? Dispersion forces generally increase in strength as the number of electrons in a molecule increases. _____

18. The strongest of the intermolecular forces are _____.

Intermolecular Attractions and Molecular Properties

19. What determines the physical properties of a compound?

_____

_____

20. Use Table 8.5 on page 245 to complete the following table.

Characteristic	Ionic Compound	Covalent Compound
Representative unit		
Physical state		
Melting point		
Solubility in water		

Review Vocabulary

Use the clues to find the vocabulary words hidden in the puzzle. Then circle the words. The terms may be appear horizonatally, vertically, or diagonally.

```
W  E  S  S  S  O  R  I  E  O  N  S  A  B  O  S  D  D  V  I  V  E
R  U  E  N  I  G  D  I  D  E  R  N  C  R  S  T  O  A  I  O  A  O
I  O  R  N  K  P  N  E  E  T  I  P  T  O  L  S  N  D  S  D  N  Y
E  L  U  C  E  L  O  M  C  I  M  O  T  A  I  D  L  E  N  N  C  I
I  R  T  S  C  S  B  M  M  L  A  T  D  E  E  C  B  O  S  Y  E  G
S  L  C  D  B  A  I  D  M  I  R  A  N  R  E  L  E  A  O  C  M  B
N  N  U  W  D  I  P  O  L  E  R  R  W  D  T  I  Y  S  O  E  R  D
M  T  R  D  P  I  O  K  O  M  M  A  C  O  W  L  R  N  O  E  O  D
S  O  T  Y  O  R  L  T  A  S  A  R  P  D  O  U  O  M  C  I  T  R
T  K  S  U  O  I  Y  O  L  L  I  Y  A  O  O  E  M  E  E  D  C  E
D  V  E  Y  U  C  A  R  S  O  S  R  C  A  D  B  S  B  M  R  P  T
E  C  C  V  E  R  T  F  O  K  O  N  S  I  U  T  M  B  C  O  A  D
N  D  N  R  L  Y  O  V  M  E  R  E  A  I  E  I  N  B  B  M  I  E
M  O  A  B  B  R  M  E  I  B  H  O  D  T  G  D  E  O  E  L  E  I
E  O  N  L  C  D  I  D  O  E  N  T  W  A  S  M  O  C  I  W  I  S
O  N  O  E  U  T  C  W  A  A  T  E  R  T  I  M  A  L  R  R  T  A
K  H  S  E  O  A  I  N  C  C  I  S  F  F  P  R  B  P  N  K  E
N  G  E  D  N  I  O  C  R  R  O  E  N  I  E  N  C  O  O  S  M  T
Y  G  R  E  N  E  N  O  I  T  A  I  C  O  S  S  I  D  D  N  O  B
N  N  L  O  O  S  M  W  N  E  O  C  R  U  O  A  V  D  E  L  D  F
```

Clues   Hidden Words

1. name given to a group of weak intermolecular attractions   _____

2. a substance with a high melting point in which all the   _____
   atoms are covalently bonded

3. two or more valid electron dot structures with the same   _____
   number of electron pairs for the same molecule or ion

4. a group of tightly bound atoms that act as a group with   _____
   either a positive or negative overall charge

5. F_2 and O_2 are examples   _____

6. the energy required to break the bond between two   _____
   covalently bonded atoms

7. electrons are found in dumbbell-shaped regions above and   _____
   below the axis of the bonding atoms

8. when electrons are found in an orbital that is symmetrical _____
   around the axis of the bonded atoms

9. a molecule that has two poles   _____

Name _____ Class _____ Date _____

9 Chemical Names and Formulas

 • ELECTRONS AND THE STRUCTURE OF ATOMS
• BONDING AND INTERACTIONS

9.1 Naming Ions

Essential Understanding Ions are named by determining their charges and applying certain rules.

 Reading Strategy

Concept Map A concept map helps you organize concepts, using visual relationships and linking words. Mapping out these connections helps you think about how information fits together.

As you read Lesson 9.1, use the concept map below. Fill in this concept map to show how to identify and name different types of ions.

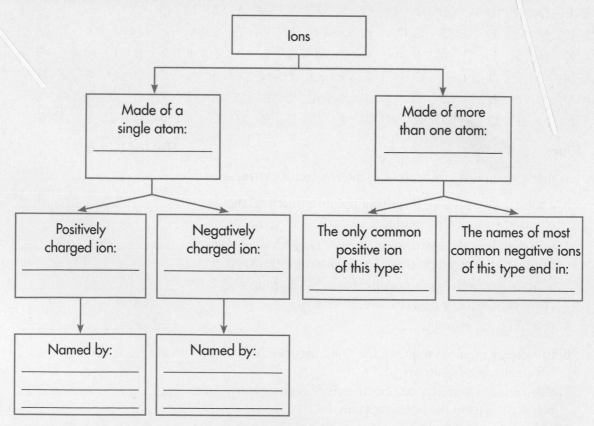

EXTENSION Extend the concept map by providing an example of each of the four types of ions.

Lesson Summary

Monatomic Ions A one-atom ion is called a monatomic ion.

▶ A monatomic ion's charge depends on its place in the periodic table.

▶ Atoms that lose electrons become positively charged ions, or cations.

▶ Atoms that gain electrons become negatively charged ions, or anions.

Polyatomic Ions Polyatomic ions contain more than one atom and behave as a unit.

▶ Negatively charged polyatomic ions are named using a root word and an *-ate* or *-ite* suffix.

After reading Lesson 9.1, answer the following questions.

Monatomic Ions

1. What are monatomic ions?

   _____

   _____

2. How is the ionic charge of a Group 1A, 2A, or 3A ion determined?

   _____

   _____

3. How is the ionic charge of a Group 5A, 6A, or 7A ion determined?

   _____

   _____

4. Circle the letter of the type of element that often has more than one common ionic charge.

   a. alkali metal

   b. alkaline earth metal

   c. transition metal

   d. nonmetal

5. The _____ of naming transition metal cations uses a Roman numeral in parentheses to indicate the numeric value of the ionic charge.

6. An older naming system uses the suffix *-ous* to name the cation with the _____ charge, and the suffix *-ic* to name the cation with the _____ charge.

7. What is a major advantage of the Stock system over the old naming system?

   _____

   _____

8. Use the periodic table to write the name and formula (including charge) for the ion formed from each element in the table below.

Element	Name	Formula
Fluorine		
Calcium		
Oxygen		

Polyatomic Ions

9. What is a polyatomic ion?

_____

_____

10. Is the following sentence true or false? The names of polyatomic anions always end in *-ide.* _____

11. What is the difference between the sulfite and sulfate anions?

_____

12. Look at Table 9.3. Circle the letter of a polyatomic ion that is a cation.

   a. ammonium

   b. acetate

   c. oxalate

   d. phosphate

13. How many atoms make up the oxalate ion and what is its charge?

_____

_____

14. What three hydrogen-containing polyatomic anions are essential components of living systems?

   a. _____

   b. _____

   c. _____

15. Look at Figure 9.5. Identify each of the ions shown below.

 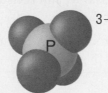 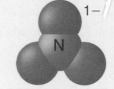

  a. _____   **b.** _____   **c.** _____

9.2 Naming and Writing Formulas for Ionic Compounds

Essential Understanding In writing names and formulas for ionic compounds, the cation is listed first, followed by the anion.

Lesson Summary

Binary Ionic Compounds Binary ionic compounds are composed of two elements, one with a positive charge and one with a negative charge.

▶ The chemical formula of a binary ionic compound includes the cation's symbol, followed by the anion's symbol, with subscripts that balance positive and negative charges.

Compounds With Polyatomic Ions Ionic compounds are named by joining the cation and anion names.

▶ To indicate more than one polyatomic ion in a chemical formula, place parentheses around the polyatomic ion and use a subscript.

▶ Roman numerals indicate the oxidation number of cations having multiple possible oxidation states.

After reading Lesson 9.2, answer the following questions.

Binary Ionic Compounds

1. Traditionally, common names were based on some _____ of a compound or its _____ .

2. What is the general name for compounds composed of two elements? They are _____ .

3. When writing the formula for any ionic compound, the charges of the ions must _____ .

4. What are two methods for writing a balanced formula?

   a. _____

   b. _____

5. What are the formulas for the compounds formed by the following pairs of ions?

   a. Fe^{2+}, Cl^- _____

   b. Cr^{3+}, O^{2-} _____

   c. Na^+, S^{2-} _____

6. What are the formulas for these compounds?

   a. lithium bromide _____

   b. cupric nitride _____

   c. magnesium chloride _____

7. The name of a binary ionic compound is written with the name of the
   _____ first, followed by the name of the _____.

8. How can you tell that cobalt(II) iodide is a binary ionic compound formed by a
   transition metal with more than one ionic charge?

   _____

   _____

9. Write the names for these binary ionic compounds.

   a. PbS _____

   b. $MgCl_2$ _____

   c. Al_2Se_3 _____

Compounds With Polyatomic Ions

10. What is a polyatomic ion?

    _____

    _____

11. How do you write the formula for a compound containing a polyatomic ion?

    _____

    _____

    _____

12. Why are parentheses used to write the formula $Al(OH)_3$?

    _____

    _____

13. Complete the table for these ionic compounds containing polyatomic ions.

Cation	Anion	Name	Formula
NH_4^+	S^{2-}		
Fe^{3+}		iron(III) carbonate	
	NO_3^-		$AgNO_3$
		potassium cyanide	KCN

9.3 Naming and Writing Formulas for Molecular Compounds

Essential Understanding Molecular compounds consist of nonmetal atoms, none of which is an ion, bonded together.

Lesson Summary

Binary Molecular Compounds Binary molecular compounds consist of two nonmetals.

▶ The prefixes in the name of a binary molecular compound show the number of atoms of each element in a molecule of the compound.

▶ The numbers related to the prefixes are used as subscripts when writing formulas of binary molecular compounds.

▶ When naming binary molecular compounds from their formulas, the subscripts in the formulas show what prefixes to use for each nonmetal in the compound.

After reading Lesson 9.3, answer the following questions.

Binary Molecular Compounds

1. Circle the letter of the type(s) of elements that form binary molecular compounds.

   a. two nonmetallic elements

   b. a metal and a nonmetal

   c. two metals

2. Is the following sentence true or false? Two nonmetallic elements can combine in only one way. _____

3. What method is used to distinguish between different molecular compounds that contain the same elements? _____

Match the prefix with the number it indicates.

_____ 4. *octa-*   **a.** 4

_____ 5. *tetra-*   **b.** 7

_____ 6. *hepta-*   **c.** 8

_____ 7. *nona-*   **d.** 9

8. What are the names of the following compounds?

   a. BF_3 _____

   b. N_2O_4 _____

   c. P_4S_7 _____

9. What are the formulas for the following compounds?

   a. carbon tetrabromide _____

   b. nitrogen triiodide _____

   c. iodine monochloride _____

   d. tetraiodine nonaoxide _____

9.4 Naming and Writing Formulas for Acids and Bases

Essential Understanding Acids and bases are ionic compounds. Their names and formulas reflect the number of hydrogen ions or hydroxide ions they contain.

Lesson Summary

Names and Formulas of Acids Names and formulas of acids are based on an acid's consisting of an anion and enough hydrogen ions to make the acid electrically neutral.

▶ The general formula for an acid is H_nX, where X is an anion, H is a hydrogen ion, and n is the number of hydrogen ions needed to make the acid neutral.

▶ Binary acids are named by using the prefix *hydro-*, the root name of the anion, and the suffix *-ic*, plus the word *acid*.

▶ Acids containing polyatomic ions are named according to the name of the anion.

Names and Formulas of Bases Bases are named like other ionic compounds.

▶ The name of a base is the name of the cation followed by the name of the anion (hydroxide).

▶ The formula of a base is written by showing the number of hydroxide ions needed to balance the positive charge on the cation.

After reading Lesson 9.4, answer the following questions.

Names and Formulas of Acids

1. Acids produce _____ ions when dissolved in water.

2. When naming acids, you can consider them to be combinations of _____ connected to as many _____ ions as are necessary to create an electrically neutral compound.

3. What is the formula for hydrobromic acid? _____

4. What are the components of phosphorous acid? What is its formula?

_____

5. Use Table 9.5 to help you complete the table about acids.

Acid Name	Formula	Anion Name
acetic acid		
carbonic acid		
hydrochloric acid		
nitric acid		
phosphoric acid		
sulfuric acid		

Names and Formulas of Bases

6. A base is a compound that produces _____ when dissolved in water.

7. How are bases named?

_____

9.5 The Laws Governing How Compounds Form

(Essential Understanding) Rules for naming and writing compound formulas are possible because laws govern how compounds are formed.

Lesson Summary

The Laws of Definite and Multiple Proportions The laws of definite and multiple proportions describe the ratios in which elements combine to form compounds.

▶ The law of definite proportions states that in any sample of a compound, the masses of the elements in the compound are always in the same proportion.

▶ The law of multiple proportions applies when the same two elements form more than one compound.

▶ When two elements form more than one compound, the law of multiple proportions says that the masses of one element combine with the same mass of the other element in simple, whole-number ratios.

Practicing Skills: Chemical Names and Formulas To name or write the formula of a compound, you must first decide what type of compound it is.

▶ Types of compounds include acids, binary compounds, compounds with polyatomic ions, and compounds containing metallic cations with different ionic charges.

BUILD Math Skills

Finding a Mass Ratio A mass ratio is a way of showing a proportion of two different masses or compounds. It tells you how much you have of one substance for every gram—or other measurement—you have of another substance.

If you had twice as much mass of compound A than you had of compound B, the ratio would be written as 2:1; which is read as "two to one."

Typically in mass ratio problems, the amount of the element you are trying to find will be based upon the amount of another element. For example, for compound A, you may have 3.28 g of C for every 2.62 g of O; and for compound B, you may have 6.32 g of C for every 1.68 g of O.

So, if you were trying to find the ratio of carbon, you would need to find how much carbon exists for 1 g of oxygen for both compounds. You would do this by simply dividing the grams of carbon by the grams of oxygen.

To find a mass ratio, follow a few simple steps:

▶ Write down the known masses of both elements in both compounds.

▶ Identify the element for which you are trying to find the ratio.

▶ Divide the element for which you're finding the mass ratio by the other known element to get both compounds in equal proportions.

▶ To compare compound A to compound B, divide the mass of A by the mass of B. To compare compound B to compound A, divide B by A to obtain the mass ratio.

▶ If the nearest whole number is requested for the ratio, the answer will need to be rounded to the nearest whole number.

Sample Problem Carbon reacts with oxygen to create two compounds. Compound A contains 4.78 g of carbon for each 5.24 g of oxygen. Compound B contains 3.63 g of carbon for each 12.6 g of oxygen. What is the mass ratio of carbon rounded to the nearest whole number?

Write down the known masses of each element for both compounds.	→	Compound A: 4.78 g C, 5.24 g O Compound B: 3.63 g C, 12.6 g O
Identify the element for which you are trying to find the ratio.	→	The question asks for the "mass ratio of carbon" so *carbon* is the element we want to compare.

Next, get the two compounds in equal proportions by dividing the element for which you are trying to find the ratio—in this case, carbon—by the other element present, oxygen.

Compound A: $\dfrac{4.78\ g\ C}{5.24\ g\ O} = \dfrac{0.912\ g\ C}{1.00\ g\ O}$

Compound B: $\dfrac{3.63\ g\ C}{12.6\ g\ O} = \dfrac{0.288\ g\ C}{1.00\ g\ O}$

Both compounds are now in g C/1.00 g O, so they are in equal proportions.

Now divide the equal proportioned amounts to get the ratio of carbon. Since it is not specified if you want to compare A to B or B to A, either proportion can be used.

Mass ratio of carbon $= \dfrac{\text{Compound A}}{\text{Compound B}}$

$= \dfrac{0.912\ g\ C\ (\text{compound A})}{0.288\ g\ C\ (\text{compound B})} = \dfrac{3.166}{1}$

Finally, round the answer to the nearest whole number.

Since .166 is less than .5 the answer rounds down to 3.00, so the mass ratio is $\dfrac{3}{1}$ or 3:1.

Hint: Remember when rounding to the nearest whole number anything equal to or greater than .5 rounds up to the next whole number, while anything less than .5 will round down.

Now it's your turn to practice finding mass ratios. Remember to get the two compounds in equal proportions before finding the mass ratio.

1. Magnesium reacts with oxygen to form two compounds. Compound A contains 7.88 g of magnesium for every 15.68 g of oxygen. Compound B contains 2.12 g of magnesium for every 6.91 g of oxygen. What is the mass ratio of magnesium rounded to the nearest whole number?

   _____

2. Chlorine reacts with oxygen to form two compounds. Compound A contains 8.43 g of chlorine for every 13.67 g of oxygen. Compound B contains 5.87 g of chlorine for every 17.33 g of oxygen. What is the mass ratio of chlorine rounded to the nearest whole number?

   _____

3. Lead forms two compounds when it reacts with oxygen. Compound A contains 8.45 g of lead for every 4.79 g of oxygen. Compound B contains 4.55 g of lead for every 0.77 g of oxygen. What is the mass ratio of oxygen rounded to the nearest whole number?

_____

4. Sulfur reacts with oxygen and creates two compounds. Compound A contains 1.34 g of sulfur for every 0.86 g of oxygen. Compound B contains 11.63 g of sulfur for every 10.49 g of oxygen. What is the mass ratio of oxygen rounded to the nearest whole number?

_____

After reading Lesson 9.5, answer the following questions.

The Laws of Definite and Multiple Proportions

5. What is the law of definite proportions?

_____

_____

_____

6. Circle the whole-number mass ratio of Li to Cl in LiCl. The atomic mass of Li is 6.9; the atomic mass of Cl is 35.5.

   a. 42:1

   b. 5:1

   c. 1:5

7. Circle the whole-number mass ratio of carbon to hydrogen in C_2H_4. The atomic mass of C is 12.0; the atomic mass of H is 1.0.

   a. 1:6

   b. 6:1

   c. 1:12

   d. 12:1

8. In the compound sulfur dioxide, a food preservative, the mass ratio of sulfur to oxygen is 1:1. An 80-g sample of a compound composed of sulfur and oxygen contains 48 g of oxygen. Is the sample sulfur dioxide? Explain.

_____

_____

9. What is the law of multiple proportions?

_____

_____

_____

10. Complete the table using the law of multiple proportions.

	Mass of Cu	Mass of Cl	Mass Ratio Cl:Cu	Whole-number Ratio of Cl
Compound A	8.3 g	4.6 g		
Compound B	3.3 g	3.6 g		

Practicing Skills: Chemical Names and Formulas

11. How can a flowchart help you to name chemical compounds?

_____

_____

12. Use the flowchart in Figure 9.18 to write the names of the following compounds:

    a. CsCl _____

    b. $SnSe_2$ _____

    c. NH_4OH _____

    d. HF _____

    e. Si_3N_4 _____

13. Complete the following five rules for writing a chemical formula from a chemical name.

    a. In an ionic compound, the net ionic charge is _____.

    b. An *-ide* ending generally indicates a(n) _____ compound.

    c. An *-ite* or *-ate* ending means that the formula contains a(n) _____ ion that includes oxygen.

    d. _____ in a name generally indicate that the compound is molecular and show the number of each kind of atom in the molecule.

    e. A(n) _____ after the name of a cation shows the ionic charge of the cation.

14. Fill in the missing labels from Figure 9.19.

Name of Compound

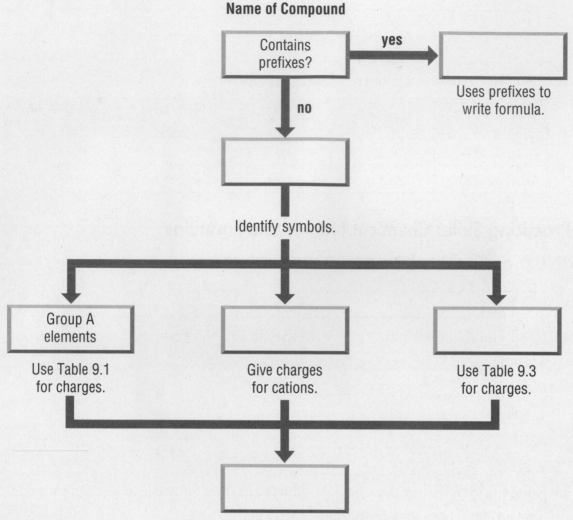

Use crisscross method. Add parentheses
for any multiple polyatomic ions.

15. Use the flowchart in Figure 9.19 to write the formulas of the following compounds:

    a. potassium silicate _____

    b. phosphorus pentachloride _____

    c. manganese(II) chromate _____

    d. lithium hydride _____

    e. diiodine pentoxide _____

Guided Practice Problems

Answer the following questions about Practice Problem 2.

How many electrons were lost or gained to form these ions?

    a. Fe^{3+} **b.** O^{2-} **c.** Cu^+ **d.** Sr^{2+}

Step 1. Determine the number of electrons based on the size of the charge.

Step 2. Determine whether the electrons were lost or gained based on the sign of the charge.

    a. _____

    b. _____

    c. _____

    d. _____

Answer the following questions about Practice Problems 10b and 10c.

Write formulas for compounds formed from these pairs of ions.

    b. Li^+, O^{2-} **c.** Ca^{2+}, N^{3-}

Li^+, O^{2-}

Analyze

Step 1. Do the ions combine in a 1:1 ratio?

_____

_____

Solve

Step 2. Use the crisscross method to balance the formula.
Write the formula. _____

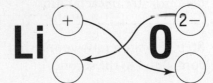

Ca^{2+}, N^{3-}

Analyze

Step 1. Will the calcium (Ca^{2+}) and nitride (N^{3-}) ions combine in a 1:1 ratio? How do you know?

_____

_____

Solve

Step 2. Use the crisscross method to balance the formula.
Write the formula. _____

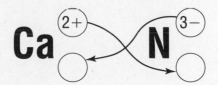

Answer the following questions about Practice Problem 15b.

Write the formula for chromium(III) nitrite.

Step 1. Is the compound ionic or molecular? Explain.

_____

_____

Step 2. Use Table 9.3 to write the formula for
the nitrite ion. _____

Step 3. Use the crisscross method to balance the formula.
Write the formula. _____

$$Cr^{3+} \quad (NO_2)^{-}$$

Answer the following questions about Practice Problem 48.

Lead forms two compounds with oxygen. One compound contains 2.98 g of lead and
0.461 g of oxygen. The other contains 9.89 g of lead and 0.763 g of oxygen. For a given mass
of oxygen, what is the lowest whole-number mass ratio of lead in the two compounds?

Complete the following steps to solve the problem.

	First compound	Second compound
Step 1. Write the ratio of lead to oxygen for each compound.	$\dfrac{\boxed{}\text{ g lead}}{0.461\text{ g oxygen}}$	$\dfrac{9.89\text{ g lead}}{\boxed{}\text{ g oxygen}}$
Step 2. Divide the numerator by the denominator in each ratio.	$\dfrac{6.46\boxed{}}{\boxed{}}$	$\dfrac{\boxed{}\text{ g lead}}{\text{g oxygen}}$
Step 3. Write a ratio comparing the first compound to the second.	$\dfrac{\boxed{}\text{ g lead/g oxygen}}{13.0\text{ g lead/g oxygen}}$	
Step 4. Simplify. Note that this ratio has no units.	$\dfrac{0.497}{1} = \text{roughly } \dfrac{1}{\boxed{}}$	

The mass ratio of lead per gram of oxygen in the two compounds is _____.

Apply the Big ideas

Copper and chlorine form copper(I) chloride, CuCl, and copper(II) chloride, $CuCl_2$.

a. How do these compounds relate to the number of electrons gained or lost by copper?

_____

_____

_____

_____

b. How does this information support the law of multiple proportions?

_____

_____

_____

_____

9 Self-Check Activity

For Questions 1–11, complete each statement by writing the correct word or words. If you need help, you can go online.

9.1 Naming Ions

1. When metals lose electrons, they form _____.

2. A(n) _____ ion contains more than one atom and acts as a unit.

9.2 Naming and Writing Formulas for Ionic Compounds

3. To write the formula for an ionic compound, write the formulas for the cation and the anion, then use subscripts to _____ charges.

4. To name an ionic compound, name the _____, then name the _____.

9.3 Naming and Writing Formulas for Molecular Compounds

5. To name a molecular compound, name the first element, add the root of the second element plus -ide, then add _____ given by the formula's subscripts.

6. To write the formula of a molecular compound, write the symbol of each element, then write _____ given by prefixes in the name of the compound.

9.4 Naming and Writing Formulas for Acids and Bases

7. Acids are named based on the _____ present in the compound.

8. Bases are named like other _____ compounds.

9.5 The Laws Governing How Compounds Form

9. If the ratio of the number of each type of atom is fixed, their _____ ratio is also fixed.

10. When naming a compound of a metal that can have more than one charge, use a(n) _____ to show the charge of the metal ion.

11. If the name of a compound ends in -ide, the compound is usually _____.

If You Have Trouble With...										
Question	1	2	3	4	5	6	7	8	9	10	11
See Page	264	268	272	274	281	282	286	287	289	292	293

Review Vocabulary

Fill in each of the blanks with a word or words that relate to each vocabulary term.

1. monatomic ion

A monatomic ion contains only one _____ and has either a positive
or a negative _____. It differs from a(n) _____
ion, which contains more than one atom. Ions with a positive charge are known as
_____, and those with a negative charge are _____.
The name of a positive monatomic ion is the _____. The name
of a negative monatomic ion is the _____
plus the suffix _____.

2. binary compound

A binary compound might contain many atoms, but it contains only _____
different types of atoms. The name of a binary _____ compound consists of
the names of the cation plus the name of the anion in the compound. _____
binary compounds are named by using _____ that show the number of each
type of atom in the compound.

3. acid

Acids contain _____ atoms and release _____ ions in
solution. They differ from bases, which release _____ ions in solution. Acids
are named according to the _____ present in the compound. The name of
a binary acid includes the prefix _____, the root of the name of the other
element present, the suffix _____, and the word _____.
Other acids are named according to the name of the _____ ion they contain.

4. law of definite proportions
5. law of multiple proportions

These two laws help show how elements combine to form compounds. The law of definite
proportions states that the _____ of elements in a specific compound are
always in the same _____. The law of multiple proportions is used when
_____ compound forms from two elements. It states that
the amount of one element that combines with a specific amount of the other element in the
compounds is in the ratio of _____.

Chemical Quantities

 THE MOLE AND QUANTIFYING MATTER

10.1 The Mole: A Measurement of Matter

Essential Understanding The mole represents a large number of very small particles.

Reading Strategy

Frayer Model The Frayer Model is a vocabulary development tool. The center of the diagram shows the concept being defined, while the quadrants around the concept are used for providing the details. Use this model when you want to understand a vocabulary term in more detail.

As you read Lesson 10.1, use the Frayer Model below. Complete the diagram for the term *mole*.

Definition in your own words	Facts/characteristics
How moles are used	**Examples**

EXTENSION Use the Frayer Model to complete a diagram for the term *molar mass.*

Definition in your own words	Facts/characteristics
How molar mass is used	Examples

Lesson Summary

Measuring Matter Matter can be measured in three ways: by count, by mass, by volume.

▶ Dimensional analysis is a tool for solving conversion problems.

What Is a Mole? A mole is Avogadro's number (6.02×10^{23}) of representative particles of something.

▶ A representative particle is the basic unit of the material, usually atoms, molecules, or formula units.

▶ The conversion factor *1 mol/6.02 × 10²³ representative particles* can be used to find the number of moles when the number of representative particles is known.

▶ The conversion factor *6.02 × 10²³ representative particles/1 mol* can be used to find the number of representative particles when the number of moles is known.

Molar Mass The molar mass of a substance is the mass in grams of a mole of that substance.

▶ For an element, molar mass is the atomic mass in grams.

▶ For a compound, molar mass is the sum of the atomic masses of each atom in a representative particle of the compound, in grams.

After reading Lesson 10.1, answer the following questions.

Measuring Matter

1. What do the questions "how much?" and "how many?" have in common?

_____

_____

2. List two or three ways to measure matter.

_____

What Is a Mole?

3. Circle the letter of the term that is an SI unit for measuring the amount of a substance.

    a. dozen   **b.** ounce   **c.** pair   **d.** mole

4. What is Avogadro's number?

_____

5. Circle the letter of the term that is NOT a representative particle of a substance.

    a. molecule   **b.** atom   **c.** grain   **d.** formula unit

6. List the representative particle for each of the following types of substances.

    a. molecular compounds   _____

    b. ionic compounds   _____

    c. elements   _____

7. Is the following sentence true or false? To determine the number of representative particles in a compound, you count the molecules by viewing them under a microscope.

_____

8. How can you determine the number of atoms in a mole of a molecular compound?

_____

_____

9. Complete the table about representative particles and moles.

Representative Particles and Moles			
	Representative Particle	Chemical Formula	Representative Particles in 1.00 mol
Atomic oxygen		O	
Oxygen gas	molecule		
Sodium ion			
Sodium chloride			

Molar Mass

10. What is the atomic mass of an element?

_____

11. Circle the letter of the phrase that completes this sentence correctly.

The atomic masses of all elements

a. are the same.

b. are based on the mass of the carbon isotope C-12.

c. are based on the mass of a hydrogen atom.

12. How do you determine the mass of a mole of a compound?

_____

_____

_____

13. Complete the labels on the diagram below.

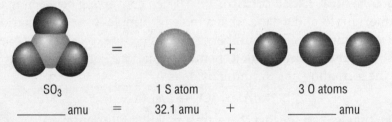

SO_3 1 S atom   3 O atoms

_____ amu   =   32.1 amu   +   _____ amu

14. What is the molar mass of a compound?

_____

15. Is the following sentence true or false? Molar masses can be calculated directly from atomic masses expressed in grams. _____

10.2 Mole-Mass and Mole-Volume Relationships

Essential Understanding A mole always contains the same number of particles. But moles of different substances have different masses.

Lesson Summary

The Mole-Mass Relationship The molar mass of a substance can be used to convert between a sample's mass and the number of moles it contains.

▶ When a sample's mass is known, find the number of moles by multiplying the mass by the conversion factor *1 mol/molar mass.*

▶ When the number of moles is known, find the sample's mass by multiplying the number of moles by the conversion factor *molar mass/1 mol.*

The Mole-Volume Relationship Mole-volume relationships are based on Avogadro's hypothesis, which says that equal volumes of gases at the same temperature and pressure contain equal numbers of particles.

▶ The volume of a gas is usually given at a standard temperature, 0°C, and a standard pressure, 1 atm or 101.3 kPa.

▶ At standard temperature and pressure (STP), a mole of gas occupies a volume of 22.4 liters.

▶ The quantities *1 mol* and *22.4 L* can be used in conversion factors that change moles to volume and volume to moles at STP.

▶ The molar mass of a gas can be found by multiplying its density at STP (in units of g/L) by *22.4 L/1 mol*.

BUILD Math Skills

Converting Between Mass and Moles When converting between mass and moles it is important to understand what a mole is. A mole is a representation of how many particles a sample has. The number of moles can be expressed as a coefficient in front of the compound or element in a chemical equation. For example, the chemical equation for the formation of aluminum oxide is:

$$4Al + 3O_2 \rightarrow 2Al_2O_3$$

From this equation we can see that there are 4 moles of aluminum, 3 moles of oxygen, and 2 moles of aluminum oxide.

The mass of a mole of a compound is equal to the total mass of all the elements of the compound. Each element has an atomic mass that can be found in the periodic table. For example, the mass of one mole of NO_2 would be equal to the atomic mass of nitrogen plus twice the atomic mass of oxygen, or 46.01 g.

The conversion factor can be written as $1 \text{ mole } \dfrac{NO_2}{46.01 \text{ g}}$. Remember, you multiply whatever you start with by any number on top, and you divide by any number on the bottom.

To convert from moles to mass or mass to moles, follow these simple steps:

▶ Determine the number of moles or grams in the given substance.

▶ Total the atomic masses for all the elements of any compound.

▶ Use the conversion process to get to the desired units.

Sample Problem Determine how many kilograms of water result from the following reaction, $2H_2 + O_2 \rightarrow 2H_2O$

| Use the chemical equation to determine how many moles of water are present. | The coefficient in front of H_2O is 2, so 2 moles of water are present. |

| Total the mass for all elements that make up one mole of water. | Mass of H: 1.01 g
Mass of O: 16 g
Total Mass: $(1.01 \times 2) + 16 = 18.02$ g |

| Determine how many grams are present in 2 moles of water. | $2 \text{ moles of } H_2O \times \dfrac{18.02 \text{ g}}{1 \text{ mole}} \text{ of } H_2O$
$= 36.04$ g |

| Convert 36.04 g of water to kilograms using the conversion method. | $36.04 \text{ g } H_2O \times \dfrac{1 \text{ kg}}{1000 \text{ g}}$
$= 0.03604$ kg of H_2O |

Hint: Remember that the atomic masses for the elements are given in grams, but the problem may require an answer in kilograms (kg) or other units. There are 1000 grams in 1 kilogram.

Now it's your turn to practice converting from moles to mass and mass to moles. Remember to multiply by numbers on the top and divide by numbers on the bottom of the conversion factor.

1. Determine how many moles are present in 0.23 kg of SO_2.

_____

2. How many grams of sodium chloride, NaCl, result from the reaction shown in the following equation, $FeCl_3 + 3NaOH \rightarrow Fe(OH)_3 + 3NaCl$?

_____

3. Determine how many moles are present in 523.46 g of glucose, $C_6H_{12}O_6$.

_____

4. How many kilograms are in 4 moles of Na_2CO_3?

_____

After reading Lesson 10.2, answer the following questions.

The Mole-Mass Relationship

5. What is the molar mass of a substance?

_____

6. What is the molar mass of KI (potassium iodide)?

_____

The Mole-Volume Relationship

7. Is the following sentence true or false? The volumes of one mole of different solid and liquid substances are the same. _____

8. Circle the letter of each term that can complete this sentence correctly. The volume of a gas varies with a change in

   a. temperature.   **c.** pressure.

   b. the size of the container.   **d.** the amount of light in the container.

9. Circle the letter of the temperature that is defined as standard temperature.

   a. 0 K   **c.** 0°C

   b. 100 K   **d.** 100°C

10. Is the following sentence true or false? Standard pressure is 101.3 kPa, or 1 atmosphere (atm). _____

11. What is the molar volume of a gas at standard temperature and pressure (STP)?

_____

12. What units do you normally use to describe the density of a gas?

_____

13. What is Avogadro's hypothesis?

_____

_____

14. Look at Figure 10.7 to help you answer this question. Why is Avogadro's hypothesis reasonable?

_____

_____

_____

15. How many gas particles occupy a volume of 22.4 L at standard temperature and pressure?

_____

16. The figure below shows how to convert from one unit to another unit. Write the missing conversion factors below.

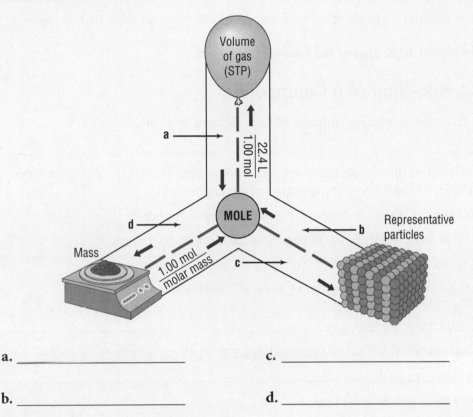

a. _____   c. _____

b. _____   d. _____

10.3 Percent Composition and Chemical Formulas

Essential Understanding   A molecular formula of a compound is a whole-number multiple of its empirical formula.

Lesson Summary

Percent Composition of a Compound Percent composition is the percent by mass of each element in a compound.

▶ To find the percent by mass of an element in a compound, use the formula:

$$\% \text{ mass of element} = \frac{\text{mass of element}}{\text{mass of compound}} \times 100\%$$

▶ To find the mass of an element in a sample of a compound, use the formula:

$$\% \text{ mass} = \frac{\text{mass of element in 1 mol compound}}{\text{molar mass of compound}} \times 100\%$$

Empirical Formulas The empirical formula of a compound is the formula with the smallest whole-number mole ratio of the elements.

▶ An empirical formula may or may not be the same as the actual molecular formula.

Molecular Formulas A molecular formula specifies the actual number of atoms in each element in one molecule or formula unit of the substance.

▶ To find a molecular formula, the molar mass of the compound must be determined.

After reading Lesson 10.3, answer the following questions.

Percent Composition of a Compound

1. How do you express relative amounts of each element in a compound?

_____

2. Circle the letter of the phrase that completes this sentence correctly. The number of percent values in the percent composition of a compound is

   a. half as many as there are different elements in the compound.

   b. as many as there are different elements in the compound.

   c. twice as many as there are different elements in the compound.

3. What is the formula for the percent by mass of an element in a compound?

_____

4. In the diagram below, which compound has a greater percent composition of chromium?

_____

How many more percentage points is this? _____

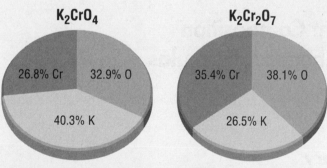

Potassium chromate, K_2CrO_4 Potassium dichromate, $K_2Cr_2O_7$

5. To calculate the percent composition of a known compound, start with the chemical formula of the compound and calculate the _____, which gives the mass of one mole of the compound.

6. Is the following sentence true or false? You can use percent composition to calculate the number of grams of an element in a given amount of a compound.

_____

7. How do you calculate the grams of an element in a specific amount of a compound?

_____

_____

Empirical Formulas

8. An empirical formula of a compound gives the _____ whole-number ratio of the atoms of the elements in a compound.

9. Is the following sentence true or false? The empirical formula of a compound is always the same as the molecular formula. _____

10. Look at Figure 10.11 and Table 10.3. Name three compounds that have an empirical formula of CH.

_____

11. Fill in the labels on the diagram below.

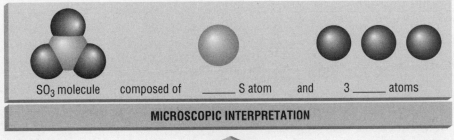

SO_3 molecule   composed of   _____ S atom   and   3 _____ atoms

MICROSCOPIC INTERPRETATION

SO3

MACROSCOPIC INTERPRETATION

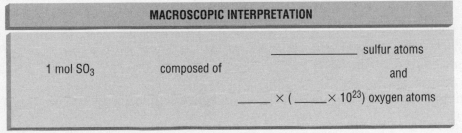

1 mol SO_3 composed of   _____ sulfur atoms

and

_____ × (_____ × 10^{23}) oxygen atoms

Molecular Formulas

12. The molecular formula of a compound is either the same as its empirical formula or a _____ of it.

13. What do you need to know to calculate the molecular formula of a compound?

_____

14. If you divide the molar mass of a compound by the empirical formula mass, what is the result?

_____

15. What factor would you use to convert the empirical formula of a compound to a molecular formula?

_____

Guided Practice Problems

Answer the following questions about Practice Problem 1.

If 0.20 bushel is 1 dozen apples and a dozen apples has a mass of 2.0 kg, what is the mass of 0.50 bushel of apples?

Analyze

Step 1. List the knowns and the unknown.

Knowns

_____

_____

_____

Unknown

_____

Use dimensional analysis to convert the number of bushels to the mass of apples, by following this sequence of conversions:

number of bushels → dozens of apples → mass of apples

Calculate

Step 2. Solve for the unknown.

The first conversion factor is _____.

The second conversion factor is _____.

Multiplying the number of bushels by these two conversion factors gives the answer in kilograms.

The mass of 0.50 bushel of apples is _____.

Evaluate

Step 3. Does the result make sense?

_____

_____

_____

Answer the following questions about Practice Problem 3.

How many moles is 2.80×10^{24} atoms of silicon?

Step 1. List what you know.

2.80×10^{24} atoms of Si

[_____] atoms in one mole

Step 2. Multiply the atoms of silicon by a mol/atoms conversion factor.

2.80×10^{24} atoms Si $\times \dfrac{1 \text{ mol}}{[\underline{}] \text{ atoms Si}}$

Step 3. Divide.

[_____] mol

Answer the following questions about Practice Problem 5.

How many atoms are in 1.14 mol of sulfur trioxide (SO_3)?

Analyze

Step 1. List the knowns and the unknown.

Knowns

_____

_____

_____

Unknown

_____

Calculate

Step 2. Solve for the unknown.

The first conversion factor is $\dfrac{6.02 \times 10^{23} \text{ molecules of SO}_3}{1 \text{ mol SO}_3}$.

The second conversion factor is $\dfrac{4 \text{ atoms}}{1 \text{ molecule SO}_3}$.

Multiply moles of SO_3 by these conversion factors:

number of atoms $= 1.14 \, \cancel{\text{mol SO}_3} \times \dfrac{6.02 \times 10^{23} \, \cancel{\text{molecules of SO}_3}}{1 \, \cancel{\text{mol SO}_3}} \times \dfrac{4 \text{ atoms}}{1 \, \cancel{\text{molecule SO}_3}}$.

$= \underline{}$

Evaluate

Step 3. Does the result make sense?

_____

_____

Answer the following questions about Practice Problem 7.

Find the molar mass of PCl_3.

Analyze

Step 1. List the knowns and the unknown.

Knowns	Unknown
_____	_____
_____	
_____	

Calculate

Step 2. Solve for the unknown.

Convert moles of phosphorus and chlorine to grams of phosphorus and chlorine. Then add to get the results.

$$1 \text{ mol P} \times \frac{31.0 \text{ g P}}{1 \text{ mol P}} = 31.0 \text{ g P}$$

$$3 \text{ mol Cl} \times \frac{35.5 \text{ g Cl}}{1 \text{ mol Cl}} = 106.5 \text{ g Cl}$$

molar mass of PCl_3 = _____

Evaluate

Step 3. Does the result make sense?

_____

_____

Answer the following questions about Practice Problem 16.

Find the mass, in grams, of 4.52×10^{-3} mol $C_{20}H_{42}$.

Analyze

Step 1. List the known and the unknown.

Known	Unknown
_____	_____

Calculate

Step 2. Solve for the unknown.

Determine the molar mass of $C_{20}H_{42}$:

$1 \text{ mol } C_{20}H_{42} = 20 \times 12.0 \text{ g} + 42 \times 1.0 \text{ g} = 282 \text{ g}$

Multiply the given number of moles by the conversion factor:

$$\text{mass} = 4.52 \times 10^{-3} \cancel{\text{mol } C_{20}H_{42}} \times \frac{282 \text{ g } C_{20}H_{42}}{1 \cancel{\text{mol } C_{20}H_{42}}} = \underline{\hspace{3cm}}$$

Evaluate

Step 3. Does the result make sense?

_____

_____

Answer the following questions about Practice Problem 18.

Find the number of moles in 3.70×10^{-1} g of boron.

Analyze

Step 1. List the known and the unknown.

Known	**Unknown**
_____	_____

The unknown number of moles is calculated by converting the known mass to the number of moles using a conversion factor of mass $\rightarrow$ moles.

Calculate

Step 2. Solve for the unknown.

Determine the molar mass of boron:

$1 \text{ mol } B = 10.8 \text{ g } B$

Multiply the given mass by the conversion factor relating mass of boron to moles of boron:

$$\text{mass} = 3.70 \times 10^{-1} \cancel{\text{g } B} \times \frac{1 \text{ mol } B}{10.8 \cancel{\text{g } B}} = \underline{\hspace{3cm}}$$

Evaluate

Step 3. Does the result make sense?

_____

_____

Answer the following questions about Practice Problems 20a and 20b.

What is the volume of these gases at STP?

a. 3.20×10^{-3} mol CO_2

b. 3.70 mol N_2

3.20×10^{-3} mol CO_2

Analyze

Step 1. List the knowns and the unknown.

Knowns   **Unknown**

_____   _____

_____

To convert moles to liters, use the relationship 1 mol CO_2 = 22.4 L CO_2 (at STP).

Calculate

Step 2. Solve for the unknown.

Multiply the given number of moles of CO_2 by the conversion factor:

volume = 3.20×10^{-3} ~~mol CO_2~~ $\times \dfrac{22.4 \text{ L } CO_2}{1 \text{ ~~mol CO_2~~}}$ = _____

Evaluate

Step 3. Does the result make sense?

_____

_____

3.70 mol N_2

Analyze

Step 1. List the knowns and the unknown.

Knowns   **Unknown**

_____   _____

_____

Use the relationship 1 mol N_2 = 22.4 L N_2 (at STP) to convert moles to liters.

Calculate

Step 2. Solve for the unknown.

Multiply the given number of moles of N_2 by the conversion factor:

$$\text{volume} = 3.70 \ \cancel{\text{mol } N_2} \times \frac{22.4 \text{ L } N_2}{1 \ \cancel{\text{mol } N_2}} = \rule{3cm}{0.4pt}$$

Evaluate

Step 3. Does the result make sense?

_____

_____

Answer the following questions about Practice Problem 22.

A gaseous compound composed of sulfur and oxygen has a density of 3.58 g/L at STP. What is the molar mass of this gas?

Analyze

Step 1. List the knowns and the unknown.

Knowns	Unknown

To convert density (g/L) to molar mass (g/mol), a conversion factor of L/mol is needed.

Calculate

Step 2. Solve for the unknown.

Multiply the density by the conversion factor relating liters and moles:

$$\text{molar mass} = \frac{3.58 \text{ g}}{1 \text{ L}} \times \frac{22.4 \text{ L}}{1 \text{ mol}} = \rule{3cm}{0.4pt}$$

Evaluate

Step 3. Does the result make sense?

_____

_____

Answer the following questions about Practice Problem 33.

A compound is formed when 9.03 g Mg combines completely with 3.48 g N. What is the percent composition of this compound?

Analyze

Step 1. List the knowns and the unknowns.

Knowns

_____

_____

_____

Unknowns

_____

_____

The percent of an element in a compound is the mass of the element in the compound divided by the mass of the compound. To be expressed as a percentage, the ratio must be multiplied by 100%.

Calculate

Step 2. Solve for the unknown.

$$\text{percent Mg} = \frac{9.03 \text{ g Mg}}{12.51 \text{ g compound}} \times 100\% = \underline{\hspace{3cm}}$$

$$\text{percent N} = \frac{3.48 \text{ g N}}{12.51 \text{ g compound}} \times 100\% = \underline{\hspace{3cm}}$$

Evaluate

Step 3. Does the result make sense?

_____

_____

Answer the following questions about Practice Problem 36.

Calculate the percent composition of these compounds.

a. ethane (C_2H_6)
b. sodium hydrogen sulfate ($NaHSO_4$)

Ethane (C_2H_6)

Analyze

Step 1. List the knowns and the unknowns.

Knowns

_____

_____

_____

Unknowns

_____

_____

Because no masses are given, the percent composition can be determined based on the molar mass of the substance. The percent of an element in a compound is the mass of the element in the compound divided by the mass of the compound. To express the ratio as a percent, the ratio is multiplied by 100%.

Calculate

Step 2. Solve for the unknown.

$$\text{percent C} = \frac{24.0 \text{ g C}}{30.0 \text{ g compound}} \times 100\% = \text{_____}$$

$$\text{percent H} = \frac{6.0 \text{ g H}}{30.0 \text{ g compound}} \times 100\% = \text{_____}$$

Evaluate

Step 3. Does the result make sense?

_____

_____

Sodium hydrogen sulfate (NaHSO$_4$)

Analyze

Step 1. List the knowns and the unknowns.

Knowns

_____

_____

_____

_____

_____

Unknowns

_____

_____

_____

_____

Because no masses are given, the percent composition can be determined based on the molar mass of the substance. The percent of an element in a compound is the mass of the element in the compound divided by the mass of the compound. To express the ratio as a percent, the ratio is multiplied by 100%.

Calculate

Step 2. Solve for the unknown.

$$\text{percent Na} = \frac{23.0 \text{ g Na}}{120.1 \text{ g compound}} \times 100\% = \underline{\hspace{3cm}}$$

$$\text{percent H} = \frac{1.0 \text{ g H}}{120.1 \text{ g compound}} \times 100\% = \underline{\hspace{3cm}}$$

$$\text{percent S} = \frac{32.1 \text{ g S}}{120.1 \text{ g compound}} \times 100\% = \underline{\hspace{3cm}}$$

$$\text{percent O} = \frac{64.0 \text{ g O}}{120.1 \text{ g compound}} \times 100\% = \underline{\hspace{3cm}}$$

Evaluate

Step 3. Does the result make sense?

_____

_____

Answer the following questions about Practice Problem 39.

Calculate the empirical formula of each compound.

a. 94.1% O, 5.9% H

b. 67.6% Hg, 10.8% S, 21.6% O

94.1% O, 5.9% H

Analyze

Step 1. List the knowns and the unknown.

Knowns   **Unknown**

_____   _____

_____

_____

Use the percent composition to convert to mass, recalling that *percent* means parts per hundred. Then use the molar mass to convert to number of moles. Finally, determine whole-number ratios based on the number of moles of each element per 100 grams of compound.

Calculate

Step 2. Solve for the unknown.

One hundred grams of compound has 5.9 g H and 94.1 g O.

Multiply by conversion factors relating moles of the elements to grams:

$$5.9 \text{ g H} \times \frac{1 \text{ mol H}}{1.0 \text{ g H}} = 5.9 \text{ mol H}$$

$$94.1 \text{ g O} \times \frac{1 \text{ mol O}}{16.0 \text{ g O}} = 5.88 \text{ mol O}$$

So, the mole ratio for 100 g of the compound is $H_{5.9}O_{5.9}$. But formulas must have whole number subscripts. Divide each molar quantity by the smaller number of moles. This will give 1 mol for the element with the smaller number of moles. In this case, the ratio is 1:1, so the empirical formula is simply H_1O_1. However, a subscript of 1 is never written, so the answer is _____.

Evaluate

Step 3. Does the result make sense?

_____

_____

67.6% Hg, 10.8% S, 21.6% O

Analyze

Step 1. List the knowns and the unknown.

Knowns

_____

_____

_____

_____

Unknown

_____

Use the percent composition to convert to mass. Then use molar mass to convert to number of moles. Finally, determine whole-number ratios based on the number of moles of each element per 100 grams of compound.

Calculate

Step 2. Solve for the unknown.

One hundred grams of compound has 67.6 g Hg, 10.8 g S, and 21.6 g O.

Multiply by a conversion factor relating moles to grams:

$$67.6 \text{ g Hg} \times \frac{1 \text{ mol Hg}}{200.6 \text{ g Hg}} = 0.337 \text{ mol Hg}$$

$$10.8 \text{ g S} \times \frac{1 \text{ mol S}}{32.1 \text{ g S}} = 0.336 \text{ mol S}$$

$$21.6 \text{ g O} \times \frac{1 \text{ mol O}}{16.0 \text{ g O}} = 1.35 \text{ mol O}$$

So, the mole ratio for 100 g of the compound is $Hg_{0.34}S_{0.34}O_{1.35}$.

Divide each molar quantity by the smaller number of moles:

$$\frac{0.34 \text{ mol Hg}}{0.34} = 1 \text{ mol Hg}$$

$$\frac{0.34 \text{ mol S}}{0.34} = 1 \text{ mol S}$$

$$\frac{1.35 \text{ mol O}}{1.35} = 4 \text{ mol O}$$

The empirical formula is _____ .

Evaluate

Step 3. Does the result make sense?

_____

_____

Answer the following questions about Practice Problem 42.

Find the molecular formula of ethylene glycol, which is used as antifreeze. The molar mass is 62.0 g/mol and the empirical formula is CH_3O.

Analyze

Step 1. List the knowns and the unknown.

Knowns   **Unknown**

_____   _____

_____

Calculate

Step 2. Solve for the unknown.

First, calculate the empirical formula mass (efm):

$$1 \text{ mol C} \times \frac{12 \text{ g C}}{1 \text{ mol C}} = 12 \text{ g C}$$

$$3 \text{ mol H} \times \frac{1.0 \text{ g H}}{1 \text{ mol H}} = 3 \text{ g H}$$

$$1 \text{ mol O} \times \frac{16 \text{ g O}}{1 \text{ mol O}} = 16 \text{ g O}$$

So, efm = 12 g + 3 g + 16 g = 31 g.

Divide the molar mass by the empirical formula mass:

Molar mass/efm = 62 g/31 g = 2

Multiply subscripts in the empirical formula by this value.

The molecular formula is _____.

Evaluate

Step 3. Does the result make sense?

_____

_____

Apply the Big idea

A student has a sample of CO_2 gas that has a mass of 22.0 g.

a. Explain how she would find the volume of the sample at STP.

_____

_____

_____

_____

b. What is the volume of 22.0 g of CO_2 at STP? Show your work.

_____

_____

10 Self-Check Activity

For Questions 1–9, complete each statement by writing the correct word or words. If you need help, you can go online.

10.1 The Mole: A Measurement of Matter

1. Knowing how the _____, mass, and volume of an item relate to a common unit allows you to convert among these units.

2. Counting the representative particles in a sample of a substance is based on the _____.

3. The molar mass of an element is its _____ expressed in units of grams.

4. The molar mass of a(n) _____ is the sum of the molar mass of all the elements in the _____ .

10.2 Mole-Mass and Mole-Volume Relationships

5. The _____ of a substance is used to convert from mass to moles or moles to mass.

6. The _____ of a gas is used to convert moles to volume or volume to moles at STP.

10.3 Percent Composition and Chemical Formulas

7. To find the percent by mass of an element in a compound, divide the mass of the element by the _____, then multiply by 100%.

8. The _____ of a compound gives the lowest whole-number ratio of the atoms or moles of the elements in a compound.

9. The _____ of a molecular compound is the same as, or a whole-number multiple of, the empirical formula of the compound.

If You Have Trouble With...								
Question	1	2	3	4	5	6	7	8	9
See Page	307	308	313	314	317	320	326	330	332

Review Key Equations

Sequence the following steps a student would use to find the percent composition of glucose, $C_6H_{12}O_6$.

    a. Divide the mass of each element by the molar mass.

    b. Find the mass of each element in one mole of glucose.

    c. Multiply each quotient by 100%.

    d. Find the molar mass of glucose.

_____

EXTENSION Use the sequence you wrote to find the percent composition of glucose.

Review Vocabulary

For each term in column 1, write the letter of the best match from column 2.

_____ **1.** mole

_____ **2.** Avogadro's number

_____ **3.** representative particle

_____ **4.** molar mass

_____ **5.** Avogadro's hypothesis

_____ **6.** standard temperature and pressure (STP)

_____ **7.** molar volume

_____ **8.** percent composition

_____ **9.** empirical formula

a. the mass of the Avogadro number of representative particles

b. 22.4 L

c. 6.02×10^{23}

d. relates volumes of gases with numbers of particles

e. atoms, molecules, or formula units

f. an SI unit used to measure amount

g. the lowest whole-number ratio of types of atoms in a compound

h. must equal 100

i. allows you to compare gases under the same physical conditions

11 Chemical Reactions

Big idea REACTIONS

11.1 Describing Chemical Reactions

Essential Understanding Chemical reactions are represented by balanced chemical equations.

Lesson Summary

Introduction to Chemical Equations A chemical equation uses symbols, and sometimes words, to show the reactants and products of a chemical reaction.

▶ A skeleton equation uses chemical formulas to represent reactants and products, but it does not indicate the relative amounts of each.

▶ Anything that enters into a reaction, such as heat or a catalyst, but is not a reactant or product is shown above or below the yields arrow in the equation.

Balancing Chemical Equations Chemical equations are balanced to show that mass is conserved during chemical reactions.

▶ A balanced equation shows the relative amounts of reactants and products, and it contains equal numbers of each type of atom on both sides of the equation.

▶ Chemical equations are balanced by using coefficients in front of the chemical formulas for the reactants and the products in a skeleton equation.

BUILD Math Skills

Balancing Equations All chemical equations must be balanced because of the law of conservation of mass, which states that matter cannot be created or destroyed. So, the number of atoms that you start with at the beginning of the reaction must equal the number of atoms that you end up with.

For example, the reaction $2Mg + O_2 \rightarrow 2MgO$ follows the law of conservation of mass because you start with 2 magnesium atoms and 2 oxygen atoms and you end up with 2 magnesium atoms and 2 oxygen atoms. You can think of the $\rightarrow$ as an = sign.

Turn the page to learn more about balancing equations.

When balancing an equation, there are a few rules to remember:

▶ The subscripts of the molecules can never be altered. Only coefficients can be added.

▶ The coefficient placed in front of a molecule applies to all elements that make up that molecule.

▶ The number of atoms can be found by multiplying the coefficient by the subscript of the element. If no subscript appears, a subscript of 1 should be assumed.

▶ Molecules made up of many elements should have coefficients added first, with single elements remaining until last.

▶ If a molecule is placed in a parentheses with a subscript outside the parentheses, the subscript applies to all elements within the parentheses. If an element within the parentheses has a subscript, then you will multiply the subscripts to get the number of atoms.

Sample Problem Balance this equation: $N_2 + H_2 \rightarrow NH_3$.

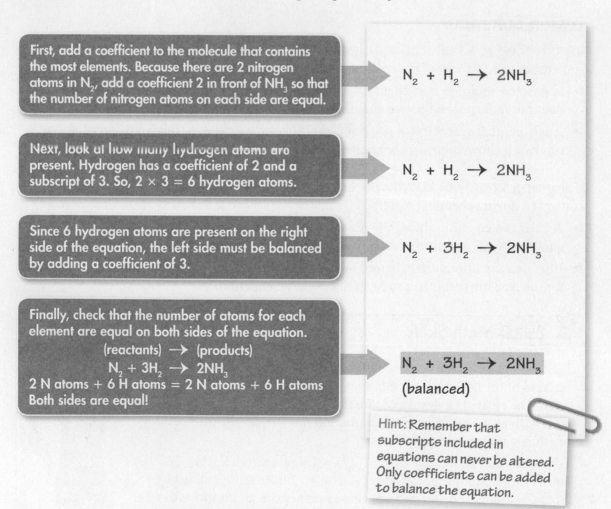

First, add a coefficient to the molecule that contains the most elements. Because there are 2 nitrogen atoms in N_2, add a coefficient 2 in front of NH_3 so that the number of nitrogen atoms on each side are equal.

$N_2 + H_2 \rightarrow 2NH_3$

Next, look at how many hydrogen atoms are present. Hydrogen has a coefficient of 2 and a subscript of 3. So, $2 \times 3 = 6$ hydrogen atoms.

$N_2 + H_2 \rightarrow 2NH_3$

Since 6 hydrogen atoms are present on the right side of the equation, the left side must be balanced by adding a coefficient of 3.

$N_2 + 3H_2 \rightarrow 2NH_3$

Finally, check that the number of atoms for each element are equal on both sides of the equation.

(reactants) $\rightarrow$ (products)
$N_2 + 3H_2 \rightarrow 2NH_3$
2 N atoms + 6 H atoms = 2 N atoms + 6 H atoms
Both sides are equal!

$N_2 + 3H_2 \rightarrow 2NH_3$
(balanced)

Hint: Remember that subscripts included in equations can never be altered. Only coefficients can be added to balance the equation.

Now it's your turn to practice balancing chemical equations. Remember that you will multiply the coefficients by the subscripts to get the total number of atoms.

1. Balance the equation for the reaction of benzene and hydrogen to form cyclohexane.

_____ C_6H_6 + _____ $H_2 \rightarrow C_6H_{12}$

2. Balance the equation for ethane, C_2H_6, burning in oxygen to form carbon dioxide and steam.

_____ C_2H_6 + _____ O_2 → _____ CO_2 + _____ H_2O

3. Balance this chemical equation.

_____ Fe_2O_3 + _____ H_2SO_4 → _____ $Fe_2(SO_4)_3$ + _____ H_2O

4. Balance the equation for aluminum burning in oxygen to form aluminum oxide.

_____ Al + _____ O_2 → _____ Al_2O_3

5. Balance the equation for ammonium carbonate so that it breaks down into gaseous ammonia, carbon dioxide, and steam.

_____ $(NH_4)_2CO_3$ → _____ NH_3 + _____ CO_2 + _____ H_2O

After reading Lesson 11.1, answer the following questions.

Introduction to Chemical Equations

6. A chemical reaction occurs when one or more _____ change into one or more new substances called _____.

7. The arrow in a reaction means _____.

8. Is the following sentence true or false? When there are two or more reactants or products, they are separated by an arrow. _____

9. Write a word equation that describes the following reactions.

   a. Acetylene reacts with oxygen to produce carbon dioxide and water.

   _____

   b. When heated, mercury(II) oxide chemically changes to form mercury and oxygen.

   _____

10. What is a chemical equation?

   _____

   _____

   _____

11. A chemical reaction that shows only the formulas but not the relative amounts of the reactants and products is a(n) _____.

12. Identify the reactant(s) and product(s) in the chemical equation $Li + Br_2$ → $LiBr$.

   a. reactant(s) _____   b. product(s) _____

13. Circle the letter of each statement that is true about a catalyst.

   a. A catalyst is the new material produced as a result of a chemical reaction.

   b. A catalyst is not used up in a chemical reaction.

   c. A catalyst adds heat to a chemical reaction.

   d. A catalyst speeds up a chemical reaction.

14. Use the symbols in Table 11.1 to write a skeleton equation for the following chemical reaction. Hydrochloric acid reacts with zinc to produce aqueous zinc(II) chloride and hydrogen gas.

_____

Balancing Chemical Equations

15. What is the law of conservation of mass?

_____

_____

16. Complete the flowchart for balancing equations.

> Determine the correct formulas and physical states for the _____ and
> _____.

↓

> Write a _____ with the formulas for the reactants on the left and
> the formulas for the products on the right of a yields sign (→).

↓

> Count the number of _____ of each element in the reactants and in
> the products.

↓

> Balance the number of atoms of the elements on the two sides of the equation by
> placing _____ in front of formulas. Never try to balance an equation
> by changing the _____ in formulas.

↓

> Check each atom or polyatomic ion to be sure the equation is _____,
> and make sure that all coefficients are in the _____ possible ratio.

17. Balance the following chemical equations.

a. _____ $Na(s)$ + _____ $H_2O(l)$ → _____ $NaOH(aq)$ + $H_2(g)$

b. _____ $AgNO_3(aq)$ + $Zn(s)$ → $Zn(NO_3)_2(aq)$ + _____ $Ag(s)$

11.2 Types of Chemical Reactions

Essential Understanding There are five types of chemical reactions: combination, combustion, decomposition, single-replacement, and double-replacement reactions.

Reading Strategy

Cluster Diagram Cluster diagrams help you show how concepts are related. To create a cluster diagram, write the main idea or topic in a center circle. Draw lines branching off the main idea, connected to circles that contain concepts related to the main concept. Continue adding facts and details to the branches.

As you read Lesson 11.2, use the cluster diagram below. Fill in each type of reaction, then add details to each.

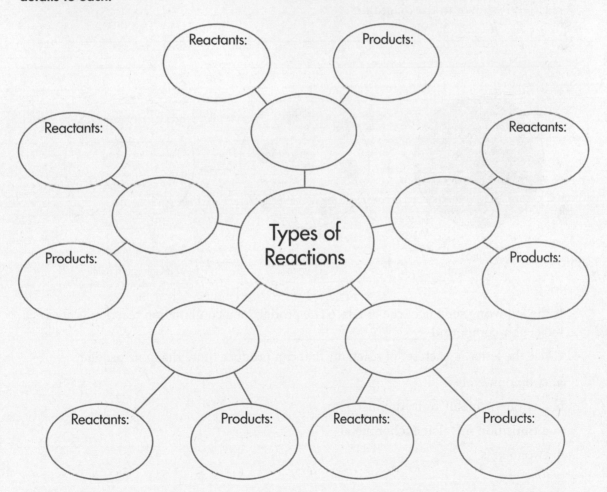

EXTENSION Write a balanced chemical equation for an example of each type of reaction.

_____

_____

_____

Lesson Summary

Classifying Reactions There are five general types of chemical reactions.

▶ A combination reaction occurs when a product is formed from two or more reactants, while a decomposition reaction involves breaking down a reactant into two or more simpler substances.

▶ In single and double-replacement reactions, elements or ions trade places in compounds.

▶ A compound or an element rapidly combines with oxygen in a combustion reaction.

After reading Lesson 11.2, answer the following questions.

Classifying Reactions

1. There are _____ general types of chemical reactions.

2. Complete the diagram of a combination reaction. Which characteristic of this type of reaction is shown in the diagram?

_____

_____

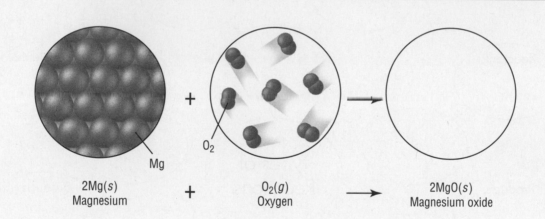

| 2Mg(s) | + | O₂(g) | → | 2MgO(s) |
| Magnesium | | Oxygen | | Magnesium oxide |

$2Mg(s) + O_2(g) \longrightarrow 2MgO(s)$

Magnesium   +   Oxygen   →   Magnesium oxide

3. Is the following sentence true or false? The product of a combination reaction is always a molecular compound. _____

4. Circle the letter of each set of reactants that can produce more than one product.

   a. two nonmetals

   b. a Group A metal and a nonmetal

   c. a transition metal and a nonmetal

   d. two metals

5. Look at Figure 11.5. Which characteristics of a decomposition reaction are shown in the diagram?

_____

_____

6. Rapid decomposition reactions can cause _____ as a result of the formation of gaseous products and heat.

7. Most decomposition reactions require the addition of _____ in the form of heat, light, or electricity.

8. Complete the diagram of a single-replacement reaction. Which characteristics of this type of reaction are shown in the diagram?

_____

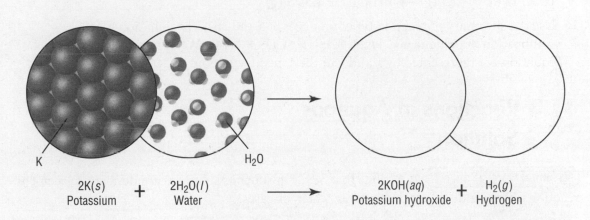

| 2K(s) | + | 2H₂O(l) | | 2KOH(aq) | + | H₂(g) |
| Potassium | | Water | | Potassium hydroxide | | Hydrogen |

$2K(s) + 2H_2O(l) \longrightarrow 2KOH(aq) + H_2(g)$

9. Using Table 11.2, state whether the following combinations will produce a reaction or no reaction.

a. Ag(s) + HCl(aq) _____

b. Cu(s) + AgNO₃(aq) _____

10. Look at Figure 11.7. Which characteristics of a double-replacement reaction are shown in the diagram?

_____

_____

11. When solutions of ionic compounds are mixed, what three circumstances might indicate that a double-replacement reaction has occurred?

a. _____

b. _____

c. _____

12. Look at the diagram of a combustion reaction in Figure 11.8. Which characteristics of this type of reaction are shown in the diagram?

_____

_____

13. Is the following sentence true or false? Hydrocarbons, compounds of hydrogen and carbon, are often the reactants in combustion reactions. _____

14. Circle the letter of each compound that can be produced by combustion reactions.

   a. oxygen

   b. carbon dioxide

   c. water

   d. glucose

15. Classify the reaction in each of the following equations.

   a. $BaCl_2(aq) + K_2CrO_4(aq) \rightarrow BaCrO_4(s) + 2KCl(aq)$ _____

   b. $Si(s) + 2Cl_2(g) \rightarrow SiCl_4(l)$ _____

   c. $2C_6H_6(l) + 15O_2(g) \rightarrow 6H_2O(l) + 12CO_2(g)$ _____

16. Use the summary of reaction types on pages 366 and 367. The equation for the combustion of pentane is $C_5H_{12} + 8O_2 \rightarrow 5CO_2 + 6H_2O$. What numbers in this equation are represented by x and y in the general equation? _____

11.3 Reactions in Aqueous Solution

Essential Understanding Reactions that occur in aqueous solutions are double-replacement reactions. The products are precipitates, water, or gases.

Lesson Summary

Net Ionic Equations Net ionic equations show what species present in solution actually are part of the chemical reaction.

▶ A complete ionic equation includes all ions present in solution, including spectator ions.

▶ A net ionic equation includes only the particles that participate in the reaction.

▶ The charges and atoms must be balanced in a net ionic equation.

Predicting the Formation of a Precipitate Solubility laws are used to predict the formation of a precipitate.

▶ A precipitate forms when one of the possible products of a double-replacement reaction is insoluble in water.

▶ In a net ionic equation for a double-replacement reaction with a precipitate, the ions that form the precipitate are the reactants and the precipitate is the product.

After reading Lesson 11.3, answer the following questions.

Net Ionic Equations

1. Many important chemical reactions take place in _____.

2. An equation that shows dissolved ionic compounds as their free ions is called a(n)
_____.

3. Is the following sentence true or false? A spectator ion is not directly involved in a
reaction. _____

4. What is a net ionic equation?

_____

_____

_____

5. Circle the letter of each sentence that is true about ionic equations.

a. A complete ionic equation shows only the ions involved in the reaction.

b. Spectator ions are left out of a net ionic equation.

c. Atoms do not need to be balanced in an ionic equation.

d. Ionic charges must be balanced in a net ionic equation.

6. Write the balanced net ionic equation for this reaction:
$Pb(NO_3)_2(aq) + KI(aq) \rightarrow PbI_2(s) + KNO_3(aq)$. Show your work.

_____

_____

_____

_____

Predicting the Formation of a Precipitate

7. What determines whether a precipitate forms when two solutions of ionic compounds
are mixed?

_____

8. Use Table 11.3 to predict whether the following compounds are soluble or insoluble.

a. $Fe(OH)_3$ _____

b. NaOH _____

c. $Ca(ClO_3)_2$ _____

d. $HgSO_4$ _____

Guided Practice Problems

Answer the following questions about Practice Problem 2.

Sulfur burns in oxygen to form sulfur dioxide. Write a skeleton equation for this chemical reaction.

Analyze

Step 1. Write the formula for each reactant and each product. Include the common STP state of each substance.

Reactants

_____

_____

Products

_____

Solve

Step 2. Write the skeleton equation using + between reactants on the left side and → to separate the reactants from the product.

_____

Answer the following questions about Practice Problem 3.

Balance the equation:

$$CO + Fe_2O_3 \rightarrow Fe + CO_2$$

Analyze

Step 1. Count the number of atoms of each element on both sides of the skeleton equation.

Left side:

_____

_____

_____

Right side:

_____

_____

_____

Solve

Step 2. Identify any necessary coefficient.

The product containing Fe needs a coefficient of 2. Two different reactants contain O. Looking at the equation, each CO takes an O from Fe_2O_3. There are 3 Os in Fe_2O_3, so CO needs a coefficient of 3. To balance C atoms, CO_2 needs a coefficient of 3.

Rewrite the equation with these coefficients and count again:

$$3CO + Fe_2O_3 \rightarrow 2Fe + 3CO_2$$

Left side: **Right side:**

_____   _____

_____   _____

_____   _____

Because the number of atoms of each element is the same on both sides, the equation is balanced.

Answer the following questions about Practice Problem 13.

Complete and balance this decomposition reaction:

$$HI \rightarrow$$

Analyze

Step 1. Identify the relevant concepts.

Remember that both hydrogen and iodine exist as diatomic molecules.

Solve

Step 2. Write the skeleton equation.

_____

Step 3. Balance the equation.

_____

Answer the following questions about Practice Problem 14.

Write and balance the equation for the formation of magnesium nitride (Mg_3N_2) from its elements.

Analyze

Step 1. Identify the relevant concepts.

Magnesium is a Group 2A metal, which means it will combine with nitrogen, a gas in Group 5A, in a 3:2 ratio. Nitrogen exists as diatomic molecules.

Solve

Step 2. Write the skeleton equation.

_____

Step 3. Balance the equation.

A coefficient of 3 is needed before the Mg reactant to balance the number of Mg atoms. N is balanced.

_____

Answer the following questions about Practice Problem 15a–c.

Complete the equations for these single-replacement reactions in aqueous solution. Balance each equation. Write "no reaction" if a reaction does not occur.

    a. $Fe(s) + Pb(NO_3)_2(aq) \rightarrow$

    b. $Cl_2(aq) + NaI(aq) \rightarrow$

    c. $Ca(s) + H_2O(l) \rightarrow$

$Fe(s) + Pb(NO_3)_2(aq) \rightarrow$

Analyze

Step 1. Identify the more active metal.

Table 11.2 shows that iron is more reactive than lead.

Solve

Step 2. Write a skeleton equation.

Fe replaces Pb.

_____

Step 3. Count to see if the equation is balanced.

Cl$_2$(aq) + NaI(aq) →

Analyze

Step 1. Identify relevant concepts.

Cl and I are Group 7A halogens, and Cl is more reactive than I. Recall that chlorine and iodine exist as diatomic molecules.

Solve

Step 2. Write a skeleton equation.

Cl replaces I.

$$Cl_2(aq) + NaI(aq) \rightarrow I_2(aq) + NaCl(aq)$$

Step 3. Balance the equation.

Ca(s) + H$_2$O(l) →

Analyze

Step 1. Identify relevant concepts.

According to Table 11.2, Ca is more reactive than H and can replace H in water. Ca has a 2+ charge and OH has a 1− charge. Also, hydrogen gas exists as a diatomic molecule.

Solve

Step 2. Write a skeleton equation.

The Ca replaces the H.

$$Ca(s) + 2H_2O(l) \rightarrow 2H_2(g) + Ca(OH)_2(aq)$$

Step 3. Balance the equation.

Answer the following questions about Practice Problem 16a and b.

Write the products of these double-replacement reactions. Balance each equation.

    a. $NaOH(aq) + Fe(NO_3)_3(aq) \rightarrow$ (Iron(III) hydroxide is a precipitate.)

    b. $Ba(NO_3)_2(aq) + H_3PO_4(aq) \rightarrow$ (Barium phosphate is a precipitate.)

$NaOH(aq) + Fe(NO_3)_3(aq) \rightarrow$

Analyze

Step 1. Write the formula for iron(III) hydroxide.

_____

Solve

Step 2. Write the skeleton equation.

$$NaOH(aq) + Fe(NO_3)_3(aq) \rightarrow Fe(OH)_3(s) + NaNO_3(aq)$$

Step 3. Balance the equation.

_____

$Ba(NO_3)_2(aq) + H_3PO_4(aq) \rightarrow$

Analyze

Step 1. Write the formula for barium phosphate.

_____

Solve

Step 2. Write the skeleton equation.

$$Ba(NO_3)_2(aq) + H_3PO_4(aq) \rightarrow Ba_3(PO_4)_2(s) + HNO_3(aq)$$

Step 3. Balance the equation.

_____

Answer the following questions about Practice Problem 19a.

Write a balanced equation for the complete combustion of glucose ($C_6H_{12}O_6$).

Analyze

Step 1. Identify the second reactant and the products.

Oxygen gas is the other reactant in a combustion reaction. The products are CO_2 and H_2O.

Step 2. Write a skeleton equation for this reaction.

_____

Solve

Step 3. Balance the equation.

_____

> **Apply the Big idea**

One way geologists identify rocks that contain the carbonate ion is to place acid on them. If the rock is a carbonate, then H_2O, bubbles of CO_2, and another compound form. Answer these questions for a reaction between HCl and $CaCO_3$, the main component of limestone.

1. This reaction is not a single reaction. Write a balanced chemical equation for each step of the reaction.

   a. the double-replacement reaction between HCl and $CaCO_3$

   _____

   b. the decomposition of one of the products of the previous reaction

   _____

2. Write a balanced equation that shows the initial reactants and the final products of the reaction.

   _____

11 Self-Check Activity

For Questions 1–12, complete each statement by writing the correct word or words. If you need help, you can go online.

11.1 Describing Chemical Reactions

1. To write a word equation, the _____ of the reactants are on the left side of the arrow, and those of the products are on the right side.

2. To write a skeleton equation, the _____ of the reactants are on the left side of the arrow, and those of the products are on the right side.

3. Use _____ to balance a skeleton equation so that it obeys the law of _____.

11.2 Types of Chemical Reactions

4. There are _____ general types of reactions.

5. The type of reaction is indicated by the number and type of _____ and products.

6. In a(n) _____ reaction, there are more than one reactant and a single product.

7. In a(n) _____ reaction, a compound breaks down into two or more products.

8. In a(n) _____ reaction, the reactants are a compound and an element, and the products are a different compound and element.

9. A(n) _____ reaction takes place between two compounds in aqueous solution.

10. Oxygen is always a reactant in a(n) _____ reaction.

11.3 Reactions in Aqueous Solution

11. A(n) _____ equation shows only the particles present that are involved in the reaction.

12. By examining solubility, you can predict whether a(n) _____ forms during a reaction.

If You Have Trouble With...											
Question	1	2	3	4	5	6	7	8	9	10	11	12
See Page	348	348	350	356	356	356	358	360	362	363	370	371

Review Vocabulary

Magnesium chloride and sodium phosphate undergo a double-replacement reaction when the solutions are mixed. Match each of the ways to express this reaction with the name of the type of equation. Use each choice only once.

Types of equations:

a. balanced equation   c. skeleton equation   e. word equation

b. complete ionic equation   d. net ionic equation

_____ 1. $3Mg^{2+} + 2PO_4^{3-} \rightarrow Mg_3(PO_4)_2$

_____ 2. $3MgCl_2 + 2Na_3PO_4 \rightarrow Mg_3(PO_4)_2 + 6NaCl$

_____ 3. magnesium chloride + sodium phosphate → magnesium phosphate
                                                   + sodium chloride

_____ 4. $MgCl_2 + Na_3PO_4 \rightarrow Mg_3(PO_4)_2 + NaCl$

_____ 5. $3Mg^{2+} + 6Cl^- + 6Na^+ + 2PO_4^{3-} \rightarrow Mg_3(PO_4)_2 + 6Na^+ + 6Cl$

Match each equation with the type of reaction it represents. You may use each type more than once. If a reaction meets the requirements of more than one type of reaction, list all types.

Types of reactions:

a. combustion   c. decomposition   e. single-replacement

b. combination   d. double-replacement

_____ 1. $2Mg(s) + O_2(g) \rightarrow 2MgO(s)$

_____ 2. $(NH_4)_2SO_4(aq) + Ba(NO_3)_2(aq) \rightarrow BaSO_4(s) + 2NH_4NO_3(aq)$

_____ 3. $H_2O(l) + CO_2(g) \rightarrow H_2CO_3(aq)$

_____ 4. $Ca(s) + 2CuNO_3(aq) \rightarrow 2Cu(s) + Ca(NO_3)_2(aq)$

_____ 5. $2NaCl(l) \xrightarrow{\text{electricity}} 2Na(s) + Cl_2(g)$

12 Stoichiometry

 THE MOLE AND QUANTIFYING MATTER, REACTIONS

12.1 The Arithmetic of Equations

Essential Understanding The law of conservation of mass applies to all chemical equations.

Reading Strategy

Vocabulary Word Map A vocabulary word map will help you learn vocabulary by associating the word with related words and images. Begin by writing the word *stoichiometry* in the top box.

As you read Lesson 12.1, use the word map below to help you get a better understanding of the meaning of the word *stoichiometry*. As you read, fill in the other boxes with terms, phrases, or images that are associated with the word.

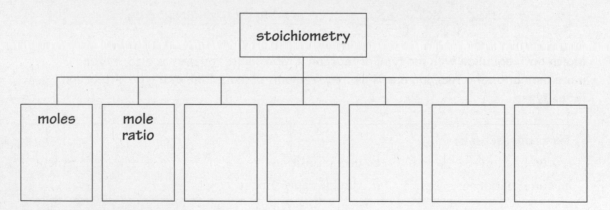

Lesson Summary

Using Equations Stoichiometric calculations tell us the amounts of reactants and products under ideal conditions.

▶ Knowing the quantity of one substance in an equation allows you to calculate the amount of any other substance consumed or created in the reaction.

Chemical Equations The solution to every stoichiometric problem requires a balanced chemical equation.

▶ In a balanced chemical equation, the total number of atoms of each element in the reactants must equal the total number of atoms of that element in the products.

▶ In a balanced chemical equation, the total mass of the reactants must equal the total mass of the products.

After reading Lesson 12.1, answer the following questions.

Using Equations

1. How can you determine the quantities of reactants and products in a chemical reaction?

_____

_____

2. Quantity usually means the _____ of a substance expressed in grams or moles.

3. A bookcase is to be built from 3 shelves (Sh), 2 side boards (Sb), 1 top (T), 1 base (B), and 4 legs (L). Write a "balanced equation" for the construction of this bookcase.

_____

4. Is the following sentence true or false? Stoichiometry is the calculation of quantities in chemical reactions. _____

5. Calculations using balanced equations are called _____.

Chemical Equations

6. From what elements is ammonia produced? How is it used?

_____

_____

7. Circle the letter of the term that tells what kind of information you CANNOT get from a chemical equation.

   a. moles

   b. mass

   c. size of particles

   d. volume

   e. number of particles

8. The coefficients of a balanced chemical equation tell you the relative number of moles of _____ and _____ in a chemical reaction.

9. Why is the relative number of moles of reactants and products the most important information that a balanced chemical equation provides?

_____

_____

10. Is the following sentence true or false? A balanced chemical equation must obey the law of conservation of mass. _____

11. Use Figure 12.2 on page 389. Complete the table about the reaction of nitrogen and hydrogen.

$N_2(g)$	$+ 3H_2(g)$	$\rightarrow 2NH_3(g)$
[____] atoms N	+ 6 atoms H	$\rightarrow$ [____] atoms N and [____] atoms H
1 molecule N_2	+ [____] molecules H_2	$\rightarrow$ [____] molecules NH_3
[____] × (6.02 × 10^{23} molecules N_2)	+ 3 × (6.02 × 10^{23} molecules H_2)	$\rightarrow$ [____] × (6.02 × 10^{23} molecules NH_3)
1 mol N_2	+ [____] mol H_2	$\rightarrow$ 2 mol NH_3
28 g N_2	+ 3 × [____] g H_2	$\rightarrow$ 2 × [____] g NH_3
	[____] g reactants	$\rightarrow$ 34 g products
Assume STP 22.4 L N_2	+ 67.2 L H_2	$\rightarrow$ [____] L NH_3

12. Circle the letter(s) of the items that are ALWAYS conserved in every chemical reaction.

    a. volume of gases   **d.** moles

    b. mass   **e.** molecules

    c. formula units   **f.** atoms

13. What reactant combines with oxygen to form sulfur dioxide? Where can this reactant be found in nature?

_____

_____

12.2 Chemical Calculations

Essential Understanding Amounts of reactants and products are always related by mole ratios.

Lesson Summary

Writing and Using Mole Ratios A mole ratio is a conversion factor derived from the coefficients of a balanced chemical equation.

▶ Mole ratios are used to convert between mass and moles in stoichiometric problems.

▶ The coefficients indicate the number of moles in a balanced equation.

Other Stoichiometric Calculations The first step in solving stoichiometric problems is writing the balanced chemical equation.

▶ Moles are always involved when solving stoichiometric problems.

▶ Several mole ratios can be created from a balanced equation.

Steps to solving a stoichiometric problem

Step 1 ▶ **Change the given quantity to moles.** Step 2 ▶ **Use the mole ratio to calculate moles of the wanted substance.** Step 3 ▶ **Convert moles of the wanted substance into the unit required by the problem.**

BUILD Math Skills

Ratios You use ratios every day, whether you realize it or not. A ratio is a term used to compare two numbers or quantities. For cxample, $3.00 per gallon of gas can be expressed as 3:1 or as $\frac{3}{1}$. Or suppose you see 35 people, and 15 of these people are men. Then the *ratio of men to women* is 15:20. Remember that order is very important. If the expression had been *the ratio of women to men*, then the numbers would have been 20:15.

The way you set up a ratio is very important. Consider a recipe for pink paint. ▶ If you write the ratio of white paint to red paint incorrectly, you'll get a different shade of pink.

These are not the same. ▶ $\frac{1 \text{ white}}{3 \text{ red}}$ = dark pink $\quad$ $\frac{3 \text{ white}}{1 \text{ red}}$ = light pink

Sample Problem Set up a ratio for a recipe using 2 parts white paint to 5 parts blue paint.

Pull out the information you need. ▶ two white to five blue

Express it as a ratio. ▶ $\frac{2}{5}$

Hint: You simply write the numbers as they are stated.

Now you try to set up the following ratios.

1. Make two cups of coffee for every one cup of tea. _____

2. Candle A is 9 cm tall. Candle B is 30 mm tall. What is the ratio of their heights? (Hint: 10 mm = 1 cm) _____

3. Miguel and Ellen have to share a prize of $50 at a ratio of $\frac{2}{3}$. How much does each get? (Hint: 1 share = $10) _____

After reading Lesson 12.2, answer the following questions.

Writing and Using Mole Ratios

4. What is essential for all calculations involving amounts of reactants and products?

    _____

5. Is the following sentence true or false? If you know the number of moles of one substance in a reaction, you need more information than the balanced chemical equation to determine the number of moles of all the other substances in the reaction.

    _____

6. The coefficients from a balanced chemical equation are used to write conversion factors called _____.

7. What are mole ratios used for?

    _____

    _____

    _____

    _____

8. The equation for the formation of potassium chloride is given by the equation

$$2K(s) + Cl_2(g) \rightarrow 2KCl(s)$$

    Write the six possible mole ratios for this equation.

    _____   _____

    _____   _____

    _____   _____

9. Is the following sentence true or false? Laboratory balances are used to measure substances directly in moles. _____

10. The amount of a substance is usually determined by measuring its mass in

    _____.

11. Is the following sentence true or false? If a sample is measured in grams, molar mass can be used to convert the mass to moles. _____

12. Complete the flow chart to show the steps for the mass–mass conversion of any given mass of G to any wanted mass of W. In the chemical equation, *a* moles of G react with *b* moles of W.

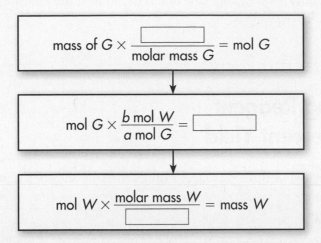

13. Use the diagram below. Describe the steps needed to solve a mass–mass stoichiometry problem.

_____

_____

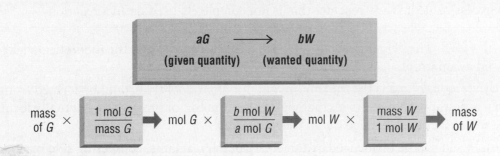

Other Stoichiometric Calculations

14. Is the following sentence true or false? From the mole ratios, you can calculate any measurement unit that is related to the mole, such as representative particles, units of mass, or volumes of gases at STP. _____

15. List two or three types of problems that can be solved with stoichiometric calculations.

_____

_____

16. In any problem relating to stoichiometric calculations, the given quantity is first converted to _____.

17. The combustion of methane produces carbon dioxide and water. The chemical equation for this reaction is $CH_4(g) + 2O_2(g) \rightarrow CO_2(g) + 2H_2O(g)$

Write the three conversion factors you would use to find the volume of carbon dioxide obtained from 1.5 L of oxygen.

_____ _____ _____

12.3 Limiting Reagent and Percent Yield

Essential Understanding   A limiting reagent limits the amount of product.

Lesson Summary

Limiting and Excess Reagents   All stoichiometric calculations must be based on the limiting reagent.

▶ The limiting reagent is the reactant that determines the amount of product that can be formed by a reaction.

▶ The reaction will stop when the limiting reagent has been used up.

▶ An excess reagent is any reactant that is not completely used up in a reaction.

Percent Yield   The percent yield is the ratio of the actual yield to the theoretical yield expressed as a percent.

▶ The theoretical yield is the maximum amount of product that could be formed from given amounts of reactants. Actual yield is the amount of product that actually forms when the reaction is carried out in the laboratory.

▶ Actual yield can be influenced by the purity of the reactants, competing side reactions, or a loss of product during collection or transfer.

After reading Lesson 12.3, answer the following questions.

Limiting Reagent and Percent Yield

1. What is a limiting reagent?

_____

_____

2. Is the following sentence true or false? A chemical reaction stops before the limiting reagent is used up. _____

3. Circle the letter of the term that correctly completes the sentence. The reactant that is not completely used up in a chemical reaction is called the _____.

    a. spectator reagent   **c.** excess reagent

    b. limiting reagent   **d.** catalyst

4. If the quantities of reactants are given in units other than moles, what is the first step for determining the amount of product?

    a. Determine the amount of product from the given amount of limiting reagent.

    b. Convert each given quantity of reactant to moles.

    c. Identify the limiting reagent.

5. In the diagram below, which reactant is the limiting reagent and why? The chemical equation for the formation of water is $2H_2 + O_2 \rightarrow 2H_2O$

_____

_____

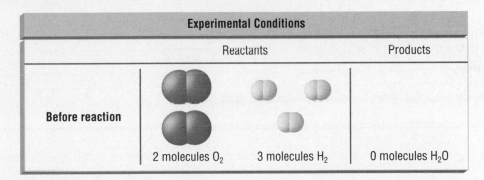

Percent Yield

6. What is the theoretical yield?

_____

_____

7. The amount of product that actually forms when a chemical reaction is carried out in a laboratory is called the _____ yield.

8. Is the following sentence true or false? The actual yield is usually greater than the theoretical yield. _____

9. Complete the equation for the percent yield of a chemical reaction.

$$\text{percent yield} = \frac{\boxed{} \text{ yield}}{\boxed{} \text{ yield}} \times 100\%$$

10. Describe four factors that may cause percent yields to be less than 100%.

_____

_____

Guided Practice Problems

Answer the following questions about Practice Problem 12.

This equation shows the formation of aluminum oxide.

$$4Al(s) + 3O_2(g) \rightarrow 2Al_2O_3(s)$$

    a. How many moles of oxygen are required to react completely with 14.8 moles of aluminum?

Analyze

1. What is the given information? _____

2. What is the unknown? _____

3. What conversion factor will you need to use? _____

Calculate

4. Complete the solution. 14.8 _____ $\times \dfrac{3 \text{ mol } O_2}{\boxed{}} =$ _____ mol O_2

Evaluate

5. Why does the answer have three significant figures?

_____

_____

_____

    b. How many moles of aluminum oxide are formed when 0.78 moles of oxygen react with an excess of aluminum?

Analyze

6. What information is given? _____

7. What information is unknown? _____

Calculate

8. Complete the solution. _____ mol $O_2 \times \dfrac{\boxed{} \text{ mol } Al_2O_3}{\boxed{}} =$ _____ mol Al_2O_3

Evaluate

9. Why does the answer have two significant figures?

_____

_____

Answer the following questions about Practice Problem 26.

The equation for the complete combustion of ethene (C_2H_4) is

$$C_2H_4(g) + 3O_2(g) \rightarrow 2CO_2(g) + 2H_2O(g)$$

If 2.70 moles of ethene reacted with 6.30 moles of oxygen, identify the limiting reagent.

Step 1. Calculate the number of moles of oxygen needed to react with 2.70 moles of ethene. Multiply by the mole ratio.

2.70 _____ $\times \dfrac{\square \text{ mol } O_2}{1 \text{ mol } C_2H_4}$

$=$ _____ mol O_2

Step 2. Compare the number of moles of oxygen needed to the number given.

_____ O_2 given is less than

_____ mol O_2 needed

Step 3. Identify the limiting reagent.

Because _____ mol O_2 are needed to react with the 2.70 mol C_2H_4 and only _____ mol O_2 are available, _____ is the limiting reagent.

Answer the following questions about Practice Problem 30.

When 84.8 g of iron(III) oxide reacts with an excess of carbon monoxide, iron is produced.

$$Fe_2O_3(s) + 3CO(g) \rightarrow 2Fe(s) + 3CO_2(g)$$

What is the theoretical yield of iron?

Step 1. Begin by finding the molar mass of Fe_2O_3.

2 mol Fe $\times$ (_____ g Fe/mol Fe)

+ 3 mol O $\times$ (_____ g O/mol O)

$=$ _____ g + 48.0 g $=$ _____ g

Step 2. Calculate the number of moles of iron(III) oxide. Multiply by the mole/mass conversion factor.

_____ g Fe_2O_3 $\times \dfrac{1 \text{ mol } Fe_2O_3}{159.6 \text{ g } Fe_2O_3}$

$=$ _____ mol

Step 3. Find the number of moles of Fe expected. Multiply by the mole ratio.

0.531 _____ $\times \dfrac{\square \text{ mol Fe}}{1 \text{ mol } Fe_2O_3}$

$=$ _____ mol Fe

Step 4. Find the mass of iron that should be produced. Multiply by the mole/mass conversion factor.

1.062 _____ $\times \dfrac{\square \text{ g Fe}}{1 \text{ mol Fe}} = 59.26 \text{ g Fe}$

Extra Practice

How many molecules of oxygen are produced by the decomposition of 1225 grams of potassium chlorate ($KClO_3$)?

$$2KClO_3(s) \rightarrow 2KCl(s) + 3O_2(g)$$

The equation for the combustion of carbon monoxide is

$$2CO(g) + O_2(g) \rightarrow 2CO_2(g)$$

How many liters of oxygen are needed to burn 10 liters of carbon monoxide?

 Apply the Big idea

1a. How many moles of chlorine gas (Cl_2) would react with 5 moles of sodium (Na) according to the following chemical equation? (Balance the equation first.)

$$Na + Cl_2 \rightarrow NaCl$$

1b. What mass of Na must be used to produce 29.2 g of NaCl?

 12 Self-Check Activity

For Questions 1–8, complete each statement by writing the correct word or words. If you need help, you can go online.

12.1 The Arithmetic of Equations

1. Chemists use balanced chemical equations as a basis to calculate how much _____ is needed or how much _____ will be formed in a reaction.

2. A balanced chemical equation can be interpreted in terms of different quantities, including numbers of atoms, molecules, or _____; mass; and _____.

12.2 Chemical Calculations

3. In chemical calculations, _____ are used to convert between a given number of moles of a reactant or product to moles of a different reactant or product.

4. In a typical stoichiometric problem, the given quantity is first converted to _____.

5. Then, the _____ from the balanced equation is used to calculate the number of moles of the wanted substance.

6. Finally, the moles are converted to any other unit of measurement related to the _____, as the problem requires.

12.3 Limiting Reagent and Percent Yield

7. In a chemical reaction, an insufficient quantity of any of the _____ will limit the amount of product that forms.

8. The percent yield is a measure of the _____ of a reaction carried out in the laboratory.

EXTENSION Fill in the missing terms in the equations below.

$$\text{Percent yield} = \frac{\boxed{}}{\boxed{}} \times \boxed{}$$

If You Have Trouble With...							
Question	1	2	3	4	5	6	7	8
See Page	386	386	390	394	394	394	400	405

Review Conversion Factors

Use what you learned about stoichiometry and conversion factors to fill in the concept map.

Mole and mass stoichiometry must have a balanced equation.

If the problem gives

moles	moles	mass	mass
use	use	use	use
$\dfrac{mole}{mole}$	$\dfrac{mole}{mole}$		$\dfrac{mole}{molar\ mass}$
In get	than	than	then
moles			
	to get	to get	then
	grams	moles	
			to get
			grams

Review Vocabulary

Answer the questions by writing the correct vocabulary term in the blanks. Then arrange the circled letters to find the hidden term.

Clues	Vocabulary Terms
ideal amount of product	O_ _ _ _ _ _ _O_ _ _O_ _ _
involved in all stoichiometric calculations	O_ _ _ _ _ _ _O
quantitative relationship between reactants and products in a balanced chemical reaction	_OO_ _OOO_O_O_
the amount of product that is measured	OO_O_O _ _ _O_
determines the amount of product formed	_O_ _O_ _ _ _ _ _ _ _ _O_
a measure of the efficiency of a chemical reaction	_ _ _O_ _ _ _O_ _ _
leftover reactants	_ _ O_ OO_ _ _O_ _ _ _

Hidden Term: _ _ _ _ _ _ _ _ _ _ _ _ _ _ _ _ _ _ _ _ _ _ _ _ _ _ _

EXTENSION Write a definition for the hidden term.

_____

_____

13 States of Matter

 KINETIC THEORY

13.1 The Nature of Gases

Essential Understanding Temperature and pressure affect gases much more than they affect any other state of matter.

Lesson Summary

Kinetic Theory and a Model for Gases The kinetic theory refers to the constant motion of particles in matter and, for gases, makes three assumptions.

▶ Particles in a gas are hard spheres and are so small that their volume is insignificant.

▶ Particles in a gas move constantly, rapidly, and randomly.

▶ When particles in a gas collide, neither particle loses any of its kinetic energy.

Gas Pressure The kinetic theory can be used to explain gas pressure.

▶ Gas pressure is the result of the simultaneous collisions of billions of gas particles with an object.

▶ The pressure air exerts on Earth is called atmospheric pressure, which is measured with a barometer.

▶ Units for measuring gas pressure include pascals (Pa), millimeters of mercury (mm Hg), and atmospheres (atm).

Kinetic Energy and Temperature Temperature is a measure of the average kinetic energy of the particles in a collection of atoms or molecules.

▶ An increase in the average kinetic energy of particles results in an increase in temperature.

▶ Particles are no longer moving at a theoretical temperature known as absolute zero (0K, −273.15°C).

▶ The Kelvin temperature of a substance is directly proportional to the kinetic energy of its particles.

BUILD Math Skills

Converting Between Units of Pressure Three of the most common units of pressure are atmospheres (atm), millimeters of mercury (mm Hg) and pascals (Pa). Atmospheres relate to the pressure exerted by our atmosphere. A device called a barometer uses the difference between heights of mercury in two different tubes to measure pressure. Pascals are the SI unit for pressure, where $1\ Pa = 1\ N/m^2$. It is important to remember that there are 1000 Pa in 1 kilopascal (kPa).

The relationship between these units is:

$$1\ atm = 760\ mm\ Hg = 101.3\ kPa$$

When converting between units:

▶ Start with the pressure in the given units.

▶ Always put the units you begin with on the bottom of the ratio by which you are going to multiply.

▶ Put the units you want to end with on the top of the ratio.

▶ You will multiply all the numbers that fall on top and divide by all the numbers that fall on the bottom.

Sample Problem Determine the number of kilopascals (kPa) present in 0.53 m of Hg.

Start with the given units.	0.53 m of Hg

Hint: Remember, you may need more than one ratio to get to the desired units.

Now you want to convert from meters to millimeters, so you can use the equivalents. The conversion is: 1×10^{-3} m = 1 mm, so *mm* will go on the top since it is the desired unit.

$$0.53\ m\ of\ Hg \times \frac{1\ mm}{1 \times 10^{-3}\ m} \rightarrow$$

$$0.53\ m\ of\ Hg \times \frac{1\ mm}{1 \times 10^{-3}\ m}$$

Next, you want to convert from mm of Hg to kilopascals, so you will use the ratio of 760 mm of Hg = 101.3 kPa.

$$0.53\ m\ of\ Hg \times \frac{1\ mm}{1 \times 10^{-3}\ m} \times \frac{101.3\ kPa}{760\ mm\ of\ Hg} \rightarrow$$

$$0.53\ m\ of\ Hg \times \frac{1\ mm}{1 \times 10^{-3}\ m} \times \frac{101.3\ kPa}{760\ mm\ of\ Hg}$$

Finally, multiply all the numbers on top and divide by all the numbers on the bottom to get the equivalent kPa.

$$\frac{(0.53 \times 101.3)}{(1 \times 10^{-3} \times 760)} = 70.64\ kPa$$

Now it's your turn to practice converting between different units of pressure.

1. Determine how many mm of Hg are equal to 5.3 atm of pressure.

_____

2. Determine how many atmospheres of pressure are equal to 65.78 kPa.

_____

3. If you have 2.86 atm of pressure, is that more or less than 2000 mm of Hg?

_____

4. What is the pressure in both mm of Hg and atmospheres if you are given 5678.32 Pa?

_____

After reading Lesson 13.1, answer the following questions.

Kinetic Theory and a Model for Gases

5. The energy an object has because of its motion is called _____.

6. Circle the letter of each sentence that is true about the assumptions of the kinetic theory concerning gases.

   a. A gas is composed of particles with insignificant volume that are relatively far apart.

   b. Strong attractive forces exist between particles of a gas.

   c. Gases tend to collect near the bottom of a container.

   d. The paths of uninterrupted travel of particles in a gas are relatively short because the particles are constantly colliding with each other or with other objects.

7. Is the following statement true or false? According to the kinetic theory, collisions between particles in a gas are perfectly elastic because kinetic energy is transferred without loss from one particle to another, and the total kinetic energy remains constant.

_____

Gas Pressure

8. Gas pressure results from the force exerted by a gas per _____.

9. Simultaneous collisions of billions of particles in a gas with an object result in

_____.

10. What force holds the particles of air in Earth's atmosphere? _____

11. What kind of pressure is measured with a barometer? _____

12. Look at Figure 13.2. What accounts for the difference in height of the two columns of mercury shown in the figure?

_____

_____

_____

_____

13. Circle the letter next to every name of a unit of pressure.

a. mm Hg   **d.** kPa

b. standard   **e.** atm

c. pascal   **f.** degree

14. Standard temperature and pressure (STP) are defined as

_____

_____

Kinetic Energy and Temperature

15. What happens to the temperature of a substance when the average kinetic energy of its particles increases?

_____

16. Is the following statement true or false? All the particles in a substance at a given temperature have the same kinetic energy. _____

17. The temperature 0 K, or –273.15°C, is called _____ zero. Theoretically, particles of matter at this temperature would have no

_____.

18. On the graph below, write the labels *lower temperature* and *higher temperature* to identify the curve that depicts the kinetic energy distribution of particles in a liquid at a lower temperature and at a higher temperature.

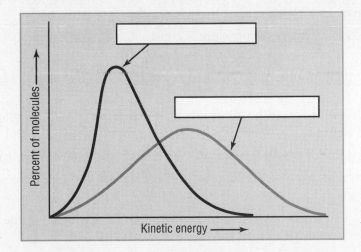

19. Circle the letter of the temperature scale that correctly completes this sentence. Temperature on the _____ scale is directly proportional to the average kinetic energy of the particles of a substance.

a. Celsius   **c.** Fahrenheit

b. Kelvin   **d.** Centigrade

13.2 The Nature of Liquids

Essential Understanding The properties and physical changes of liquids are the result of the particle motion and the attraction between particles in a liquid.

Lesson Summary

A Model for Liquids The properties of liquids are the result of both the disruption caused by particle motion and the attraction between particles in a liquid.

▶ Liquids flow because their particles can slide by each other.

▶ Liquids have a definite volume because of the attraction between their particles.

▶ Particles are close together in a liquid, so a change in pressure has little effect on a liquid.

Evaporation Evaporation is the change of a liquid to a gas at the surface of a liquid that is not boiling.

▶ The kinetic energy of a particle at the surface of a liquid determines whether or not the particle evaporates.

▶ Evaporation increases when the temperature of the liquid increases.

▶ Evaporation is a cooling process because the higher-energy particles in the liquid are the particles that evaporate.

Vapor Pressure Vapor pressure is the force exerted by a gas above a liquid in a closed container.

▶ In a closed container containing a liquid, gas particles eventually condense at the same rate as liquid particles vaporize.

▶ In a closed system, when vapor pressure is constant, a dynamic equilibrium has been reached.

▶ Increasing the temperature of a contained liquid increases its vapor pressure.

Boiling Point Boiling point is the temperature at which particles throughout a liquid have enough energy to vaporize.

▶ At the boiling point of a liquid, vapor pressure equals the external pressure on the liquid.

▶ Boiling point is affected by external pressure; as external pressure decreases, boiling point decreases.

▶ The normal boiling point of a liquid is the temperature at which the liquid boils when the external pressure is 101.3 kPa.

After reading Lesson 13.2, answer the following questions.

A Model for Liquids

1. Is the following sentence true or false? The kinetic theory states that there are no attractions between the particles of a liquid. _____

2. Circle the letter next to each sentence that is true about the particles of a liquid.

   a. Most of the particles in a liquid have enough kinetic energy to escape into a gaseous state.

   b. Liquids are much denser than gases because intermolecular forces reduce the amount of space between the particles in a liquid.

   c. Increasing pressure on a liquid has almost no effect on its volume.

   d. Liquid particles are free to slide past one another.

Evaporation

3. The conversion of a liquid to a gas or vapor is called _____.

4. When vaporization occurs at the surface of a liquid that is not boiling, the process is called _____.

5. As a liquid evaporates, why do only some of the particles break away from the surface of the liquid? Why does the liquid evaporate faster if the temperature is increased?

   _____

   _____

   _____

   _____

6. Is the following sentence true or false? Evaporation is a cooling process because the particles in a liquid with the highest kinetic energy tend to escape first, leaving the remaining particles with a lower average kinetic energy and, thus, a lower temperature.

   _____

Questions 7–10 refer to either container A or container B below. Think of each container as a system involving both liquid water and water vapor.

 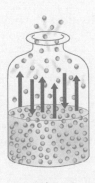

(a)   (b)

7. From which of the containers are water molecules able to escape? _____

8. In which container can a dynamic equilibrium be established between water molecules in the liquid state and water molecules in the vapor state? _____

9. In which container will the water level remain constant? _____

10. From which container is it possible for all of the liquid water to disappear through evaporation? _____

11. What causes the chill you may feel after stepping out of a swimming pool on a warm, windy day?

_____

_____

Vapor Pressure

12. Circle the letter next to each sentence that is true about vapor pressure.

  a. Vapor pressure exists when particles of a liquid in a closed, partly filled container vaporize and collide with the walls of the container.

  b. After a time in a closed, partly filled container, a liquid will evaporate and its vapor will condense at equal rates.

  c. Look at Figure 13.6b. Condensation on the inside of the terrarium indicates that there is no liquid-vapor equilibrium in the sealed terrarium.

  d. When the temperature of a contained liquid increases, its vapor pressure increases.

13. Look at Figure 13.7. How does the vapor pressure of the ethanol in the manometer change when the temperature is increased from 0°C to 20°C? Circle the letter of the correct answer.

  a. The vapor pressure decreases by more than 4 kPa.

  b. The vapor pressure remains constant.

  c. The vapor pressure increases by more than 4 kPa.

  d. There is no way to detect a change in vapor pressure with a manometer.

Boiling Point

14. The boiling point of a liquid is the temperature at which the vapor pressure of the liquid is just equal to the _____.

15. Look at Figure 13.8. Why does the boiling point decrease as altitude increases?

_____

_____

_____

16. Use Figure 13.9. At approximately what temperature would ethanol boil atop Mount Everest, where the atmospheric pressure is 34 kPa? Circle the letter next to the best estimate.

  a. 50°C   **b.** 100°C   **c.** 0°C   **d.** 85°C

17. Is the following sentence true or false? After a liquid reaches its boiling point, its temperature continues to rise until all the liquid vaporizes. _____

13.3 The Nature of Solids

Essential Understanding The properties of solids are related to their structure.

Lesson Summary

A Model for Solids The properties of solids reflect the arrangement and fixed locations of their particles.

▶ Particles in a solid vibrate in place and do not move past each other.

▶ At its melting point, the particles in a solid overcome the attraction between them, and they start to flow.

▶ For any substance, freezing point is the same temperature as the melting point, and equilibrium between liquid and solid exist at this temperature.

Crystal Structure and Unit Cells The shape of a crystal reflects the arrangements of the particles in the solid.

▶ Based on their shape, crystals are classified into seven crystal systems.

▶ Solid substances that can exist in more than one form are allotropes.

▶ Solids that have no crystal form are amorphous solids.

After reading Lesson 13.3, answer the following questions.

A Model for Solids

1. Is the following sentence true or false? Although particles in solids have kinetic energy, the motion of particles in solids is restricted to vibrations about fixed points.
   _____

2. A solid melts when _____.

3. Is the following sentence true or false? The temperature at which the liquid and solid states of a substance are in equilibrium is the same as the melting point *and* the freezing point of the substance. _____

Crystal Structure and Unit Cells

4. How are particles arranged in a crystal?

   _____

5. What type of solid has a relatively low melting point?

   _____

6. Do all solids melt when heated? Explain.

   _____

7. Circle the letter next to each sentence that is true about solids.

    a. Most solid substances are not crystalline.

    b. All crystals have sides, or faces, that intersect at angles that are characteristic for a given substance.

    c. There are seven groups, or crystal systems, into which all crystals can be classified.

    d. The orderly array of sodium ions and chloride ions gives crystals of table salt their regular shape.

Identify the unit cell in each figure below as *simple cubic*, *body-centered cubic*, or *face-centered cubic*.

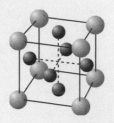 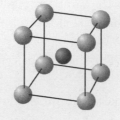 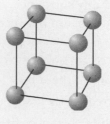

8. _____ **9.** _____ **10.** _____

11. Is the following sentence true or false? Some solid substances can exist in more than one form. Give an example to support your answer.

_____

_____

12. Two or more different molecular forms of the same element in the same physical state are called _____.

13. What is an amorphous solid?

_____

14. Circle the letter next to each solid that is an amorphous solid.

    a. table salt

    b. rubber

    c. plastic

    d. glass

15. How does glass differ from a crystalline solid?

_____

_____

_____

13.4 Changes of State

Essential Understanding Changes of state depend on changes in energy of the particles involved.

Reading Strategy

Concept Map A concept map helps you organize concepts using visual relationships and linking words. Mapping out these connections helps you think about how information fits together.

As you read Lesson 13.4, use the concept map below. On each arrow, fill in the appropriate change of state.

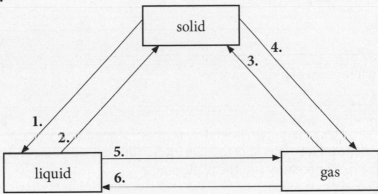

EXTENSION Give a real-life example of each change of state shown in the concept map.

_____

_____

_____

Lesson Summary

Sublimation Sublimation is the change of state from a solid to a vapor without passing through the liquid state.

▶ Sublimation occurs when the solid has a vapor pressure that is greater than atmospheric pressure at or near room temperature.

▶ The process that is the opposite of sublimation is deposition.

▶ There are useful applications for sublimation such as separating mixtures and purifying compounds.

Phase Diagrams A phase diagram relates the solid, liquid, and gas states of a particular substance to the temperature and the pressure at which the states exist in equilibrium.

▶ The triple point on the diagram is the set of temperature and pressure at which all three states exist in dynamic equilibrium.

▶ A phase diagram can be used to show how a change in temperature or pressure might affect the state of a substance.

After reading Lesson 13.4, answer the following questions.

Sublimation

1. The process by which wet laundry dries on an outdoor clothesline in winter is called
_____.

2. Is the following sentence true or false? Solids have vapor pressure because some particles
near the surface of a solid substance have enough kinetic energy to escape directly into
the vapor phase. _____

Phase Diagrams

3. What does a phase diagram show?

_____

_____

4. What is the triple point of a substance?

_____

_____

5. In the phase diagram for water shown below, label the melting point and boiling point at
normal atmospheric pressure, and the triple point.

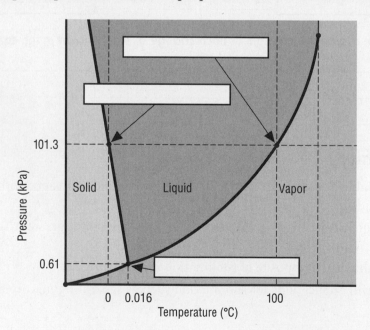

6. Use the phase diagram above to answer the following question. Why is a laboratory
required to produce the conditions necessary for observing water at the triple point?

_____

_____

_____

Guided Practice Problems

Answer the following questions about Practice Problem 2.

The pressure at the top of Mount Everest is 33.7 kPa. Is that pressure greater than or less than 0.25 atm?

Analyze

Step 1. To convert kPa to atm, what conversion factor do you need to use?

_____

Step 2. Why can you use an estimate to solve this problem?

_____

_____

Calculate

Step 3. Write the expression needed to find the answer.

_____

Step 4. Which common fraction is this number close to?

_____

Step 5. What is this fraction written as a decimal? Is this number greater than or less than 0.25?

_____

Evaluate

Step 6. Are you confident your estimate gave a correct answer to this problem?

_____

_____

Extra Practice

What pressure, in atmospheres, does a gas exert at 152 mm Hg?

What is this pressure in kilopascals?

Apply the Big idea

Ahmed's yard is covered with snow. Use the kinetic theory to explain the changes that occur in the snow when the air temperature increases above the freezing point of water.

_____

_____

_____

_____

_____

_____

_____

13 Self-Check Activity

For Questions 1–11, complete each statement by writing the correct word or words. If you need help, you can go online.

13.1 The Nature of Gases

1. The _____ makes three assumptions about the volume, the motion, and the collisions of gas particles.

2. When many particles in a gas simultaneously collide with an object, _____ results.

3. The _____ temperature of a substance is directly proportional to the average kinetic energy of the particles of the substance.

13.2 The Nature of Liquids

4. The _____ of liquids depend on both the disruption of the particles in the liquid and the attraction between the particles.

5. During _____, particles with enough energy escape at the surface of a liquid.

6. When a closed system has constant vapor pressure, a(n) _____ exists between the liquid and its vapor.

7. When the particles throughout a liquid have enough energy to vaporize, _____ occurs.

13.3 The Nature of Solids

8. The arrangement and location of its particles affect the _____ of a solid.

9. A crystalline solid has a certain arrangement of particles, which is reflected in its _____.

13.4 Changes of State

10. When the vapor pressure of a solid equals or exceeds atmospheric pressure at room temperature, _____ occurs.

11. A(n) _____ relates the solid, liquid, and gas states of a substance to temperature and pressure.

If You Have Trouble With...											
Question	1	2	3	4	5	6	7	8	9	10	11
See Page	420	421	424	425	426	427	428	431	432	436	438

Review Vocabulary

For each set of vocabulary terms, write a sentence that includes all the terms and explains the relationship among them.

1. vaporization, evaporation, sublimation

_____

_____

_____

_____

2. boiling point, normal boiling point

_____

_____

_____

_____

3. atmospheric pressure, barometer, pascal (Pa), standard atmosphere (atm)

_____

_____

_____

_____

4. phase diagram, triple point, melting point, boiling point

_____

_____

_____

_____

5. kinetic energy, gas pressure, vacuum

_____

_____

_____

_____

14 The Behavior of Gases

 KINETIC THEORY

14.1 Properties of Gases

Essential Understanding Kinetic theory is an attempt to explain some of the properties of gases by describing how particles interact with one another.

Reading Strategy

Cause and Effect Identifying cause and effect can help you understand the relationship among events. A cause is the reason something happens. The effect is what happens. In science, many actions cause other actions to happen.

As you read Lesson 14.1, use the cause and effect chart below. Record three causes for an increase in gas pressure.

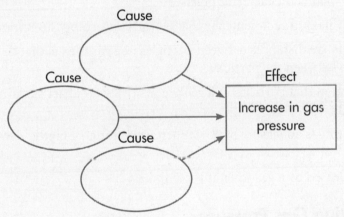

EXTENSION Below each cause, use kinetic theory to explain how it will increase the gas pressure.

Lesson Summary

Compressibility Gases can expand to fill its volume, and gases can be squeezed into a smaller volume.
- ▶ Gases do not have definite shape or volume.
- ▶ Gases are easily compressed because of the space between molecules in a gas.

Factors Affecting Gas Pressure Gases exert pressure.
- ▶ Collisions between molecules of gases and the walls of its container cause the pressure in a closed container of gas.
- ▶ Factors that affect the gas pressure (P) of an enclosed gas are its temperature (T), its volume (V), and the number of molecules.

Effect of factor on gas pressure	(T)	(V)	Number of molecules	(P)
Increasing (T) will increase (P) if (V) and number of molecules are constant.	↑	constant	constant	↑
Decreasing (V) will increase (P) if (T) and number of molecules are constant.	constant	↓	constant	↑
Increasing the number of molecules will increase (P) if (V) and (T) are constant.	constant	constant	↑	↑

After reading Lesson 14.1, answer the following questions.

Compressibility

1. Look at Figure 14.1. Explain how an automobile air bag protects the people in the car from being hurt as a result of impact.

   _____

   _____

   _____

2. What theory explains the behavior of gases? _____

3. Circle the letter next to each sentence that is true concerning the compressibility of gases.

   a. The large relative distances between particles in a gas means that there is considerable empty space between the particles.

   b. The assumption that particles in a gas are relatively far apart explains gas compressibility.

   c. Compressibility is a measure of how much the volume of matter decreases under pressure.

   d. Energy is released by a gas when it is compressed.

Factors Affecting Gas Pressure

4. List the name, the symbol, and a common unit for the four variables that are generally used to describe the characteristics of a gas.

   a. _____

   b. _____

   c. _____

   d. _____

5. What keeps the raft in Figure 14.3 inflated?

   _____

   _____

6. How do conditions change inside a rigid container when you use a pump to add gas to the container?

_____

_____

7. The diagrams below show a sealed container at three pressures. Complete the labels showing the gas pressure in each container.

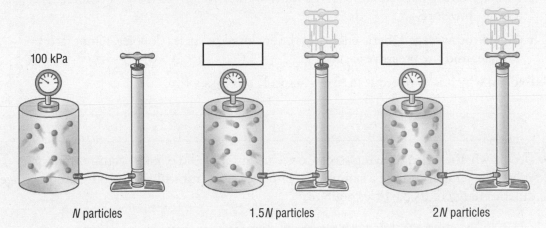

N particles   1.5N particles   2N particles

8. What can happen if too much gas is pumped into a sealed, rigid container?

_____

_____

9. Is the following sentence true or false? When a sealed container of gas is opened, gas will flow from the region of lower pressure to the region of higher pressure. _____

10. Look at Figure 14.5. What happens when the push button on an aerosol spray can is pressed?

_____

_____

_____

11. In the diagram, complete the labels showing the pressure on the piston and the gas pressure inside the container.

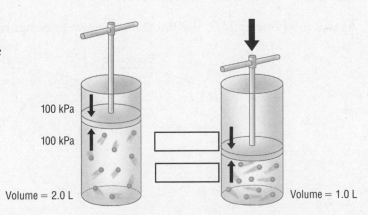

100 kPa

100 kPa

Volume = 2.0 L

Volume = 1.0 L

12. When the volume of a gas is reduced by one half, what happens to its pressure?

_____

13. Is the following sentence true or false? Raising the temperature of a contained gas causes its pressure to decrease. _____

14. Circle the letter next to each sentence that correctly describes how gases behave when the temperature increases.

    a. The average kinetic energy of the particles in the gas increases as the particles absorb energy.

    b. Faster-moving particles impact the walls of their container with more force, exerting greater pressure.

    c. When the average kinetic energy of the enclosed particles doubles, temperature doubles and the pressure is cut in half.

15. Explain why it is dangerous to throw aerosol cans into a fire.

_____

_____

16. Decide whether the following sentence is true or false, and explain your reasoning. When the temperature of a sample of steam increases from 100°C to 200°C, the average kinetic energy of its particles doubles.

_____

_____

14.2 The Gas Laws

Essential Understanding The gas laws are a set of mathematical tools to help predict the behavior of gases under specific conditions of pressure *(P)*, temperature *(T)*, volume *(V)*, and number of moles of gas *(n)*.

Reading Strategy

Compare and Contrast A Venn diagram is a useful tool in visually organizing related information. A Venn diagram shows which characteristics the concepts share and which characteristics are unique to each concept.

As you read Lesson 14.2, use the Venn diagram to compare Boyle's law and Charles's law.

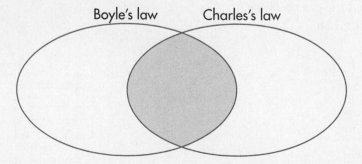

Boyle's law   Charles's law

EXTENSION Use a three-circle Venn diagram to compare Boyle's law, Charles's law, and the combined gas law.

Lesson Summary

Boyle's Law: Pressure and Volume Boyle's law states that the pressure and volume of a gas are inversely proportional to each other (constant T, n).

▶ The equation for Boyle's law is $P_1 \times V_1 = P_2 \times V_2$

Charles's Law: Temperature and Volume Charles's law states that the volume of a gas is directly proportional to its Kelvin temperature (constant P, n).

▶ The equation for Charles's law is $\dfrac{V_1}{T_1} = \dfrac{V_2}{T_2}$

Gay-Lussac's Law: Pressure and Temperature Gay-Lussac's law states that the pressure of a gas is directly proportional to its Kelvin temperature (constant V, n).

▶ The equation for Gay-Lussac's law is $\dfrac{P_1}{T_1} = \dfrac{P_2}{T_2}$

The Combined Gas Law The combined gas law describes the relationship among the pressure, volume, and Kelvin temperature of a gas (constant n).

▶ The equation for the combined gas law is $\dfrac{P_1 \times V_1}{T_1} = \dfrac{P_2 \times V_2}{T_2}$

Gas law	(T)	(V)	(n)	(P)
Boyle's law	constant	↓	constant	↑
Charles's law	↑	↑	constant	constant
Gay-Lussac's law	↑	constant	constant	↑

BUILD Math Skills

Isolating a Variable Remember that all equations have two sides— a left side and a right side. The first step in isolating a variable is to get any term with the variable in it on one side of the equation. The next step is to get rid of everything else on the same side of the equation as the variable.

In order to get rid of the 'extra' variables, you must undo its association with that side of the equation. To do this, you do the opposite operation to both sides.

Turn to the next page to learn more about isolating a variable.

Sample Problem Solve for x in $x + 2 = 14$.

The key to solving this equation is to isolate x.

$$x + 2 = 14$$

Hint: It is important that you subtract 2 from both sides, otherwise you can't use an equals sign.

On the left side of the equation, x is added to 2. To undo addition, you must subtract 2 from both sides of the equation.

$$(x + 2) - 2 = 14 - 2$$
$$x = 12$$

Sample Problem Isolate V_1 in the equation: $\dfrac{V_1}{T_1} = \dfrac{V_2}{T_2}$

You need to get V_1 by itself on the left side. So you need to move T_1 to the right side.

$$\frac{V_1}{T_1} = \frac{V_2}{T_2}$$

To undo the division of V_1 by T_1, you just multiply both sides by T_1.

$$\frac{T_1}{1} \times \frac{V_1}{T_1} = \frac{V_2 \times T_1}{T_2} \quad \text{so} \quad V_1 = \frac{V_2 \times T_1}{T_2}$$

Isolate the variables in the problems below.

1. Isolate V_2 in the equation: $\dfrac{V_1}{T_1} = \dfrac{V_2}{T_2}$ _____

2. Isolate T_2 in the equation: $\dfrac{P_1}{T_1} = \dfrac{P_2}{T_2}$ _____

3. Isolate P_2 in the equation: $\dfrac{P_1}{T_1} = \dfrac{P_2}{T_2}$ _____

After reading Lesson 14.2, answer the following questions.

Boyle's Law: Pressure and Volume

4. Circle the letter of each sentence that is true about the relationship between the volume and the pressure of a contained gas at constant temperature?

a. When the pressure increases, the volume decreases.

b. When the pressure decreases, the volume increases.

c. When the pressure increases, the volume increases.

d. When the pressure decreases, the volume decreases.

5. _____ law states that for a given mass of gas at constant temperature, the volume of the gas varies inversely with pressure.

Questions 6, 7, 8, and 9 refer to the graph. This graph represents the relationship between pressure and volume for a sample of gas in a container at a constant temperature.

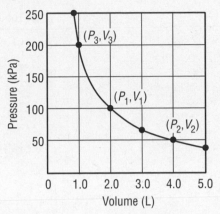

6. $P_1 \times V_1 =$ _____

7. $P_2 \times V_2 =$ _____

8. $P_3 \times V_3 =$ _____

9. What do you notice about the product of pressure times volume at constant temperature?

_____

Charles's Law: Temperature and Volume

10. Look at the graph in Figure 14.10. What two observations did Jacques Charles make about the behavior of gases from similar data?

_____

_____

11. What does it mean to say that two variables are directly proportional?

_____

_____

12. Is the following sentence true or false? Charles's law states that when the pressure of a fixed mass of gas is held constant, the volume of the gas is directly proportional to its Kelvin temperature. _____

13. Charles's law may be written $\dfrac{V_1}{T_1} = \dfrac{V_2}{T_2}$ at constant pressure if the temperatures are

measured on what scale? _____

Gay-Lussac's Law: Pressure and Temperature

14. Complete the following sentence. Gay-Lussac's law states that the pressure of a gas is

_____

_____

15. Gay-Lussac's law may be written $\dfrac{P_1}{T_1} = \dfrac{P_2}{T_2}$ if the volume is constant and if the

temperatures are measured on what scale? _____

16. Complete the missing label in the diagram below showing the pressure change when a gas is heated at constant volume.

100 kPa

300 K

600 K

The Combined Gas Law

17. Is the following sentence true or false? The gas laws of Boyle, Charles, and Gay-Lussac can be combined into a single mathematical expression. _____

Questions 18–21 refer to the following equation:

$$\frac{P_1 \times V_1}{T_1} = \frac{P_2 \times V_2}{T_2}$$

18. What law does this mathematical equation represent?

_____

19. Which gas law does this equation represent if temperature is held constant so that $T_1 = T_2$? _____

20. Which gas law does this equation represent if pressure is held constant so that $P_1 = P_2$?

_____

21. Which gas law does this equation represent if volume is held constant so that $V_1 = V_2$?

_____

22. In which situations does the combined gas law enable you to do calculations when the other gas laws do not apply?

_____

_____

14.3 Ideal Gases

Essential Understanding The gas laws are combined into the ideal gas law, which mathematically relates the four gas variables.

Lesson Summary

Ideal Gas Law The combined gas law can be modified to include the number of moles, n.
▶ The ideal gas law is $PV = nRT$.

Ideal Gases and Real Gases At many conditions of temperature and pressure, real gases behave like ideal gases.

▶ Real gas particles have volume and exert forces on each other.

▶ Real gases differ most from ideal gases at low temperatures and high pressures.

After reading Lesson 14.3, answer the following questions.

Ideal Gas Law

1. In addition to pressure, temperature, and volume, what fourth variable must be considered when analyzing the behavior of a gas?

_____

2. Is the number of moles in a sample of gas directly proportional or inversely proportional to the number of particles of gas in the sample?

_____

3. At a specified temperature and pressure, is the number of moles of gas in a sample directly proportional or inversely proportional to the volume of the sample?

_____

4. Circle the letter next to the correct description of how the combined gas law must be modified to introduce the number of moles.

   a. Multiply each side of the equation by the number of moles.

   b. Add the number of moles to each side of the equation.

   c. Divide each side of the equation by the number of moles.

5. For what kind of gas is $(P \times V) / (T \times n)$ a constant for all values of pressure, temperature, and volume under which the gas can exist? _____

6. What constant can you calculate when you know the volume occupied by one mole of gas at standard temperature and pressure? _____

7. Use what you know about the ideal gas law to answer the question. What would be the units for R if P is in pascals, T is in Kelvins, V is in liters, and n is in moles?

_____

8. Complete the table about the ideal gas law. Write what each symbol in the ideal gas law represents, the unit in which it is measured, and the abbreviation of the unit.

Symbol	Quantity	Unit	Abbreviation for Unit
P			
V			
n			
R			
T			

9. When would you use the ideal gas law instead of the combined gas law?

_____

_____

Ideal Gases and Real Gases

10. Circle the letter of each sentence that is true about ideal gases and real gases.

a. An ideal gas does not follow the gas laws at all temperatures and pressures.

b. An ideal gas does not conform to the assumptions of the kinetic theory.

c. There is no real gas that conforms to the kinetic theory under all conditions of temperature and pressure.

d. At many conditions of temperature and pressure, real gases behave very much like ideal gases.

11. Is the following sentence true or false? If a gas were truly an ideal gas, it would be impossible to liquefy or solidify it by cooling or by applying pressure. _____

12. Real gases differ most from an ideal gas at _____ temperatures and _____ pressures.

13. Circle the letter(s) that complete the statement. Ideal gas particles

a. move randomly.

b. have no kinetic energy.

c. repel each other at high pressure.

d. have no mass.

14.4 Gases: Mixtures and Movements

Essential Understanding Gas pressure depends only on (1) the number of particles in a given volume and (2) their average kinetic energy. The kind of particle is not important.

Lesson Summary

Dalton's Law Dalton's law states that in a mixture of gases, the total pressure is the sum of the partial pressures of the component gases.

▶ Dalton's law is expressed as $P_{total} = P_1 + P_2 + P_3 \ldots$.

Graham's Law Gases of lower molar mass diffuse and effuse faster than gases of higher molar mass.

▶ The diffusion and effusion of a gas depends on the type of gas molecule.

▶ Graham's law states that the rates of effusion of two gases are inversely proportional to the square roots of their molar masses.

▶ To compare the rates of effusion of two gases use $\dfrac{Rate_A}{Rate_B} = \sqrt{\dfrac{molar\ mass_B}{molar\ mass_A}}$

After reading Lesson 14.4, answer the following questions.

Dalton's Law

1. Is the following statement true or false? Gas pressure depends only on the number of particles in a given volume and on their average kinetic energy. The type of particle does not matter. _____

2. The contribution of the pressure of each gas in a mixture to the total pressure is called the _____ exerted by that gas.

3. Container (T) in the figure below contains a mixture of the three different gases in (a), (b), and (c) at the pressures shown. Write in the pressure in container (T).

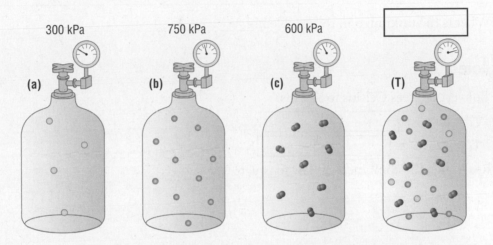

4. Is the following sentence true or false? If two objects with different masses have the same kinetic energy, the one with the greater mass must move faster. _____

Graham's Law

5. What is Graham's law of effusion?

_____

_____

Guided Practice Problems

Answer the following questions about Practice Problem 15.

A gas at 155 kPa and 25°C has an initial volume of 1.00 L. The pressure of the gas increases to 605 kPa as the temperature is raised to 125°C. What is the new volume?

Analyze

    a. Temperature can be converted from Celsius to Kelvin by adding _____ .

    b. What is the expression for the combined gas law?

    _____

    c. What is the unknown in this problem? _____

Calculate

    d. Convert degrees Celsius to kelvins.

$$T_1 = 25°C + \boxed{} = \boxed{} \, K$$

$$T_2 = 125°C + \boxed{} = \boxed{} \, K$$

    e. Rearrange the combined gas law to isolate V_2

$$V_2 =$$

    f. Substitute the known quantities into the equation and solve.

$$V_2 = \frac{1.00 \, L \times \boxed{} \, kPa \times 398 \, K}{605 \, kPa \times \boxed{} \, K} = \boxed{}$$

Evaluate

    g. Explain why you think your answer is reasonable.

    _____

    _____

    _____

    _____

    h. Are the units in your answer correct? How do you know?

    _____

Answer the following questions about Practice Problem 33.

Determine the total pressure of a gas mixture that contains oxygen, nitrogen, and helium if the partial pressures of the gases are as follows:

$$P_{O_2} = 20.0 \text{ kPa} \qquad\qquad P_{N_2} = 46.7 \text{ kPa} \qquad\qquad P_{He} = 26.7 \text{ kPa}.$$

Analyze

a. What is the expression for Dalton's law of partial pressure? _____

b. What is the unknown in this problem? _____

Calculate

c. Substitute the known quantities into the equation and solve.

Evaluate

d. Why is your answer reasonable?

_____

_____

Extra Practice

A gas has a pressure of 7.50 kPa at 420 K. What will the pressure be at 210 K if the volume does not change?

 Apply the Big idea

A student analyzes a problem and lists the following knowns and unknowns.

KNOWNS	UNKNOWN
V_1 = 500 mL	V_2
T_1 = 25°C	
T_2 = 40°C	

He calculates V_2 and gets −80 mL. Is this value correct? Explain why or why not.

_____

_____

14 Self-Check Activity

For Questions 1–10, complete each statement by writing the correct word or words. If you need help, you can go online.

14.1 Properties of Gases

1. Gases are easily compressed because of the _____ in a gas.

2. The amount of gas (n), volume (V), and temperature (T) are factors that affect _____ .

14.2 The Gas Laws

3. As the pressure of a gas increases, the _____ decreases, if the temperature is constant.

4. As the _____ of an enclosed gas increases, the volume increases, if the pressure is constant.

5. As the temperature of an enclosed gas increases, the _____ increases, if the volume is constant.

6. The _____ allows you to do calculations for situations in which only the amount of gas is constant.

14.3 Ideal Gas Laws

7. Calculating the number of moles of a contained gas requires an expression that contains the variable _____ .

8. Real gases differ most from an ideal gas at _____ temperatures and _____ pressures.

14.4 Gases: Mixtures and Movements

9. In a mixture of gases, the total pressure is the sum of the _____ of the gases.

10. Gases of lower molar mass diffuse and effuse faster than gases of _____ molar mass.

If You Have Trouble With...									
Question	1	2	3	4	5	6	7	8	9	10
See Page	413	414	418	420	422	424	426	428	432	435

Review Key Equations

Read the answer and find the question that matches.

Answer

_____ **1.** This equation $PV = nRT$ shows the relationship between a variety of gas properties.

_____ **2.** This variable must remain constant for the combined gas law to be true.

_____ **3.** Gay-Lussac's law relates these two gas variables.

_____ **4.** This gas law relates volume and temperature.

_____ **5.** This law allows you to compare the rates of effusion of two gases.

_____ **6.** This gas law relates pressure and volume.

_____ **7.** In Dalton's law, the partial pressures of the component gases are related to the total pressure by this function.

Question

A. What is Charles's law?

B. What is the number of moles?

C. What is the sum?

D. What is the ideal gas law?

E. What are the temperature and pressure?

F. What is Graham's law of effusion?

G. What is Boyle's law?

EXTENSION As you choose the question, write the equation that identifies the gas law.

Review Vocabulary

Choose a synonym from the list below for each of the four vocabulary words. Then come up with a way that will help you remember the meaning of the words. One has been done for you.

flow out	incomplete force	spread out	ability to give to pressure

Vocabulary	Synonym	How I'm Going to Remember the Meaning
compressibility		ss in *compress* reminds me of the ss in *pressure*
partial pressure		
diffusion		
effusion		

15 Water and Aqueous Systems

 BONDING AND INTERACTIONS

15.1 Water and Its Properties

Essential Understanding The bonding between water molecules differs when water is in different states, giving it different properties.

 Reading Strategy

Compare and Contrast Organizing information in a table helps you compare and contrast several topics at one time. Compare water in the liquid state to water in the solid state. As you read, ask yourself, "How are they similar? How are they different?"

As you read Lesson 15.1, use the compare and contrast table below.

Attributes of water	Water in the liquid state	Water in the solid state
Physical properties		
How atoms bond		
Relative density		

EXTENSION Make a Venn diagram of the information in the compare and contrast table.

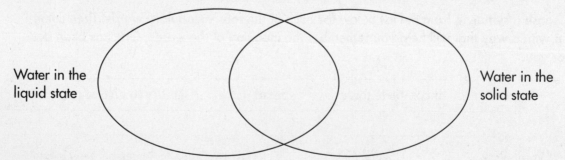

Water in the liquid state

Water in the solid state

Lesson Summary

Water in the Liquid State The polarity of water molecules causes its high surface tension, low vapor pressure, and high boiling point.

▶ The O—H bonds in a water molecule are polar because oxygen is more electronegative than hydrogen.

▶ Hydrogen bonding between water molecules occurs because a hydrogen atom is weakly bonded to an unshared electron pair of another water molecule's oxygen atom.

Water in the Solid State Hydrogen bonding gives ice unique properties.

▶ Hydrogen bonds hold water molecules in place in the solid phase, so ice is less dense than water.

▶ Because ice is less dense than liquid water, ice floats on liquid water.

After reading Lesson 15.1, answer the following questions.

Water in the Liquid State

1. What unique substance is essential to all life on Earth? _____

2. Approximately what fraction of Earth's surface is covered in water? _____

3. Circle the letter next to each sentence that is true concerning water molecules.

   a. Each O—H covalent bond in a water molecule is nonpolar.

   b. In a water molecule, the less electronegative hydrogen atoms acquire a partial positive charge and the oxygen atom acquires a partial negative charge.

   c. Because the water molecule has an H—O—H bond angle of 105°, the molecule as a whole is polar.

4. The diagram below depicts a water molecule. Complete the labels showing the locations of the hydrogen atoms, the oxygen atom, and the regions of positive and negative charge.

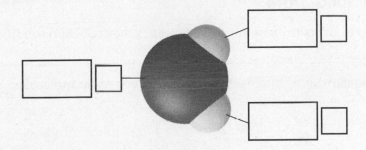

5. The diagram below depicts a collection of water molecules. Draw dotted lines showing where hydrogen bonding occurs.

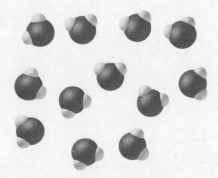

6. Circle the letter next to each sentence that describes a result of the surface tension of water.

   a. In a full glass of water, the water surface seems to bulge over the rim of the glass.

   b. Water beads up into small, nearly spherical drops on a paper towel.

   c. Water forms nearly spherical drops at the end of an eyedropper.

   d. An insect called a water strider is able to "walk" on water.

7. Using Figure 15.4, explain why a water drop has surface tension.

   _____

   _____

   _____

8. Do liquids that have higher surface tension produce drops that are flatter or more nearly spherical than liquids with lower surface tension?

   _____

   _____

9. What is the name for an agent, such as a detergent, that has the ability to reduce surface tension? _____

Water in the Solid State

10. What happens to the density of most substances as they cool and solidify?

   _____

11. The diagrams below show hydrogen bonding between water molecules.

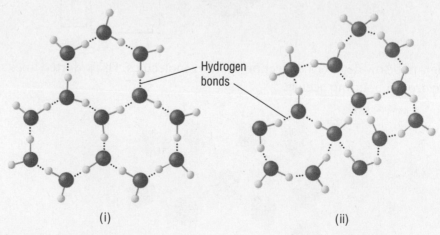

Hydrogen bonds

(i)   (ii)

   a. Which diagram depicts ice? _____

   b. Which diagram depicts liquid water? _____

   c. Why is ice less dense than liquid water? Refer to the diagrams to help you explain.

   _____

   _____

   _____

12. Look at Table 15.1. To four significant figures, list the density of

    a. liquid water at 4°C _____

    b. liquid water at 0°C _____

    c. ice at 0°C _____

13. What is unusual about the data in Question 12? Will ice float on liquid water?

_____

_____

_____

15.2 Homogeneous Aqueous Systems

(Essential Understanding) Water forms aqueous solutions with other compounds, and usually those compounds are ionic or polar covalent.

Reading Strategy

Combination Notes Combination notes help you to convey ideas in words and pictures at the same time. Write *Solutions* at the top of the T. In the left column, write brief phrases about solutions and the solution process. In the right column, draw pictures that help you visualize these concepts.

As you read Lesson 15.2, use the T-chart below. As you read about solutions and solvation, write notes on the left side of the T and illustrate them with molecular diagrams on the right side.

EXTENSION Complete another T-chart that shows the differences in ionic concentration and movement for nonelectrolytes, weak electrolytes, and strong electrolytes.

Lesson Summary

Solutions A solution consists of a dissolving medium, called a solvent, and dissolved particles, called the solute.

▶ Ionic and polar covalent compounds form aqueous solutions most easily.

▶ During the process of solvation, charged ions of an ionic solid are surrounded by solvent molecules.

Electrolytes and Nonelectrolytes A compound is classified as an electrolyte or a nonelectrolyte based on how well it conducts an electric current when it is in solution or melted.

▶ An electrolyte conducts an electric current when it is dissolved in water or molten. All ionic compounds are electrolytes.

▶ A nonelectrolyte does not conduct an electric current when it is dissolved in water or molten. Many molecular compounds are nonelectrolytes.

▶ An electrolyte is a strong electrolyte if many ions exist in solution, and it is a weak electrolyte if it produces some, but not many, ions in solution.

Hydrates A hydrate is a compound that contains water molecules in its crystal structure.

▶ The water in a hydrate is called water of hydration.

▶ Water of hydration is not held tightly to the compound, so the water molecules can be easily lost and regained.

 BUILD Math Skills

Calculating a Percent of a Hydrate A percent is a way of expressing the proportion you have of something compared to the total amount. The percent equation is

$$\% = \frac{\text{part}}{\text{whole}} \times 100$$

The term *hydrate* is used to describe a molecule or compound that contains water as part of its structure. The hydrate formula is written with the compound or molecule formula first, followed by a dot, then the number of water molecules present for every one unit of the compound. For example, the formula for calcium sulfate trihydrate is $CaSO_4 \cdot 3H_2O$. So, for every mole of calcium sulfate, there are 3 moles of water.

To find the percent of water by mass for any given hydrate, just follow these steps:

▶ Write out the formula for the hydrate.

▶ Calculate the mass of water and multiply it by the number of moles indicated in the hydrate formula.

▶ Calculate the mass of the compound.

▶ Add the mass of the compound to the mass of the water to get the total mass for the hydrate.

▶ Use the equation: $\% = \frac{\text{mass of water}}{\text{mass of hydrate}} \times 100\%$

to obtain percent of water by mass for the hydrate.

Sample Problem Determine the percent by mass of the hydrate copper sulfate pentahydrate, $CuSO_4 \cdot 5H_2O$.

First, write out the hydrate formula.	$CuSO_4 \cdot 5H_2O$
Calculate the mass of water and multiply it by the number of moles indicated in the hydrate formula.	mass of H: 1.01 g × 2 = 2.02 g mass of O: 16 g mass of water: (2.02 + 16) × 5 = 90.1 g
Calculate the mass of the compound ($CuSO_4$).	mass of Cu: 63.55 g mass of S: 32.07 g mass of O: 16 g × 4 = 64 g mass of compound: 63.55 + 32.07 + 64 = 159.62 g
Add the mass of the compound to the mass of the water to get the total hydrate mass.	total hydrate mass: 90.1 + 159.62 = 249.72 g
Use the equation: $\dfrac{\text{mass of water}}{\text{mass of hydrate}} \times 100$ to get mass percent of water.	mass % of water: $\dfrac{90.1\ g}{249.72\ g} \times 100 =$ 0.3608 × 100 = 36.08%

Now it's your turn to practice finding the mass percent of water for a given hydrate. Remember to multiply the mass of water by the number of moles indicated in the hydrate formula.

1. Determine the mass percent of water for magnesium carbonate pentahydrate, $MgCO_3 \cdot 5H_2O$.

   _____

2. Determine the mass percent of water for gypsum or calcium sulfate dihydrate, $CaSO_4 \cdot 2H_2O$.

   _____

3. Determine the mass percent of water for lithium perchlorate trihydrate, $LiClO_4 \cdot 3H_2O$.

   _____

4. Determine the mass percent of water for cobalt (II) chloride hexahydrate, $CoCl_2 \cdot 6H_2O$.

   _____

After reading Lesson 15.2, answer the following questions.

Solutions

5. Water samples containing dissolved substances are called _____.

Match each term to its description by writing its letter on the line next to the description.

_____ **6.** dissolving medium   **a.** solution

_____ **7.** dissolved particles   **b.** solute

_____ **8.** homogeneous mixture of particles   **c.** solvent
           in a dissolving medium

9. Is the following sentence true or false? After sodium chloride dissolves in a container of water, the sodium chloride will eventually settle to the bottom of the container if the solution remains undisturbed at a constant temperature. _____

10. Circle the letter next to each sentence that is true about aqueous solutions.

   a. Solute particles can be either ionic or molecular, and their average diameters are usually less than 1 nanometer.

   b. When a solution is filtered, both solute and solvent will pass through the filter paper.

   c. Ionic compounds and substances containing polar covalent molecules readily dissolve in water.

   d. Nonpolar covalent molecules, such as those found in oil, grease, and gasoline, readily dissolve in water.

11. What happens when a solid crystal of sodium chloride is placed in water?

_____

_____

12. What process occurs when solute ions become surrounded by solvent molecules?

_____

13. Look at the model of solvation in Figure 15.8. If enough solvent is present, what will eventually happen to the ionic solid depicted at the bottom of the diagram?

_____

_____

14. When a compound cannot be solvated to any significant extent, it is called

_____.

15. Circle the letter next to the one sentence that best explains why the ionic compounds barium sulfate ($BaSO_4$) and calcium carbonate ($CaCO_3$) are nearly insoluble in water.

  a. The attractions between the ions in the crystals of these ionic compounds are weaker than the attractions between the ions and water molecules.

  b. The attractions between the ions in the crystals of these ionic compounds are stronger than the attractions between the ions and water molecules.

  c. There is no difference in the strength of the attractions between the ions in the crystals and the attractions between the ions and water molecules.

  d. These ionic compounds are easily dissolved in water.

16. What saying sums up the observation that, as a rule, polar solvents dissolve ionic compounds and polar molecules, but nonpolar solvents dissolve nonpolar compounds?

_____

Electrolytes and Nonelectrolytes

17. What types of compounds can carry an electric current in the molten state or in aqueous solution? _____

18. Is the following sentence true or false? All ionic compounds are electrolytes.

_____

19. Compounds that do not conduct an electric current in either aqueous solution or the molten state are called _____.

Look at the light bulbs in Figure 15.10 to answer Questions 20, 21, and 22.

_____ **20.** Which bulb, *a*, *b*, or *c*, indicates that the solution is nonconductive?

_____ **21.** Which bulb, *a*, *b*, or *c*, indicates that the solution is weakly conductive?

_____ **22.** Which bulb, *a*, *b*, or *c*, indicates that the solution is highly conductive?

Hydrates

23. Water in a crystal that is an integral part of the crystal structure is called

_____.

24. A compound that contains water as an integral part of its crystal structure is called

_____.

25. What does "·$5H_2O$" mean when included in a chemical formula?

_____

_____

26. Circle the letter next to each sentence that is true about hydrated compounds. Use Figures 15.12 and 15.13 to help you.

   a. Crystals of copper sulfate pentahydrate always contain five molecules of water for each copper and sulfate ion pair.

   b. Heating blue crystals of copper sulfate pentahydrate above 100°C drives off the water of hydration, leaving a white anhydrous powder.

   c. It is possible to regenerate copper sulfate pentahydrate by treating anhydrous copper sulfate with water.

   d. Anhydrous cobalt(II) chloride is a good indicator for the presence of water because it changes from pink to blue when exposed to moisture.

27. If a hydrate has a vapor pressure greater than that of the water in the surrounding air, the hydrate will lose water to the air, or _____.

28. Hygroscopic substances that remove water from the air are used as drying agents called _____.

29. Look at Figure 15.15. What happens to dry sodium hydroxide pellets that are exposed to normally moist air? What kind of compound exhibits this behavior?

   _____

   _____

   _____

15.3 Heterogeneous Aqueous Systems

Essential Understanding Particles larger than the particles in a solution form heterogeneous aqueous systems, such as suspensions and colloids.

Lesson Summary

Suspensions The particles in a suspension will eventually settle out if left undisturbed.
▶ The particles in a suspension can be removed by filtration.

Colloids The particles in a colloid cannot be separated by settling or filtration.
▶ Milk is an example of a colloid.
▶ Both the dispersed phase and the dispersion medium in a colloid can be any state of matter.
▶ Colloids exhibit both the Tyndall effect and Brownian motion.

After reading Lesson 15.3, answer the following questions.

Suspensions

1. Is the following sentence true or false? Heterogeneous mixtures are not true solutions.

_____

2. Heterogeneous mixtures in which particles settle out upon standing are called

_____.

3. Is the following sentence true or false? When a suspension of clay particles in water is filtered, both clay and water will pass through the filter paper. _____

Colloids

4. Heterogeneous mixtures in which particles are of intermediate size between those of true solutions and suspensions are called _____.

5. The scattering of light in all directions by colloidal particles is known as the

_____.

6. Identify each type of system shown in the figure below.

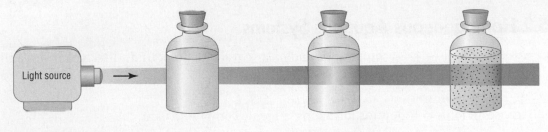

_____   _____   _____

Apply the Big idea

A student is examining three different aqueous systems.

    a. From what you know about aqueous systems, explain how the student can decide which sample is a solution, which is a suspension, and which is a colloid.

_____

_____

_____

_____

    b. Sequence *solution, suspension,* and *colloid* according to how much the polarity of water molecules affects the particles in the system. Explain your answer.

_____

_____

_____

15 Self-Check Activity

For Questions 1–8, complete each statement by writing the correct word or words. If you need help, you can go online.

15.1 Water and Its Properties

1. Many of the unique properties of water result from the _____ bonding between water molecules.

2. The unique properties of water include its low _____ and its high surface tension and boiling point.

3. Both liquid water and solid water have hydrogen bonds, but in solid water, they form a(n) _____ arrangement.

15.2 Homogeneous Aqueous Systems

4. _____ compounds and polar covalent compounds dissolve most readily in water.

5. Because all ionic compounds form ions, all ionic compounds are _____.

6. The water molecules in _____ are easily gained or lost because they are held in place by weak bonds.

15.3 Heterogeneous Aqueous Systems

7. The particles in a(n) _____ are relatively large and will settle out over time.

8. _____ contain particles smaller than those in suspensions but larger than those in solutions.

If You Have Trouble With...							
Question	1	2	3	4	5	6	7	8
See Page	489	490	492	494	496	498	504	505

Review Key Equations

From the choices below, write in each box the term that correctly completes the equation.

> mass of water   percent by mass H_2O mass of hydrate

$$\boxed{} = \frac{\boxed{}}{\boxed{}} \times 100\%$$

EXTENSION Choose a hydrate from Table 15.2 and find its percent by mass H_2O.

Review Vocabulary

Answer the following questions.

1. Use the terms *weak electrolyte, electrolyte, nonelectrolyte,* and *strong electrolyte* to complete this diagram.

Greatest number of ions	← ———————————————————————	No ions

_____ - _____ - _____

_____

2. Complete the following paragraph with vocabulary terms from Lesson 15.2.

   Sheryl was working with a sample of $MgSO_4 \cdot 7H_2O$ in the lab. She knew the compound was a(n) _____ because it contained water molecules in its formula. She placed the compound in a test tube and heated it, driving off the _____. The resulting compound was _____. Because this compound is now _____, which means it absorbs water from its environment, it could be used as a(n) _____ to remove water from other compounds.

3. Sequence the following terms according to the size of the particles they contain, from smallest to largest: *colloid, solution, suspension.*

   _____

Name _____ Class _____ Date _____

16 Solutions

 THE MOLE AND QUANTIFYING MATTER

16.1 Properties of Solutions

Essential Understanding The properties of solutions depend on the amount of solute dissolved in the solvent or the concentration of particles in the solution.

Lesson Summary

Solution Formation Agitation, temperature, and particle size all affect the speed at which a solute dissolves in a solvent.

▶ Agitation (stirring or shaking) increases the speed at which a solute dissolves.

▶ In general, increasing temperature increases how quickly a solute dissolves, and decreasing temperature decreases the rate.

▶ The smaller the particles, the quicker the rate of dissolving.

Solubility Solubility reflects the amount of solute that will dissolve in a certain amount of solvent at a specified temperature.

▶ A solution that can hold no more of the solute at a particular temperature is said to be a saturated solution at that temperature.

▶ An unsaturated solution is a solution that contains less solute than is required to saturate it at that temperature.

▶ Miscible liquids are capable of mixing in any ratio without separation of two phases.

Factors Affecting Solubility Temperature and pressure can affect the solubility of a solute in a solvent.

▶ A supersaturated solution contains more solute than usually would dissolve at that temperature.

▶ In general, increasing temperature increases the solubility of a solid in a liquid and decreases the solubility of a gas in a liquid.

▶ Increased pressure increases the solubility of a gas in a liquid but does not affect the solubility of a liquid or a solid in a liquid.

Henry's Law	Cause	Effect
$\frac{S_1}{S_2} = \frac{P_1}{P_2}$	increased pressure above solution	increased solubility of gas
	decreased pressure above solution	decreased solubility of gas

After reading Lesson 16.1, answer the following questions.

Solution Formation

Look at Figure 16.1 to help you answer Questions 1 and 2.

1. Underline the condition that causes sugar to dissolve *faster* in water.

   a. as a whole cube   or   in granulated form?

   b. when allowed to stand   or   when stirred?

   c. at a higher temperature   or   at a lower temperature?

2. Name three factors that influence the rate at which a solute dissolves in a solvent.

   a. _____

   b. _____

   c. _____

3. Is the following sentence true or false? Finely ground particles dissolve more rapidly than larger particles because finer particles expose a greater surface area to the colliding solvent molecules. _____

Solubility

4. Complete the following table showing the steps in a procedure to determine the total amount of sodium chloride that will dissolve in 100 g of water at 25°C.

Procedure	Amount dissolved	Amount not dissolved
Add 36.0 g of sodium chloride to the water	36.0 g	0.0 g
Add an additional 1.0 g of sodium chloride		
Determine the total amount that dissolves		

5. The amount of a substance that dissolves in a given quantity of solvent at a constant temperature is called the substance's _____ at that temperature.

6. If a solution contains the *maximum* amount of solute for a given quantity of solvent at a constant temperature, it is called a(n) _____ solution.

7. Look at Figure 16.2. Circle the letter of each sentence that is true about a saturated solution.

   a. The total amount of dissolved solute remains constant.

   b. The total mass of undissolved crystals remains constant.

   c. When the rate of solvation equals the rate of crystallization, a state of dynamic equilibrium exists.

   d. If more solute were added to the container, the total amount of dissolved solute would increase.

8. If two liquids dissolve each other, they are said to be _____.

9. Look at Figure 16.4. Why does the oil float on water?

_____

_____

Factors Affecting Solubility

10. Is the following sentence true or false? The solubility of sodium chloride in water increases to 39.2 g per 100 g of water at 100°C from 36.2 g per 100 g of water at 25°C.

_____

11. Circle the letter of the sentence that best answers the following question. How does the solubility of solid substances change as the temperature of the solvent increases?

a. The solubility increases for all solids.

b. The solubility increases for most solids.

c. The solubility remains constant.

12. Look at Table 16.1. Which solid substance listed in the table is nearly insoluble at any temperature? _____

13. How does the solubility of a gas change with an increase in temperature?

_____

14. The directly proportional relationship between the solubility of a gas in a liquid and the pressure of the gas above the liquid is known as _____.

15. Describe the two diagrams of a bottled carbonated beverage shown below as *greater pressure* or *lower pressure*, and then as *greater solubility* or *lower solubility*. How do these two examples illustrate the relationship between the solubility of a gas and its vapor pressure?

_____

_____

_____

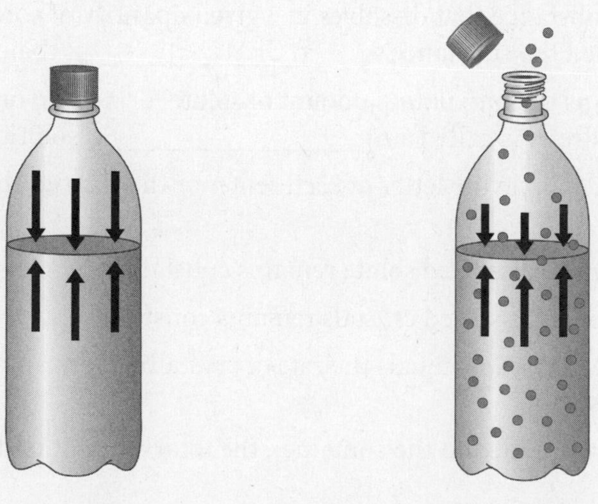

_____   _____

16. How does a solution become supersaturated?

_____

_____

_____

_____

16.2 Concentrations of Solutions

Essential Understanding The concentration of a solution can be expressed in several ways, including molarity, percent by mass, and percent by volume.

 Reading Strategy

Venn Diagram A Venn diagram is a useful tool in visually organizing related information. A Venn diagram shows which characteristics the concepts share and which characteristics are unique to each concept.

As you read Lesson 16.2, use the Venn diagram below. Fill in the diagram to compare and contrast different measures of concentration by percent.

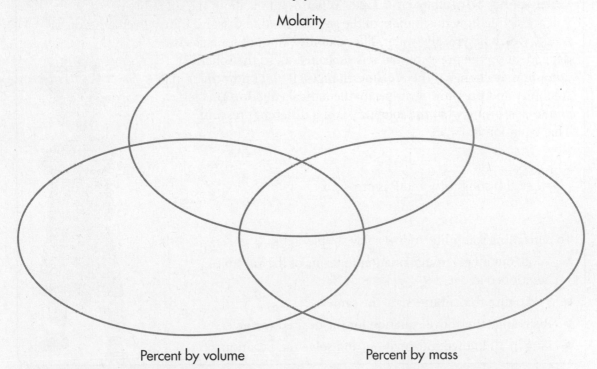

EXTENSION Choose one measure of concentration. Explain how diluting a solution affects the calculation of that measure of concentration.

_____

_____

Lesson Summary

Molarity The most important quantitative unit of concentration in chemistry is molarity.

▶ Molarity is the number of moles of solute dissolved per liter of solution.

Making Dilutions Diluting a solution involves adding additional solvent, which decreases the amount of solute per volume of solution.

▶ Diluting a solution does not affect the amount of solute in the solution, just the volume of solution.

▶ Because the amount of solute does not change, the product of the molarity and the volume before dilution equals the product of the molarity and the volume after dilution.

Percent Solutions Concentration can also be measured as percent by volume or percent by mass.

▶ Percent by volume equals the volume of solute divided by the volume of solution, multiplied by 100%.

▶ Percent by mass equals the mass of solute divided by the mass of the solution, multiplied by 100%.

📌 BUILD Math Skills

Calculating Solubility of a Gas When you talk about the solubility of a gas, you are saying how much mass of the gas you need to dissolve it in a given amount of liquid, which is typically water. The solubility amount for a gas is dependent on the pressure that it is subjected to, so the solubility amount may change if the pressure changes. If you know the initial solubility and pressure, a simple mathematical equation enables you to determine what the solubility is at a different pressure. That equation is:

$$\frac{S_1}{P_1} = \frac{S_2}{P_2}.$$ S is solubility, and P is pressure.

To determine solubility, follow a few simple steps:

▶ Write out all given information in terms of the variables mentioned above.

▶ Make sure that all units are the same.

▶ Rearrange the above equation for the desired variable.

▶ Plug in all known information, and solve the equation.

Sample Problem A gas has a solubility of 0.83 g/L in water at a pressure of 1.5 atm. What is the solubility of the gas at a pressure of 0.23 atm?

Write out the given information in terms of the appropriate variables.	$S_1 = 0.83$ g/L; $P_1 = 1.5$ atm; $P_2 = 0.23$ atm
You are trying to find S_2, so the equation should be rearranged for S_2.	$S_2 = \dfrac{(S_1 \times P_2)}{P_1}$
Plug in the known information, and solve.	$S_2 = \dfrac{(0.83 \times 0.23)}{1.5} = 0.12726$ g/L
Report your answer to the correct number of significant figures.	Since all of the given information has 2 significant digits, $S_2 = 0.13$ g/L

Hint: Remember to report your answer with the correct number of significant figures.

Now it's your turn to practice determining solubility. Remember to check that all information is given in the same units.

1. A gas has a solubility of 0.67 g/L at a pressure of 2.3 atm. If the pressure changes to 0.78 atm, what is the new solubility of the gas?

_____

2. At a pressure of 1.13 atm, a gas has a solubility of 0.13 g/L. If the solubility changes to 0.543 g/L, what has the pressure changed to?

_____

3. At a pressure of 1.56 atm, the solubility of a gas in unknown. It is known that at a pressure of 1.05 atm, the solubility is 1.68 g/L. What is the initial solubility?

_____

4. A gas has a solubility of 0.89 g/L at an unknown pressure. The same gas has a solubility of 0.34 g/L at a pressure of 2.0 atm. What is the unknown pressure?

_____

After reading Lesson 16.2, answer the following questions.

Molarity

5. A measure of the amount of solute dissolved in a given quantity of solvent is the _____ of a solution.

6. The most important unit of concentration in chemistry is _____.

7. Is the following sentence true or false? Molarity is the number of moles of dissolved solute per liter of solvent. _____

8. Look at Figure 16.8. Circle the letter of the best procedure for making a 0.50-molar (0.50M) solution in a 1-L volumetric flask.

   a. Add distilled water exactly to the 1-L mark, add 0.50 mol of solute, and then agitate to dissolve the solute.

   b. Place 0.50 mol of solute in the flask, add distilled water to the 1-L mark, and then agitate to dissolve the solute.

   c. Combine 0.50 mol of water with 0.50 mol of solute in the flask, and then agitate to dissolve the solute.

   d. Fill the flask with distilled water until it is about half-full, add 0.50 mol of solute, agitate to dissolve the solute, and then carefully fill the flask with distilled water to the 1-L mark.

9. List the information needed to find the molarity of a 2.0-L solution containing 0.50 mol of sodium chloride.

Knowns   **Unknown**

_____ of solution   molarity = ?

_____ of sodium chloride

$$\text{molarity }(M) = \frac{\boxed{}}{\text{liters of solution}}$$

Making Dilutions

10. How do you make a solution less concentrated?

_____

11. On the diagrams below, assume that each beaker contains an equal number of moles of solute. Label each solution as *concentrated* or *dilute*. Then indicate the approximate relative volumes of each solution by drawing in the surface level on each beaker.

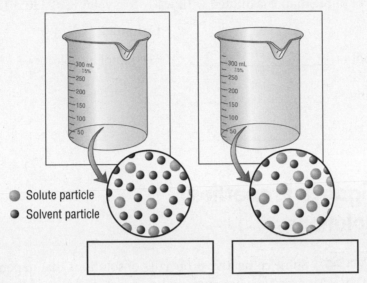

Solute particle
Solvent particle

Questions 12 and 13 refer to the following situation. Solvent is added to a solution until the total volume of the solution doubles.

12. What happens to the number of moles of solute present in the solution when the volume doubles?

_____

13. Circle the letter of the correct description of the change in molarity of a solution when the volume doubles.

a. The molarity of the solution is cut in half.

b. The molarity of the solution doubles.

c. The molarity of the solution remains constant.

d. The molarity of the solution increases slightly.

14. List the information you need to find how many milliliters of a stock solution of $2.00M$ $MgSO_4$ you would need to prepare 100.0 mL of $1.00M$ $MgSO_4$.

Knowns

$M_1 = $ _____

$M_2 = $ _____

$V_2 = $ _____

$M_1 \times$ _____ $=$ _____ $\times$ _____

Unknown

$V_1 = ?$ mL of $2.00M$ $MgSO_4$

Percent Solutions

15. List the information needed to find the percent by volume of ethanol in a solution when 50 mL of pure ethanol is diluted with water to a volume of 250 mL.

Knowns

Volume of ethanol = _____

Volume of solution = _____

% (v/v) = _____

Unknown

% ethanol by volume = ? %

16.3 Colligative Properties of Solutions

Essential Understanding Some colligative properties of solutions that depend on the number of solute particles are vapor pressure, boiling point, and freezing point.

Lesson Summary

Describing Colligative Properties Colligative properties depend on the number of solute particles present in solution.

▶ It is the number of particles, not the identity of the solute, that changes the colligative property.

▶ Increasing the amount of solute in solution decreases the vapor pressure, decreases the freezing point, and increases the boiling point of the solution.

After reading Lesson 16.3, answer the following questions.

Describing Colligative Properties

1. Properties of a solution that depend only on the number of particles dissolved, but not the identity of solute particles in the solution, are called _____.

2. Is the following sentence true or false? A nonvolatile substance is one that does not vaporize easily. _____

3. Look at Figure 16.11. What happens to the vapor pressure equilibrium when a nonvolatile solute is added to a pure solvent?

_____

_____

_____

4. How is the decrease in vapor pressure of a solution with a nonvolatile solute related to the number of particles per formula unit of solute?

_____

_____

_____

_____

5. Assume 3 mol each of three different solutes have been added to three identical beakers of water, as shown below. If the beakers are covered to form closed systems at constant temperature, rank the vapor pressures in each container from 1 (lowest) to 3 (highest).

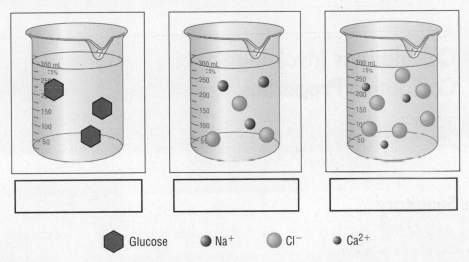

6. Circle the letter of each sentence that is true about the freezing point of a solution formed by a liquid solvent and a nonvolatile solute.

   a. When a substance freezes, the arrangement of its particles becomes less orderly.

   b. The presence of a solute in water disrupts the formation of orderly patterns as the solution is cooled to the freezing point of pure water.

   c. More kinetic energy must be withdrawn from a solution than from a pure solvent in order for the solution to solidify.

   d. The freezing point of the solution is lower than the freezing point of the pure solvent.

7. One mole of which substance, glucose or sodium chloride, will produce more freezing-point depression when added to equal amounts of water? Why?

_____

_____

_____

8. Circle the letter next to each sentence that is true concerning the boiling point of a solution formed by a liquid solvent and a nonvolatile solute.

   a. The boiling point is the temperature at which the vapor pressure equals atmospheric pressure.

   b. Adding a nonvolatile solute decreases the vapor pressure.

   c. Because of the decrease in vapor pressure, additional kinetic energy must be added to raise the vapor pressure of the liquid phase to atmospheric pressure.

   d. The boiling point of the solution is higher than the boiling point of the pure solvent.

9. The difference between the boiling point of a solution and that of the pure solvent is called the _____.

16.4 Calculations Involving Colligative Properties

Essential Understanding The colligative properties of a solution can be quantified by using the number of solute particles produced in solution, the amount of solution, and certain constants.

Lesson Summary

Molality and Mole Fraction Both the molality and mole fraction relate the ratio of solute to solvent in a solution.

▶ Molality is the number of moles of solute per kilogram of solvent.

▶ Mole fraction is the ratio of moles of solute to total moles of solute and solvent.

Freezing-Point Depression and Boiling-Point Elevation The amount a freezing point is lowered or a boiling point is elevated depends on the molality of the solution and related constants.

▶ The freezing-point depression of a solution is the product of the molality of the solution and the molal freezing-point depression constant.

▶ The boiling-point elevation of a solution is the product of the molality of the solution and the molal boiling-point elevation constant.

After reading Lesson 16.4, answer the following questions.

Molality and Mole Fraction

1. For a solution, the ratio of moles of solute to mass of solvent in kilograms, represented by m, is the solution's _____.

2. Is the following sentence true or false? Molarity and molality are always the same for a solution. _____

3. What is the molality of a solution prepared by adding 1.0 mol of sodium chloride to 2.0 kg of water? _____

4. The circle graph below shows the ratio of ethylene glycol (EG) to water in one antifreeze solution. Write the mole fractions for each substance.

Mole fraction EG = $\dfrac{\boxed{}}{\boxed{} + \boxed{}} = \dfrac{\boxed{}}{\boxed{}} = \boxed{}$

Mole fraction H_2O = $\dfrac{\boxed{}}{\boxed{} + \boxed{}} = \dfrac{\boxed{}}{\boxed{}} = \boxed{}$

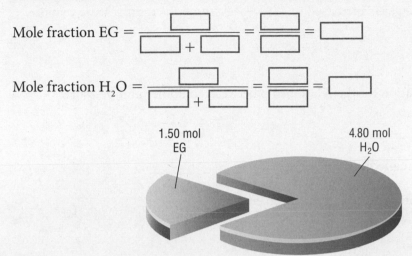

1.50 mol
EG

4.80 mol
H_2O

Freezing-Point Depression and Boiling-Point Elevation

5. Assuming a solute is molecular and not ionic, the magnitude of the boiling-point elevation of the solution, ΔT_b, is directly proportional to _____

_____.

6. Look at Table 16.2. What is the molal boiling-point elevation constant, K_b, for water?

_____

7. You need to find the freezing point of a $1.50m$ aqueous NaCl solution. You calculate ΔT_f to be $1.86°C/m \times 3.00m$, or $5.86°C$. What is the temperature at which the solution freezes? _____

Guided Practice Problems

Answer the following questions about Practice Problem 1.

The solubility of a gas in water is 0.16 g/L at 104 kPa of pressure. What is the solubility when the pressure of the gas is increased to 288 kPa? Assume the temperature remains constant.

Analyze

Step 1. What is the equation for the relationship between solubility and pressure?

_____

Step 2. What is this law called? _____

Step 3. What are the known values in this problem?

$P_1 =$ _____

$S_1 =$ _____

_____ $= 288$ kPa

Step 4. What is the unknown in this problem? _____

Calculate

Step 5. Rearrange the equation to solve for the unknown.

$S_2 =$ _____

Step 6. Substitute the known values into the equation and solve.

$$S_2 = \frac{\boxed{}\ \text{g/L} \times \boxed{}\ \text{kPa}}{\boxed{}\ \text{kPa}} = \boxed{}$$

Evaluate

Step 7. How do you know that your answer is correct?

_____

_____

Step 8. Are the units correct? Explain.

_____

_____

Answer the following questions about Practice Problem 10.

A solution has a volume of 2.0 L and contains 36.0 g of glucose ($C_6H_{12}O_6$). If the molar mass of glucose is 180 g/mol, what is the molarity of the solution?

Step 1. What is the equation for molarity of a solution?

Molarity (M) = _____

Step 2. How many moles of glucose are in the solution?

$$\boxed{} \text{ g} \times \frac{1 \text{ mol}}{\boxed{} \text{ g}} = \boxed{} \text{ mol glucose}$$

Step 3. Substitute the known values into the equation for molarity.

$$M = \frac{\boxed{}}{2.0 \; \boxed{}}$$

Step 4. Solve.

$M = $ _____

Answer the following questions about Practice Problem 11.

A solution has a volume of 250 mL and contains 0.70 mol NaCl. What is its molarity?

Analyze

Step 1. List the knowns and the unknown.

Knowns   **Unknown**

_____   _____

_____

The units of molarity, M, is mol solute/L solution.

Calculate

Step 2. Solve for the unknown.
As long as the units are correct, division gives the result.

$$\text{Molarity} = \frac{\text{mol solute}}{\text{solution volume}} = \frac{0.70 \text{ mol NaCl}}{0.250 \text{ L}} = \underline{\hspace{3cm}}$$

Evaluate

Step 3. Does the result make sense?

_____

_____

Answer the following questions about Practice Problem 14.

How many milliliters of a solution of 4.00M KI are needed to prepare 250.0 mL of 0.760M KI?

Analyze

Step 1. List the knowns and the unknown.

Knowns   **Unknown**

_____   _____

_____

_____

_____

Calculate

Step 2. Solve for the unknown.

Rearranging the equation above will give the result

$$V_1 = \frac{M_2 V_2}{M_1} = \frac{0.760M \text{ KI} \times 250.0 \text{ mL}}{4.00M \text{ KI}} = \underline{\hspace{4cm}}$$

Evaluate

Step 3. Does the result make sense?

_____

_____

_____

Answer the following questions about Practice Problem 16.

If 10 mL of propanone (or acetone, [C_3H_6O]) is diluted with water to a total solution volume of 200 mL, what is the percent by volume of propanone in the solution?

_____

Step 1. What is the equation for calculating percent by volume?

% (v/v) = _____ × 100%

Step 2. What are the knowns in this problem?

_____

_____

Step 3. Substitute the known values into the equation and solve.

$$\% \text{ (v/v)} = \frac{\boxed{} \text{ mL}}{\boxed{} \text{ mL}} \times 100\% = \boxed{} \%$$

Answer the following questions about Practice Problem 34.

How many grams of sodium fluoride are needed to prepare a 0.400*m* NaF solution that contains 750 g of water?

Analyze

Step 1. List the knowns and the unknown.

Knowns   **Unknown**

_____   _____

_____

_____

The final solution must contain 0.400 mol of NaF per 1000 g of water. This information will provide a conversion factor. The process of conversion will be:

$$\text{grams of water} \rightarrow \text{mol NaF} \rightarrow \text{grams NaF}.$$

Calculate

Step 2. Solve for the unknown.

Multiply by the appropriate conversion factors:

$$750 \text{ g H}_2\text{O} \times \frac{0.400 \text{ mol NaF}}{100 \text{ g H}_2\text{O}} \times \frac{42.0 \text{ g NaF}}{1 \text{ mol NaF}} = \underline{\hspace{2in}}$$

Evaluate

Step 3. Does the result make sense?

_____

_____

_____

Answer the following questions about Practice Problem 38.

What is the freezing-point depression of an aqueous solution of 10.0 g of glucose ($C_6H_{12}O_6$) in 50.0 g H_2O?

Analyze

Step 1. List the knowns and the unknown.

Knowns

_____

_____

_____

_____

Unknown

_____

To use the given equation, first convert the mass of solute to the number of moles, then calculate the molality, m.

Calculate

Step 2. Solve for the unknown.

Calculate the molar mass of $C_6H_{12}O_6$: $1\,mol\ C_6H_{12}O_6 = $ _____

Calculate the number of moles of solute using this conversion:

$$1\ mol\ C_6H_{12}O_6 = 10.0\ g\ C_6H_{12}O_6 \times \frac{1\ mol\ C_6H_{12}O_6}{180\ g\ C_6H_{12}O_6} = \underline{\hspace{4cm}}$$

Calculate the molality:

$$m = \frac{mol\ solute}{kg\ solvent} = \frac{0.0556\ mol\ C_6H_{12}O_6}{0.0500\ kg\ H_2O} = \underline{\hspace{3cm}}$$

Calculate the freezing-point depression using the known formula:

_____

Evaluate

Step 3. Does the result make sense?

_____

_____

_____

Answer the following questions about Practice Problem 40.

What is the boiling point of a solution that contains 1.25 mol $CaCl_2$ in 1400 g of water?

Step 1. What is the concentration m of the $CaCl_2$ solution?

$$\frac{1.25 \text{ mol}}{\boxed{} \text{ g}} \times \frac{\boxed{} \text{ g}}{1 \text{ kg}} = \boxed{} \, m$$

Step 2. How many particles are produced by the ionization of each formula unit of $CaCl_2$?

$CaCl_2(s) \rightarrow Ca^{2+} + \boxed{} Cl^-$

Therefore, _____ particles are produced.

Step 3. What is the total molality of the solution?

_____ $\times$ $0.89m = 2.7m$

Step 4. What is the molal boiling point elevation constant (K_b) for water?

K_b(water) $=$ _____ °C/m

Step 5. Calculate the boiling-point elevation.

$\Delta T_b =$ _____ °C/m $\times$ 2.7 _____ $= 1.4$ _____

Step 6. Add ΔT_b to 100°C to find the new boiling point.

_____ °C $+$ 100°C $=$ _____ °C

Answer the following questions about Practice Problem 41.

What mass of NaCl would have to be dissolved in 1.000 kg of water to raise the boiling point by 2.00°C?

Analyze

Step 1. List the knowns and the unknown.

Knowns   **Unknown**

_____   _____

_____

_____

_____

First, calculate the molality, m, using the given equation. Then, use a molar mass conversion to determine the mass of solute.

Calculate

Step 2. Solve for the unknown.

Calculate the molality by rearranging $\Delta T_b = K_b \times m$:

$$m = \Delta T_b/K_b = \frac{2.00°C}{1.86°C/m} = \underline{\hspace{3cm}}$$

Calculate the molar mass of NaCl:

1 mol NaCl = 58.5 g = _____ kg NaCl

Determine the number of moles of solute using the molality and the amount of solvent:

moles NaCl = mass of solvent × molality

$$= 1.000 \text{ kg H}_2\text{O} \times \frac{1.08 \text{ mol NaCl}}{1 \text{ kg H}_2\text{O}} = \underline{\hspace{3cm}}$$

Finally, convert the number of moles of NaCl to mass:

$$1.08 \text{ mol NaCl} \times \frac{5.85 \times 10^{-2} \text{ kg NaCl}}{1 \text{ mol NaCl}} = \underline{\hspace{3cm}}$$

Evaluate

Step 3. Does the result make sense?

_____

_____

Apply the Big idea

When is the molarity of a solution the same as its molality? When are they different? Explain your answer.

_____

_____

_____

_____

16 Self-Check Activity

For Questions 1–9, complete each statement by writing the correct word or words. If you need help, you can go online.

16.1 Properties of Solutions

1. A solute dissolves faster if it is stirred, temperature is _____, or particle size is _____.

2. If the temperature stays the same in a(n) _____ solution, a dynamic equilibrium exists between any undissolved solute and the solution.

3. _____ affects the solubility of any solute, but _____ affects solubility only if the solute is a gas.

16.2 Concentrations of Solutions

4. The number of moles of solute divided by the _____ is equal to molarity.

5. Diluting a solution increases the _____ of the solution, but the amount of _____ in the solution stays the same.

6. Percent by _____ is the ratio of the volume of solute to the volume of solution.

16.3 Colligative Properties of Solutions

7. Vapor-pressure lowering, freezing-point depression, and boiling-point elevation are all _____ properties.

16.4 Calculations Involving Colligative Properties

8. The ratio of solute to solvent is expressed as _____ or mole fraction.

9. The amount that freezing point is depressed or boiling point is elevated is proportional to the _____ of the solution.

If You Have Trouble With...								
Question	1	2	3	4	5	6	7	8	9
See Page	518	520	521	525	528	529	534	538	542

Review Key Equations

Match each formula in the first column with what it is used to calculate in the second column.

_____ 1. $\dfrac{\text{moles of solute}}{\text{kilogram of solvent}}$

_____ 2. $\Delta T_f = K_f \times m$

_____ 3. $\dfrac{S_1}{P_1} = \dfrac{S_2}{P_2}$

_____ 4. $\dfrac{\text{moles of solute}}{\text{liter of solution}}$

_____ 5. $\dfrac{n_A}{(n_A + n_B)}$

_____ 6. $\Delta T_b = K_b \times m$

_____ 7. $\dfrac{\text{volume of solute}}{\text{volume of solution}} \times 100\%$

a. boiling-point elevation

b. percent by volume

c. Henry's law

d. molarity

e. molality

f. mole fraction

g. freezing-point depression

Review Vocabulary

Look at the groups of terms below. Three of the terms in each group are related, while one does not belong. Circle the one that does not belong, and explain the relationship among the others.

1. moles, molarity, mass, volume

_____

_____

2. solute addition, elevation, freezing point, depression

_____

_____

3. saturated, mole, dissolved, solubility

_____

_____

4. solubility, freezing point, colligative, vapor pressure

_____

_____

17 Thermochemistry

Big idea MATTER AND ENERGY

17.1 The Flow of Energy

Essential Understanding All processes, whether physical or chemical, absorb or release energy according to the law of conservation of energy.

Reading Strategy

Cause and Effect A cause and effect chart is a useful tool when you want to describe how, when, or why one event causes another. As you read, draw a cause and effect chart that shows the relationship between heat flow and endothermic and exothermic processes.

As you read Lesson 17.1, use the cause and effect chart below. Complete the chart with the terms *system* and *surroundings*.

Process	Cause	Effect
endothermic	_____ lose(s) heat	_____ gain(s) heat
exothermic	_____ lose(s) heat	_____ gain(s) heat

EXTENSION Provide an example of each of the causes and effects in the chart.

_____

_____

Lesson Summary

Energy Transformations Thermochemistry is the study of energy transformations, or changes, that happen during chemical reactions or changes in state.

▶ Energy changes can involve heat transfer and/or work.

▶ Heat is the energy transferred from a warmer object to a cooler object.

Endothermic and Exothermic Processes Endothermic and exothermic processes involve the gain and loss of heat between a system and its surroundings.

▶ The system is the area of focus, and the surroundings are everything else in the universe.

▶ During any energy change, the total amount of energy is conserved.

▶ In an endothermic process, energy from the surroundings is absorbed by the system; in an exothermic process, energy from the system is released to the surroundings.

▶ Calories and joules are two units used to measure heat flow.

Heat Capacity and Specific Heat

An object's heat capacity and specific heat describe how much heat must be absorbed to raise the temperature of the object by a specific amount.

▶ Heat capacity is the amount of heat needed to raise the temperature of an object 1°C.

▶ Specific heat is the amount of heat needed to raise the temperature of 1 g of a substance 1°C.

▶ To calculate specific heat, use the formula $C = \frac{q}{m} \times \Delta T$ where q is heat, m is mass, and ΔT is the change in temperature.

BUILD Math Skills

Algebraic Equations An algebraic equation is a way of writing a mathematical relationship that includes an equal sign and at least one variable. We usually write a variable as a letter, and the value of a variable depends on the information in the problem.

Algebraic equations can contain more than one variable, or the whole equation may have only variables, such as $x^2 + 3y = z$. It's best to rearrange these kinds of equations so that the variable you're solving for is the only thing on one side of the equal sign.

$x^2 + 3y = z$ can be rewritten as $y = \frac{(z - x^2)}{3}$

There are a few rules to follow when rearranging algebraic expressions:

Rule	Example	Solution
To move a variable in the *denominator* to the opposite side, *multiply* both sides of the equation by that variable.	$\frac{2}{x} = y$	$\frac{2}{x} = y$ $x \bullet \left(\frac{2}{x}\right) = y \bullet x$ $2 = yx$
To move a variable in the *numerator* to the opposite side, *divide* both sides of the equation by that variable.	$\frac{x}{2} = y$	$\frac{x}{2} = y$ $\left(\frac{1}{x}\right) \bullet \left(\frac{x}{2}\right) = \frac{y}{x}$ $\frac{1}{2} = \frac{y}{x}$
To move a variable that is by itself, do the opposite of its sign to both sides of the equation.	$x + 4y = z$	$x + 4y = z$ $x + 4y - 4y = z - 4y$ $x = z - 4y$
If the variable has an exponent, raise both sides of the equation to the reciprocal of the exponent.	$x^2 = 3 + y$	$x^2 = 3 + y$ $(x^2)^{\frac{1}{2}} = (3 + y)^{\frac{1}{2}}$ Recall that $\frac{1}{2}$ is the reciprocal of 2.

Turn the page to learn more about algebraic equations.

Sample Problem Rearrange the following equation for x: $\frac{4x^3}{5y} + 6 = z$.

Start with any variables or numbers that are not multiplied or divided by the variable you want to isolate. In this case, it would be the number 6.	$\frac{4x^3}{5y} + 6 = z$ $\frac{4x^3}{5y} + 6 - 6 = z - 6$ $\frac{4x^3}{5y} = z - 6$
Multiply both sides by $5y$ since it is in the denominator.	$5y \cdot \left(\frac{4x^3}{5y}\right) = (z - 6) \cdot 5y$ $5y \cdot \left(\frac{4x^3}{5y}\right) = (z - 6) \cdot 5y$ $4x^3 = (z - 6) \cdot 5y$
Now divide both sides by 4 since x has a coefficient of 4.	$\frac{4x^3}{4} = \frac{(z-6) \cdot 5y}{4}$ $\frac{4x^3}{4} = \frac{(z-6) \cdot 5y}{4}$ $x^3 = \frac{(z-6) \cdot 5y}{4}$
Finally, since x has an exponent, raise both sides to its reciprocal, which, in this case, is $\frac{1}{3}$.	$(x^3)^{\frac{1}{3}} = \left(\frac{(z-6) \cdot 5y}{4}\right)^{\frac{1}{3}}$ $(x^3)^{\frac{1}{3}} = \left(\frac{(z-6) \cdot 5y}{4}\right)^{\frac{1}{3}}$ $x = \left(\frac{(z-6) \cdot 5y}{4}\right)^{\frac{1}{3}}$

Now it's your turn to practice rearranging algebraic equations. Remember that whatever operation you perform, you must apply it to both sides of the equation.

1. Rearrange the following equation for y: $x^2 + \frac{3y}{2z} = 7$

_____

2. Write the following equation so that only x appears on one side: $\frac{3zx^4}{5 + z} = 2y$

_____

3. Rewrite the following equation for the variable z: $\frac{2x}{3y} - 12 + 3z^2 = 5x^3$

_____

4. Rearrange the following equation for the variable y: $6x^3 + \frac{2z}{3y} = z^2$

_____

After reading Lesson 17.1, answer the following questions.

Energy Transformations

5. What area of study in chemistry is concerned with the heat transfers that occur during chemical reactions? _____

6. Where the use of energy is concerned (in a scientific sense), when is work done?

_____

7. Circle the letter next to each sentence that is true about energy.

a. Energy is the capacity for doing work or supplying heat.

b. Energy is detected only because of its effects.

c. Heat is energy that transfers from one object to another because they are at the same temperature.

d. Gasoline contains a significant amount of chemical potential energy.

8. Circle the letter next to each sentence that is true about heat.

a. One effect of adding heat to a substance is an increase in the temperature of that substance.

b. Heat always flows from a cooler object to a warmer object.

c. If two objects remain in contact, heat will flow from the warmer object to the cooler object until the temperature of both objects is the same.

Endothermic and Exothermic Processes

9. What can be considered the "system" and what are the "surroundings" when studying a mixture of chemicals undergoing a reaction? Write your answers where indicated below.

System:

_____

_____

Surroundings:

_____

_____

10. In thermochemical calculations, is the direction of heat flow given from the point of view of the system, or of the surroundings?

_____

11. What universal law states that energy can neither be created nor destroyed and can always be accounted for as work, stored potential energy, or heat?

_____

Questions 12 through 16 refer to the systems and surroundings illustrated in diagrams (a) and (b) below.

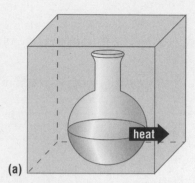 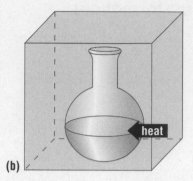

(a) (b)

12. Which diagram illustrates an endothermic process? _____

13. Is heat flow positive or negative in diagram (a)? _____

14. Which diagram illustrates an exothermic process? _____

15. Is heat flow positive or negative in diagram (b)? _____

16. What does a negative value for heat represent?

_____

To answer Questions 17 and 18, use Figure 17.2.

17. A system is a person sitting next to a fire. Is this system endothermic or exothermic? Explain why.

_____

_____

18. A system is a person who is perspiring. Is this system endothermic or exothermic? Explain why.

_____

_____

_____

19. Heat generated by the human body is usually measured in units called

_____.

20. Describe the chemical reaction that generates heat in the human body.

_____

21. What is the definition of a calorie?

_____

_____

22. How is the calorie (written with a lowercase *c*) related to the dietary Calorie (written with a capital *C*)?

_____

23. Circle the letter next to the SI unit of heat and energy.

  a. calorie

  b. Calorie

  c. joule

  d. Celsius degree

Heat Capacity and Specific Heat

24. Is the following sentence true or false? Samples of two different substances having the same mass always have the same heat capacity. _____

25. Compare the heat capacity of a 2-kg steel frying pan and a 2-g steel pin. If the heat capacities of these objects differ, explain why.

_____

26. Is the following sentence true or false? The specific heat of a substance varies with the mass of the sample. _____

17.2 Measuring and Expressing Enthalpy Changes

Essential Understanding The amount of heat absorbed or released in a chemical reaction can be measured in a calorimeter and expressed in a chemical equation.

Lesson Summary

Calorimetry Calorimetry is the measurement of the amount of heat absorbed or released in a chemical or physical process.

▶ The device used to measure this heat change is a calorimeter.

▶ At constant pressure, the enthalpy (*H*) of a system accounts for the heat flow in the system.

▶ To calculate the enthalpy change in a calorimeter experiment, multiply the mass of the water by its specific heat and the change in temperature.

Thermochemical Equations Thermochemical equations include the enthalpy change.

▶ The heat of reaction is the enthalpy change for a chemical reaction exactly as it is written.

▶ An exothermic reaction has a negative heat of reaction, and an endothermic reaction has a positive heat of reaction.

▶ The heat of reaction depends on the number of moles and the state of matter of each reactant present.

▶ The heat of combustion is the heat of reaction for the complete combustion of one mole of a substance.

After reading Lesson 17.2, answer the following questions.

Calorimetry

1. The property that is useful for keeping track of heat transfers in chemical and physical processes at constant pressure is called _____.

2. What is calorimetry?

_____

_____

3. Use Figure 17.6. Circle the letter next to each sentence that is true about calorimeters.

   a. The calorimeter container is insulated to minimize loss of heat to, or absorption of heat from, the surroundings.

   b. Because foam cups are excellent heat insulators, they can be used as simple calorimeters.

   c. A stirrer is used to keep temperatures uneven in a calorimeter.

   d. In the calorimeter shown in Figure 17.6, the chemical substances dissolved in water constitute the system, and the water is part of the surroundings.

4. Is the following sentence true or false? For systems at constant pressure, heat flow and enthalpy change are the same thing. _____

5. Complete the table below to show the direction of heat flow and type of reaction for positive and negative change of enthalpy.

Sign of enthalpy change	Direction of heat flow	Is reaction endothermic or exothermic?
ΔH is positive ($\Delta H > 0$)		
ΔH is negative ($\Delta H < 0$)		

6. Name each quantity that is represented in the equation for heat change in an aqueous solution.

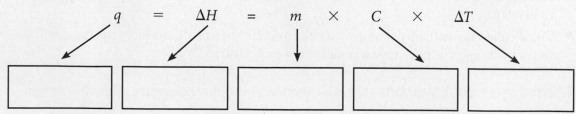

$$q \quad = \quad \Delta H \quad = \quad m \quad \times \quad C \quad \times \quad \Delta T$$

Thermochemical Equations

7. What happens to the temperature of water after calcium oxide is added?

_____

8. A chemical equation that includes the heat change is called a(n) _____ equation.

9. Why is it important to give the physical state of the reactants and products in a thermochemical equation?

_____

_____

10. Complete the enthalpy diagram for the combustion of natural gas. Use the thermochemical equations in this section as a guide.

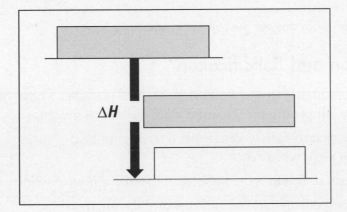

17.3 Heat in Changes of State

Essential Understanding Energy is either absorbed or released during all changes of state.

Lesson Summary

Heats of Fusion and Solidification For any substance, the molar heat of fusion equals the molar heat of solidification, but they have opposite signs.

▶ The molar heat of fusion for a substance is the amount of heat absorbed when one mole of a solid melts at a constant temperature.

▶ The molar heat of solidification for a substance is the amount of heat released when one mole of a liquid solidifies at a constant temperature.

▶ The molar heat of fusion has a positive value, and the molar heat of solidification has a negative value.

Heats of Vaporization and Condensation For any substance, the molar heat of vaporization equals the molar heat of condensation, but with opposite signs.

▶ The molar heat of vaporization for a substance is the amount of heat absorbed when one mole of a liquid vaporizes at a constant temperature.

▶ The molar heat of condensation for a substance is the amount of heat released when one mole of a vapor condenses at its normal boiling point.

▶ The molar heat of vaporization has a positive value, and the molar heat of condensation has a negative value.

Heat of Solution Heat is either released or absorbed during the solution process.

▶ The molar heat of solution is the amount of energy released or absorbed when one mole of the substance dissolves.

▶ If the temperature of the solution rises when the solute dissolves, the solution process is exothermic.

▶ If the temperature of the solution lowers when the solute dissolves, the solution process is endothermic.

After reading Lesson 17.3, answer the following questions.

Heats of Fusion and Solidification

1. Is the following sentence true or false? A piece of ice placed in a bowl in a warm room will remain at a temperature of 0°C until all of the ice has melted. _____

2. Circle the letter next to each sentence that is true about heat of fusion and heat of solidification of a given substance.

   a. The molar heat of fusion is the negative of the molar heat of solidification.

   b. Heat is released during melting and absorbed during freezing.

   c. Heat is absorbed during melting and released during freezing.

   d. The quantity of heat absorbed during melting is exactly the same as the quantity of heat released when the liquid solidifies.

3. Use Table 17.3. Determine ΔH for each of these physical changes.

   a. $H_2(s) \rightarrow H_2(l)$ $\Delta H =$ _____

   b. $NH_3(s) \rightarrow NH_3(l)$ $\Delta H =$ _____

   c. $O_2(s) \rightarrow O_2(l)$ $\Delta H =$ _____

Heats of Vaporization and Condensation

4. Is the following sentence true or false? As liquids absorb heat at their boiling points, the temperature remains constant while they vaporize. _____

Use the heating curve for water shown below to answer Questions 5, 6, and 7.

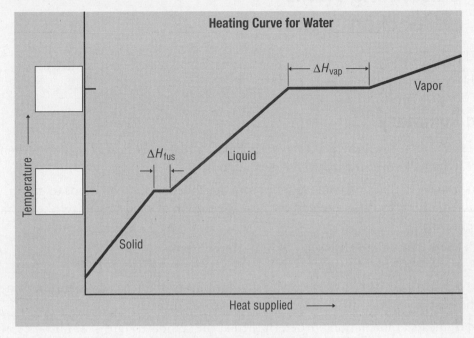

Heating Curve for Water

5. Label the melting point and boiling point temperatures on the graph.

6. What happens to the temperature during melting and vaporization?

_____

_____

7. Circle the letter next to the process that *releases* the most heat.

   a. Melting of 1 mol of water at 0°C

   b. Freezing of 1 mol of water at 0°C

   c. Vaporization of 1 mol of water at 100°C

   d. Condensation of 1 mol of water at 100°C

Use Table 17.3 to help you answer Questions 8 and 9.

8. How many of the 6 substances listed have a higher molar heat of vaporization than water? Which one(s)? _____

9. It takes _____ of energy to convert 1 mol of methanol molecules in the solid state to 1 mol of methanol molecules in the liquid state at the normal melting point.

Heat of Solution

10. The heat change caused by dissolution of one mole of a substance is the

   _____.

11. How does a cold pack containing water and ammonium nitrate work?

_____

_____

_____

17.4 Calculating Heats of Reaction

Essential Understanding Heats of reaction can be calculated when it is difficult or impossible to measure them directly.

Lesson Summary

Hess's Law Hess's law provides a way to calculate a reaction's heat of reaction when each heat of reaction is known for intermediate reactions.

▶ Hess's law states that if you add two or more thermochemical equations to get an overall equation, you also can add the heat of reaction of each step to get the overall heat of reaction.

▶ Hess's law is also called Hess's law of heat summation.

Standard Heats of Formation Using standard heats of formation is another way to determine heat of reaction when it cannot be measured directly.

▶ Standard heats of formation are determined at the standard state of a substance, which is its stable form at 25°C and 101.3 kPa.

▶ A compound's standard heat of formation is the change in enthalpy when one mole of the compound is formed from its elements with all substances in their standard states.

▶ For any reaction, the standard heat of reaction is calculated by subtracting the sum of the standard heats of formation of all the reactants from the sum of the standard heats of formation of all the products.

After reading Lesson 17.4, answer the following questions.

Hess's Law

1. For reactions that occur in a series of steps, Hess's law of heat summation says that if you add the thermochemical equations for each step to give a final equation for the reaction, you may also _____

   _____.

2. Is the following sentence true or false? Graphite is a more stable form of elemental carbon than is diamond at 25°C, so diamond will slowly change to graphite over an extremely long period of time. _____

3. Look at Figures 17.14 and 17.15. According to Hess's law, the enthalpy change from diamond to carbon dioxide can be expressed as the sum of what three enthalpy changes?

   a. _____

   b. _____

   c. _____

Standard Heats of Formation

4. The change in enthalpy that accompanies the formation of one mole of a compound from its elements with all substances in their standard states at 25°C and 101.3 kPa is called the _____.

5. Is the following sentence true or false? Chemists have set the standard heat of formation of free elements, including elements that occur in nature as diatomic molecules, at zero.

_____

6. Complete the enthalpy diagram below by finding the heat of formation when hydrogen and oxygen gases combine to form hydrogen peroxide at 25°C. Use the data in Table 17.4 and the equation $\Delta H^0 = \Delta H_f^0$ (products) $- \Delta H_f^0$ (reactants) to find the answer.

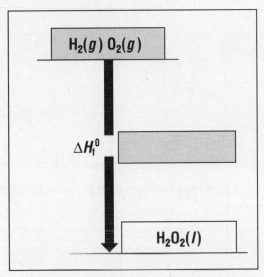

7. Look at Table 17.4. Methane burns to form carbon dioxide and water vapor.

$$CH_4(g) + 2O_2(g) \rightarrow CO_2(g) + 2H_2O(g)$$

a. Will the heat of this reaction be positive or negative? How do you know?

_____

_____

_____

b. How does your experience confirm that your answer to Question 7a is reasonable?

_____

_____

_____

Guided Practice Problems

Answer the following questions about Practice Problem 3.

When 435 J of heat is added to 3.4 g of olive oil at 21°C, the temperature increases to 85°C. What is the specific heat of the olive oil?

Analyze

a. What is the formula for calculating specific heat? _____

b. What are the knowns and the unknown in this problem?

Knowns   **Unknown**

$m =$ _____   _____

$q =$ _____

$\Delta T =$ _____

Calculate

c. Substitute the known values into the equation for specific heat, and solve.

$C_{\text{olive oil}} = \boxed{} = 2.0\ \boxed{}$

Evaluate

d. Explain why you think your answer is reasonable. Think about the time it takes to fry foods in olive oil versus the time it takes to cook foods in boiling water.

_____

_____

_____

_____

_____

e. Are the units in your answer correct? How do you know?

_____

_____

Answer the following questions about Practice Problem 12.

When 50.0 mL of water containing 0.50 mol HCl at 22.5°C is mixed with 50.0 mL of water containing 0.50 mol NaOH at 22.5°C in a calorimeter, the temperature of the solution increases to 26.0°C. How much heat (in kJ) is released by this reaction?

a. Calculate the final volume of the water. V_{final} = 50.0 mL + 50.0 mL = _____

b. Calculate the total mass of the water, using the density of water. m = _____ mL × [＿＿] g / mL = _____ g

c. Calculate ΔT. ΔT = 26.0°C – _____ °C = _____ °C

d. Substitute the known quantities into the equation for changes in enthalpy (ΔH). ΔH = – (_____ g) × (4.18 _____) × _____ °C

e. Solve. _____ J

f. Convert joules to kilojoules (kJ) and round to three significant figures. _____ J × $\frac{1\ kJ}{1000\ J}$ = _____ kJ

Answer the following questions about Practice Problem 22.

How many grams of ice at 0°C could be melted by the addition of 0.400 kJ of heat?

a. Write the conversion factors from ΔH_{fus} and the molar mass of ice. $\frac{1\ mol\ ice}{[＿＿]\ kJ}$ and $\frac{[＿＿]\ g\ ice}{1\ mol\ ice}$

b. Multiply the known heat change by the conversion factors.

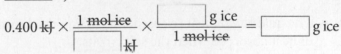

$0.400\ \text{kJ} × \frac{1\ \text{mol ice}}{[＿＿]\ \text{kJ}} × \frac{[＿＿]\ g\ ice}{1\ \text{mol ice}} = [＿＿]\ g\ ice$

> **Apply the Big idea**

A student dissolved a compound in water. The molar heat of solution of the compound is –54.3kJ/mol. The enthalpy of the solution changed by approximately 27 kJ.

Write three statements that you know to be true about dissolving this compound in water.

_____

_____

_____

_____

17 Self-Check Activity

For Questions 1–10, complete each statement by writing the correct word or words. If you need help, you can go online.

17.1 The Flow of Energy

1. Energy changes occur as heat _____ and/or work.

2. The total amount of energy in the universe _____ during any physical or chemical process.

3. The _____ of an object depends on its chemical composition and also on its mass.

17.2 Measuring and Expressing Enthalpy Changes

4. The enthalpy change of a reaction can be determined by measuring the heat flow of the reaction at constant _____.

5. In a(n) _____, enthalpy change can be written as a reactant, or it can be written as a(n) _____.

17.3 Heat in Changes of State

6. The quantity of heat released when a liquid solidifies _____ the quantity of heat absorbed when the solid melts.

7. The quantity of heat released when a vapor condenses equals the quantity of heat absorbed when the _____.

8. When a solute dissolves in a solvent, heat is either _____ or released.

17.4 Calculating Heats of Reaction

9. Using _____, heat of reaction can be determined indirectly by using known heats of reaction of more than one thermochemical equation.

10. Heat of reaction can be calculated using standard heats of formation if the reaction occurs at _____.

If You Have Trouble With...									
Question	1	2	3	4	5	6	7	8	9	10
See Page	556	557	559	562	565	569	572	574	578	580

Review Key Equations

Match each of these problems with the equation you most likely would use to solve it. Use each equation only once.

a. $C = \dfrac{q}{m \times \Delta T}$

b. $q_{sys} = \Delta H = -q_{surr} = -m \times C \times \Delta T$

c. $\Delta H^0 = \Delta H_f^0 \text{ (products)} - \Delta H_f^0 \text{ (reactants)}$

_____ 1. What is the change in enthalpy if 50.0 mL of an aqueous solution of HCl at 20°C and 50.0 mL of an aqueous KOH solution at 20°C react in a calorimeter, and the temperature increases to 24°C?

_____ 2. What is the standard heat of reaction for the reaction of $SO_2(g)$ with $O_2(g)$ to form $SO_3(g)$?

_____ 3. The temperature of a piece of iron with a mass of 53 g increases from 10°C to 28°C when the iron absorbs 439 J of heat. What is the heat capacity of iron?

EXTENSION What else do you need to know to solve Problem 2?

_____

_____

Review Vocabulary

In each set of three terms below, underline the term that does not belong with the other two terms. In the blanks provided, explain your answer.

4. molar heat of fusion, molar heat of solidification, molar heat of solution

_____

_____

_____

5. heat capacity, heat of reaction, specific heat

_____

_____

_____

6. Hess's law of heat summation, heat of combustion, heat of reaction

_____

_____

_____

18 Reaction Rates and Equilibrium

 CHEMICAL REACTIONS MATTER AND ENERGY

18.1 Rates of Reaction

Essential Understanding Collision theory explains why some reactions happen faster than others.

Lesson Summary

Describing Reaction Rates The rate of a reaction is determined by the number of effective collisions per unit of time.

▶ Collision theory states particles must collide for a reaction to occur.

▶ Activation energy is the minimum amount of kinetic energy colliding particles must have for a reaction to occur.

Factors Affecting Reaction Rates Temperature, concentration, surface area, and catalysts affect the rate of reaction.

▶ Temperature change affects reaction rate by changing the speed of the colliding particle.

▶ Concentration and particle size affect reaction rate by controlling the number of particles and the surface area available for collisions.

▶ A catalyst speeds up a reaction without being used up in the reaction.

After reading Lesson 18.1, answer the following questions.

Describing Reaction Rates

1. How are rates of chemical change expressed?

_____

_____

2. Look at Figure 18.3. In a typical reaction, as time passes, the amount of _____ decreases and the amount of _____ increases.

3. What does collision theory say about the energies of atoms, ions, or molecules reacting to form products when they collide?

_____

_____

_____

4. Look at the figures below. One shows a collision that results in the formation of product. Label it *effective collision*. Label the other collision *ineffective collision*.

_____   _____

5. Is the following sentence true or false? Particles lacking the necessary kinetic energy to react bounce apart unchanged when they collide. _____

6. Look at Figure 18.5. Which arrangement of atoms contains the least amount of energy?

    a. reactants

    b. activated complex

    c. products

7. Circle the letter of the term that completes the sentence correctly. The minimum amount of energy that particles must have in order to react is called the _____ .

    a. kinetic energy

    b. activation energy

    c. potential energy

    d. collision energy

8. An activated complex is the arrangement of atoms at the _____ of the activation-energy barrier.

9. Circle the letter of the term that best describes the lifetime of an activated complex.

    a. 10^{-15} s

    b. 10^{13} s

    c. 10^{-13} s

    d. 10^{-1} s

10. Why is an activated complex sometimes called the transition state?

_____

_____

Factors Affecting Reaction Rates

11. Changes in the rate of chemical reactions depend on conditions such as

_____ .

12. The main effect of increasing the temperature of a chemical reaction is to _____ the number of particles that have enough kinetic energy to react when they collide.

13. What happens when you put more reacting particles into a fixed volume?

_____

_____

14. Is the following sentence true or false? The smaller the particle size, the larger the surface area of a given mass of particles. _____

15. What are some ways to increase the surface area of solid reactants?

_____

16. A _____ is a substance that increases the rate of a reaction without being used up itself during the reaction.

17. What does a catalyst do?

_____

_____

The graph below shows the reaction rate of the same reaction with and without a catalyst. Use it to help you answer Questions 18 and 19.

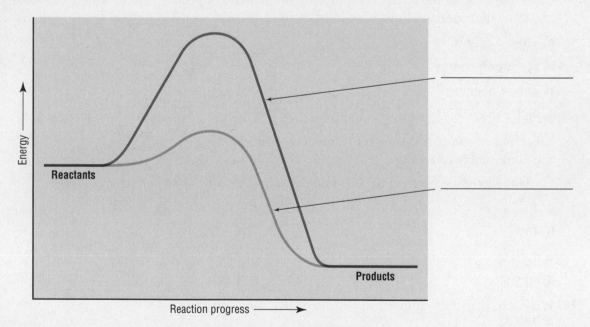

18. Label each curve as *with catalyst* or *without catalyst*.

19. What does the graph show about the effect of a catalyst on the rate of a reaction?

_____

_____

20. In a chemical equation, how do you show that catalysts are not consumed or chemically altered during a reaction?

_____

_____

21. A(n) _____ is a substance that interferes with the action of a catalyst.

18.2 The Progress of Chemical Reactions

Essential Understanding The rate of a reaction depends on the concentrations of the reactants, and is limited by the slowest step in a sequence of steps.

Lesson Summary

Rate Laws Rate laws express reaction rate in terms of the concentrations of the reactants.

▶ The specific rate constant, k, times the concentration of a reactant equals the reaction rate.

▶ In a first-order reaction, reaction rate depends on the concentration of only one reactant.

▶ In a higher-order reaction, reaction rate depends on the concentrations of more than one reactant.

Order	Reaction	Rate
first-order	$A \rightarrow B$	$k[A]$
higher-order	$aA + bB \rightarrow cC + dD$	$k[A]^a[B]^b$

Reaction Mechanisms Most reactions occur in more than one step, with the speed of the reaction determined by the speed of the slowest step.

▶ In elementary reactions, reactants form products in a single step.

▶ Most reactions take place in several steps, each step being an elementary reaction.

▶ In a multi-step reaction, the rate of the slowest step determines the rate of the reaction.

After reading Lesson 18.2, answer the following questions.

Rate Laws

1. Is the following sentence true or false? A rate law is an expression relating the rate of a reaction to the concentration of products. _____

2. What is a specific rate constant (k) for a reaction?

   _____

   _____

3. The _____ of a reaction is the power to which the concentration of a reactant must be raised to give the experimentally observed relationship between concentration and rate.

4. In a first-order reaction, the reaction rate is directly proportional to the concentration of _____.

   a. two or more reactants

   b. both reactants and products

   c. only one reactant

5. How do you determine the reaction mechanism of a reaction?

_____

Reaction Mechanisms

6. A(n) _____ reaction is one in which reactants are converted to products in a single step.

7. What is a reaction progress curve?

_____

_____

8. Is the following sentence true or false? A reaction mechanism includes all of the elementary reactions of a complex reaction. _____

9. What is an intermediate of a reaction?

_____

_____

10. What determines the rate of a multi-step chemical reaction?

_____

_____

11. Look at Figure 18.11. What is one difference between this graph and the chemical equation for this reaction?

_____

_____

_____

_____

18.3 Reversible Reactions and Equilibrium

Essential Understanding   All reactions are reversible. Reactants go to products in the forward direction. Products go to reactants in the reverse direction.

Reading Strategy

Cause and Effect A cause and effect chart is a useful tool when you want to describe how, when, or why one event causes another. As you read, draw a cause and effect chart that shows the relationship between stresses on a chemical system at equilibrium and the shift in the equilibrium of the system.

As you read Lesson 18.3, use the cause and effect chart below. List two changes in concentration that result in a shift in equilibrium toward more product.

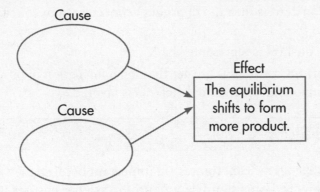

Cause

Cause

Effect

The equilibrium shifts to form more product.

EXTENSION Add another cause to the cause and effect chart that shows how a change in pressure results in more product in this reaction: $N_2(g) + 3H_2(g) \rightarrow 2NH_3(g)$.

Lesson Summary

Reversible Reactions A reversible reaction is a chemical reaction that does not go to completion and can occur in both the forward and reverse directions.

▶ During a reversible reaction, reactants form from products at the same time products form from reactants.

▶ When forward and reverse reactions occur at the same rate, equilibrium exists.

Factors Affecting Equilibrium: Le Châtelier's Principle Any stress on an equilibrium causes the equilibrium to shift in the direction that releases the stress.

▶ A change in concentration of any reactant or product will shift the equilibrium.

▶ Changing the temperature of an equilibrium causes the equilibrium to shift.

▶ Changes in pressure or volume change the equilibrium of reactions that involve gases.

Stresses and Their Effects on Equilibrium		
Stress		**Shift**
Reactant concentration	increase	right
Reactant concentration	decrease	left
Product concentration	increase	left
Product concentration	decrease	right
Temperature	increase	left
Temperature	decrease	right
Pressure	increase	toward side with fewer moles of gas
Volume	decrease	toward side with fewer moles of gas

Equilibrium Constants Equilibrium constants can be used to calculate concentrations and solubilities.

▶ An equilibrium constant is the ratio of product concentrations to reactant concentrations at equilibrium.

▶ The equilibrium constant is represented by K_{eq}.

▶ When the equilibrium constant is greater than one, formation of products is favored. When it is less than one, formation of reactants is favored.

BUILD Math Skills

Significant Figures Significant figures are important because they tell us how precise our data really is. Using significant figures in science ensures that everyone understands the *precision* of the measurements. Remember, significant digits apply only to measurements. They do not apply to pure numbers or definitions, such as 60 s/min.

How to Determine Significant Figures in a Number

Step 1 Does your number have a decimal point? If it does not have a decimal point, go to Step 2. If it does have a decimal point, go to Step 3.

Step 2 Counting significant figures with no decimal point: start at the right-hand side of the number. Begin going to the left until you reach a non-zero number. Once you reach a non-zero number, that number and all other numbers to the left of it (including zeros) count as significant figures.

Step 3 Counting significant figures with a decimal point: start at the left-hand side of the number. Begin going to the right until you reach a non-zero number. Once you reach a non-zero number, that number and all other numbers to the right of it (including zeros) count as significant figures.

Sample Problem How many significant figures are in 23500?

There's no decimal, so start at the right and move left.
→ 23500

Move left until you reach a non-zero number. Five is the first non-zero number.
→ 23500

All numbers to the left are significant.
→ 23500 *or three significant figures*

Sample Problem How many significant figures are in 0.00075?

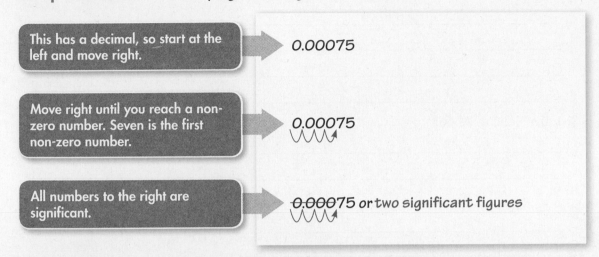

This has a decimal, so start at the left and move right. → *0.00075*

Move right until you reach a non-zero number. Seven is the first non-zero number. → *0.00075*

All numbers to the right are significant. → *0.00075 or two significant figures*

Now it's your turn to identify significant figures in the numbers below.

1. 0.0145009 _____

2. 34.9 _____

3. 600.0 _____

4. 200.000 _____

Significant Figures in Calculations

Multiplication or Division The number of significant figures in the answer is the same as that in the quantity with the *smallest* number of significant figures.

> For example, suppose you divide 25.624 grams by 25 mL. The answer should have only 2 significant figures because 25 mL has the *smallest* number of significant figures. The answer is 1.0 g/mL, not 1.0000 g/mL or 1.000 g/mL.

Addition and Subtraction The number of decimal places in the answer is equal to the number of decimal places in the quantity with the *smallest number of decimal places*.

> For example, suppose you add 14.16 + 3.2. You get 17.36, but this is not the final answer. Since the smallest number of decimal places is 1, you have to round to get only 1 decimal place. The correct answer is 17.4.

Now it's your turn to do some calculations with significant figures. Be sure that each answer is expressed to the correct number of significant figures.

5. 46.6 kg + 5.72 kg = _____

6. 4.62×0.19 = _____

For questions 7–9, write the final answer and explain your reasoning.

7. $22.37 \text{ cm} \times 3.10 \text{ cm} \times 85.75 \text{ cm} = 5946.50525 \text{ cm}^3$

_____

_____

_____

8. 91.68 mL − 19.1 mL = 72.50 mL

_____

_____

_____

_____

9. 1.473 ÷ 2.6 = 0.5665

_____

_____

_____

_____

After reading Lesson 18.3, answer the following questions.

Reversible Reactions

10. What happens in a reversible reaction?

_____

_____

11. Is the following sentence true or false? Chemical equilibrium is a state in which the forward and reverse reactions take place at different rates. _____

12. The equilibrium position of a reaction is given by the relative _____ of the system's components at equilibrium.

13. Fill in the missing labels on the diagram below with either the words *at equilibrium* or *not at equilibrium*. At equilibrium, how many types of molecules are present in the mixture? _____

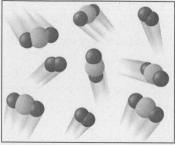 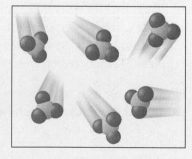

SO$_2$ and O$_2$ →   2SO$_2$ + O$_2$ ⇌ 2SO$_3$ ←   SO$_3$

_____   _____   _____

14. Use Figure 18.13 to answer these questions.

   a. Which graph, left or right, shows an initial concentration of 100% SO_3 and no SO_2?

   _____

   b. Compare the initial concentrations of the substances shown in the other graph.

   _____

   c. What is the favored substance at equilibrium? How can you tell?

   _____

Factors Affecting Equilibrium: Le Châtelier's Principle

15. What is Le Châtelier's principle?

   _____

   _____

16. Circle the letters of the terms that complete the sentence correctly. Stresses that upset the equilibrium of a chemical system include changes in _____.

   a. concentration   **c.** pressure

   b. the amount of catalyst   **d.** temperature

17. When you add a product to a reversible chemical reaction, the reaction is always pushed in the direction of _____. When you remove a product, the reaction is pulled in the direction of _____.

18. Is the following sentence true or false? Increasing the temperature of a chemical reaction causes the equilibrium position of a reaction to shift in the direction that absorbs heat. _____

19. How does increasing pressure affect a chemical system?

   _____

   _____

20. Decreasing the pressure on the system shown in Figure 18.16 results in a shift of equilibrium to favor _____.

Equilibrium Constants

21. The equilibrium constant (K_{eq}) is the ratio of _____ concentrations to _____ concentrations at equilibrium, with each concentration raised to a power equal to the number of _____ of that substance in the balanced chemical equation.

22. What are the exponents in the equilibrium-constant expression?

   _____

23. What do the square brackets indicate in the equilibrium-constant expression?

   _____

   _____

24. Is the following sentence true or false? The value of K_{eq} for a reaction depends on the temperature. _____

25. A value of K_{eq} greater than one means that _____ are favored over _____ . A value of K_{eq} less than one means that _____ are favored over _____ .

18.4 Solubility Equilibrium

Essential Understanding Equilibrium between ions in solution and undissolved compounds reflect the solubility of an ionic compound.

Lesson Summary

The Solubility Product Constant The solubility product constant of an ionic compound reflects the number of ions the compound forms in solution.

▶ Even ionic compounds that appear to be insoluble produce some ions in solution.

▶ The solubility product constant, K_{sp}, reflects only the concentrations of the dissolved ions raised to the power that is the coefficient of that ion in the equation.

$$K_{sp} = [A^+]^a[\,B^-]^b$$

The Common Ion Effect The common ion effect is a shift in equilibrium that happens because the concentration of an ion that is part of the equilibrium is changed.

▶ A common ion is an ion that is found in more than one compound in solution.

▶ The addition of a common ion to a solution reduces the solubility of the dissolved compound.

▶ A precipitate forms if the concentration of two ions in solution is greater than the K_{sp} for the compound formed from the ions.

After reading Lesson 18.4, answer the following questions.

The Solubility Product Constant

1. What is the solubility product constant (K_{sp})?

_____

_____

_____

2. Look at Table 18.1. Which ionic compounds are exceptions to the general insolubility of carbonates, phosphates, and sulfites?

_____

3. Look at Table 18.2. Which salt is more soluble in water, silver bromide (AgBr) or silver chromate (Ag_2CrO_4)? _____

The Common Ion Effect

4. A common ion is an ion that is present in both _____ in a solution.

5. Is the following sentence true or false? Raising the solubility of a substance by the addition of a common ion is called the common ion effect. _____

6. A solubility product can be used to predict whether a _____ will form when solutions are mixed.

18.5 Entropy and Free Energy

Essential Understanding Whether a reaction occurs spontaneously depends on heat changes involved in the reaction and the randomness of the particles involved.

Lesson Summary

Free Energy and Spontaneous Reactions Spontaneous reactions occur naturally and release free energy.

▶ Free energy is energy available to do work.

▶ In a reversible reaction, the favored reaction is considered to be the spontaneous reaction.

Entropy Entropy measures the degree of disorder, or randomness, of a system.

▶ According to the law of disorder, systems naturally move in the direction of maximum disorder.

▶ Reactions are favored if entropy increases in the reaction.

Enthalpy and Entropy Enthalpy and entropy together determine whether a reaction is spontaneous.

▶ A reaction is spontaneous if heat is released and entropy increases.

▶ A reaction is nonspontaneous if heat is absorbed and entropy decreases.

▶ If the change in either entropy or enthalpy is favorable and the other change is not, the size of each change must be known to determine if the reaction is spontaneous.

Free Energy Change Free energy change is calculated from enthalpy change, entropy change, and temperature.

▶ Free energy change equals enthalpy change minus the product of the temperature and the entropy change.

$$\Delta G = \Delta H - T\Delta S$$

▶ When free energy change is negative, a reaction is spontaneous.

▶ A change in temperature can make a formerly nonspontaneous reaction spontaneous.

After reading Lesson 18.5, answer the following questions.

Free Energy and Spontaneous Reactions

1. Free energy is energy that is available to do _____.

2. Is the following sentence true or false? A process can be made 100% efficient. _____

3. Make a concept map about balanced chemical reactions.

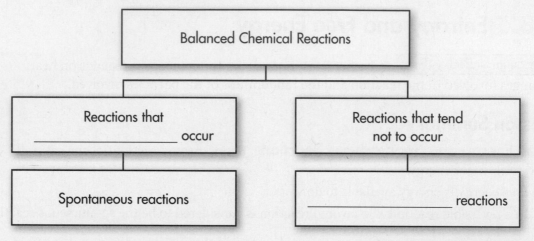

4. Spontaneous reactions are reactions that occur naturally and that favor the formation of _____ at the specified conditions.

5. Describe four spontaneous reactions mentioned in this section.

   a. _____

   b. _____

   c. _____

   d. _____

6. What are nonspontaneous reactions?

   _____

   _____

7. Is the following sentence true or false? Some reactions that are non-spontaneous at one set of conditions may be spontaneous at other conditions. _____

Entropy

8. Some factor other than _____ change must help determine whether a physical or chemical process is spontaneous.

9. What is entropy? _____

10. The law of disorder states that processes move in the direction of _____ disorder or randomness.

11. Is the following sentence true or false? Entropy decreases when a substance is divided into parts. _____

12. Number the diagrams below from 1 to 3 to show the increasing entropy of the system. Diagram 1 should show the least amount of entropy.

Liquid	Solid	Gas

_____   _____   _____

13. Does entropy tend to increase or decrease in chemical reactions in which the total number of product molecules is greater than the total number of reactant molecules?

_____

14. Entropy tends to _____ when temperature increases.

Enthalpy and Entropy

15. What determines whether a reaction is spontaneous?

_____

_____

16. Why is an exothermic reaction accompanied by an increase in entropy considered a spontaneous reaction? _____

17. Is the following sentence true or false? A nonspontaneous reaction, one in which the products are not favored, has heat changes, entropy changes, or both, working against it.

_____

Free Energy Change

18. What is the symbol for a change in entropy? _____

19. The Gibbs free-energy change (ΔG) is an indication as to whether a process is _____ at a given temperature.

20. What is the equation used to calculate the Gibbs free-energy change?

_____

_____

21. The numerical value of ΔG is _____ in spontaneous processes because the system loses free energy; the numerical value of ΔG is _____ in nonspontaneous processes because the system requires that work be expended to make them go forward at the specified conditions.

Guided Practice Problems

Show that the unit of k for a first-order reaction is a reciprocal unit of time, such as a reciprocal second (s^{-1}). Begin with the expression Rate $= k[A]$.

1. Analyze

Plan a problem-solving strategy. The definition of the reaction rate is the change in concentration of a reactant per unit of time. So using a unit, "concentration," for the numerator and "time" for the denominator, the reaction rate has units [concentration/time]. Use this knowledge algebraically to show the unit for k.

2. Solve

Apply the problem-solving strategy. Because the change in concentration per unit time is proportional to the initial concentration, setting up an equation with units will show this proportionality.

$$\frac{A[\text{concentration}]}{t[\text{time}]} = k[A]\,[\text{concentration}]$$

Canceling the unit "concentration" from both sides of the equation gives the result:

$$\frac{1}{[\text{time}]} = k$$

The unit of k is $[\text{time}]^{-1}$

Answer the following questions about Practice Problem 17.

How is the equilibrium position of this reaction affected by the following changes?

$$C(s) + H_2O(g) + \text{heat} \rightleftharpoons CO(g) + H_2(g)$$

   a. lowering the temperature

   b. increasing the pressure

   c. removing hydrogen

   d. adding water vapor

1. Analyze

Identify the relevant concepts. According to Le Châtelier's principle, the equilibrium position will shift in a direction that minimizes the imposed stress.

2. Solve

Apply the concepts to this problem. Use Le Châtelier's principle to analyze the shift in the system effected by each stress.

   a. _____

   _____

b. _____
_____

c. _____
_____

d. _____
_____

Answer the following questions about Practice Problem 18.

The reaction in which ammonia is formed is $N_2(g) \rightleftharpoons 3H_2(g) + 2NH_3(g)$. At equilibrium, a 1-L flask contains 0.15 mol H_2, 0.25 mol N_2, and 0.10 mol NH_3. Calculate K_{eq} for the reaction.

1. Analyze

List the knowns and the unknown.

Knowns

Unknown

_____   _____

_____

_____

2. Calculate

Solve for the unknowns.

Use the concentrations given and the coefficients from the balanced equation to determine K_{eq}:

$$K_{eq} = \frac{[NH_3]^2}{[N_2] \times [H_2]^3}$$

$$= \frac{0.10^2}{0.25 \times 0.15^3}$$

$$= 11.85$$

Answer the following questions about Practice Problem 20.

Suppose the following system reaches equilibrium.

$$N_2(g) + O_2(g) \rightleftharpoons 2NO(g)$$

Analysis of the equilibrium mixture in a 1-L flask gives the following results: 0.50 mol of N_2, 0.50 mol of O_2, 0.020 mol of NO. Calculate K_{eq} for the reaction.

1. Analyze

List the knowns and the unknowns.

Knowns   **Unknown**

$[N_2] =$ _____ $K_{eq} = ?$

$[O_2] =$ _____

$[NO] = 0.020$ mol/L

2. Calculate

Write the K_{eq} for the reaction. $K_{eq} =$
It should have three variables.

Substitute the known values in the expression.

$$K_{eq} = \frac{(\boxed{}\ mol/L)^2}{\boxed{}\ mol/L \times \boxed{}\ mol/L}$$

Solve. Write your answer in scientific notation. $K_{eq} = 0.0016 = \boxed{}$

Answer the following questions about Practice Problem 32.

What is the concentration of calcium ions in a saturated calcium carbonate solution at 25°C ? Use the K_{sp} value for calcium carbonate from Table 18.2.

1. Analyze

List the knowns and the unknown.

Knowns   **Unknown**

_____   _____

_____

_____

At equilibrium $[Ca^{2+}] = [CO_3^{2-}]$. This fact will be used to solve for the unknown.

2. Calculate

Solve for the unknown.

$K_{sp} = [Ca^{2+}][CO_3^{2-}]$

Make a substitution based on the equilibrium condition stated above:

$K_{sp} = [Ca^{2+}] \times [Ca^{2+}] = [Ca^{2+}]^2 = 4.5 \times 10^{-9}$

Now solve for the unknown:

$[Ca^{2+}] =$ _____

Answer the following questions about Practice Problem 33.

What is the concentration of sulfide ion in a 1.0-L solution of iron(II) sulfide to which 0.04 mol of iron(II) nitrate is added? The K_{sp} of FeS is 8×10^{-19}.

1. Analyze

List the knowns and the unknown.

Knowns   **Unknown**

_____   _____

_____

_____

_____

_____

Let $x = [S^{2-}]$ so that $x + 0.04 = [Fe^{2+}]$

2. Calculate

Solve for the unknown.

Because K_{sp} is very small, simplify by assuming $x \ll 0.04$, and becomes negligible. Thus, $[Fe^{2+}]$ is approximately equal to 0.04 M.

Solve for x in the equation:
$K_{sp} = [Fe^{2+}] \times [S^{2-}] = [Fe^{2+}] \times x = 8 \times 10^{-19}$

Rearranging for x gives the result:

$$x = \frac{8 \times 10^{-19}}{[Fe^{2+}]} = \frac{8 \times 10^{-19}}{0.04 \text{ mol}} = 2 \times 10^{-17} M$$

So $[S^{2-}] =$ _____

Apply the Big idea

Use the Reaction Mechanism to answer questions 1–5.

Reaction Mechanism					
Step 1	_fast_	**Step 2**	_slow_	**Step 3**	_fast_
A + B ⟶ C		A + D ⟶ E		C + E ⟶ F	

1. What is the overall balanced equation? _____

2. The highest activation energy is in which step? _____

3. What is the rate law for this reaction mechanism? rate = _____

4. Which letters, if any, represent intermediates in the reaction mechanism shown?

_____

5. What term describes step 2, the slowest step in the reaction mechanism?

_____

18 Self-Check Activity

For Questions 1–11, complete each statement by writing the correct word or words. If you need help, you can go online.

18.1 Rates of Reaction

1. Reaction rate is usually expressed as the change in concentration of _____ per unit time.

2. Temperature, particle size, _____, and the use of a catalyst can affect reaction rate.

18.2 The Progress of Chemical Reactions

3. The value of *k*, which represents the _____, is large when products form quickly and small when reactants form quickly.

4. Two or more _____ reactions make up most chemical reactions.

18.3 Reversible Reactions and Equilibrium

5. At equilibrium, both the forward and the reverse reactions continue, but the _____ of the reactants stay the same.

6. Stresses that upset chemical equilibrium include changes in concentration, _____, and pressure.

18.4 Solubility Equilibrium

7. Compounds that have low solubility have _____ solubility product constants.

8. A(n) _____ forms if the product of the concentrations of two ions in a mixture is greater than the K_{sp} of the compound the ions form.

18.5 Entropy and Free Energy

9. _____ reactions release free energy and produce large amounts of products.

10. A reaction is spontaneous based on the size and direction of entropy changes and _____ changes.

11. When the value of ΔG is _____, a process is spontaneous.

If You Have Trouble With...										
Question	1	2	3	4	5	6	7	8	9	10	11
See Page	543	546	552	555	558	560	570	572	576	580	582

Review Key Equations

Match items in column A to those in column B.

Column A

_____ 1. $k\,[A]$

_____ 2. $k\,[A]^a[B]^b$

_____ 3. $\dfrac{[C]^c[D]^d}{[A]^a[B]^b}$

_____ 4. $[A]^a[B]^b$

_____ 5. $\Delta H - T\Delta S$

Column B

A. K_{sp}, the solubility product constant

B. the rate of a higher-order reaction

C. K_{eq}, the equilibrium constant

D. ΔG, change in free energy

E. the rate of a first-order reaction

Review Vocabulary

Each cell has a vocabulary term from the chapter. Write how you'll remember the definition of each term on the table. A few have been done for you.

rate	inhibitor	activation energy	entropy	activated complex	
rate law	specific rate constant	first-order reaction A → B	elementary reaction	reaction mechanism	intermediate product of step 1 is reactant in step 2
reversible reaction ⟷	chemical equilibrium	equilibrium position	equilibrium constant	Le Châtelier's principle	
solubility product constant	common ion effect	common ion	nonspontaneous reaction		
free energy	spontaneous reaction happens naturally	collision theory	law of disorder		

 Acids, Bases, and Salts

Big idea ▶ REACTIONS

19.1 Acid-Base Theories

Essential Understanding Acids and bases can be classified in terms of hydrogen ions or hydroxide ions, or in terms of electron pairs.

◤ Reading Strategy

Use Prior Knowledge When you use prior knowledge, you think about your own experience before you read. You will learn new material better if you can relate it to something you already know.

Before you read Lesson 19.1, write your definition for *acid* and *base* in the table below. After you read, write the scientific definition for each term, and compare it to your own definition.

Term	Your definition	Scientific definition
Acid		
Base		

EXTENSION Name the theory that matches the scientific definition in the table. List three compounds that are acids and three that are bases according to that definition.

Lesson Summary

Arrhenius Acids and Bases Compounds are classified as Arrhenius acids or bases based on whether they ionize to yield hydrogen or hydroxide ions.

▶ Arrhenius acids contain a hydrogen atom that is released in water to form a hydronium ion (H_3O^+).

▶ Arrhenius bases contain a hydroxide group which is released in water to form a hydroxide ion (OH^-).

Brønsted-Lowry Acids and Bases Brønsted-Lowry acids are hydrogen ion donors, while bases are hydrogen ion acceptors.

▶ Brønsted-Lowry acids and bases include all the Arrhenius acids and bases plus additional substances that accept or donate hydrogen ions.

▶ The transfer of a hydrogen ion from one compound to another creates two conjugate acid-base pairs.

▶ An amphoteric compound, such as water, can be either a Brønsted-Lowry acid or base.

Lewis Acids and Bases Lewis classified substances as acids or bases depending on whether they accepted or donated a pair of electrons.

▶ The Lewis definitions are the most general for acids and bases since they are not limited to hydrogen ions.

▶ It is often necessary to write the electron dot formula of a compound to determine whether it is a Lewis acid or base.

After reading Lesson 19.1, answer the following questions.

Arrhenius Acids and Bases

1. Circle the letters of all the terms that complete the sentence correctly. The properties of acids include _____.

   a. reacting with metals to produce oxygen

   b. giving foods a sour taste

   c. forming solutions that conduct electricity

   d. causing indicators to change color

2. Bases are compounds that react with acids to form _____ and a(n) _____.

3. Circle the letters of all the terms that complete the sentence correctly. The properties of bases include _____.

   a. tasting bitter

   b. feeling slippery

   c. changing the color of an indicator

   d. always acting as a strong electrolyte

4. Match the number of ionizable hydrogens with the type of acid.

   _____ one   a. diprotic

   _____ two   b. triprotic

   _____ three   c. monoprotic

5. Hydrogen is joined to a very _____ element in a very polar bond.

6. Alkali metals react with water to produce _____ solutions.

7. How do concentrated basic solutions differ from other basic solutions?

   _____

Brønsted-Lowry Acids and Bases

8. How does the Brønsted-Lowry theory define acids and bases?

_____

_____

9. Is the following sentence true or false? Some of the acids and bases included in the Arrhenius theory are not acids and bases according to the Brønsted-Lowry theory.

_____

10. Is the following sentence true or false? A conjugate acid is the particle formed when a base gains a hydrogen ion. _____

11. A conjugate _____ is the particle that remains when an acid has donated a hydrogen ion.

12. What is a conjugate acid–base pair?

_____

_____

13. A substance that can act as both an acid and a base is said to be _____.

14. In a reaction with HCl, is water an acid or a base?

_____

Lewis Acids and Bases

15. What is a Lewis acid?

_____

_____

16. A Lewis base is a substance that can _____ a pair of electrons to form a covalent bond.

17. Is the following sentence true or false? All the acids and bases included in the Brønsted-Lowry theory are also acids and bases according to the Lewis theory.

_____

18. Complete this table of acid-base definitions.

Acid–Base Definitions		
Type	**Acid**	**Base**
Brønsted-Lowry		H^+ acceptor
	electron-pair acceptor	
	H^+ producer	

19.2 Hydrogen Ions and Acidity

Essential Understanding Water-based solutions may be acidic, basic, or neutral depending on the concentration of hydrogen ions present.

Lesson Summary

Hydrogen Ions From Water Water self-ionizes into equal numbers of H^+ and OH^- ions.

▶ In aqueous solutions, $[H^+] \times [OH^-] = 1.0 \times 10^{-14} M = K_w$, the ion product constant for water.

▶ If the concentration of hydrogen ions is greater than the concentration of hydroxide ions, the solution is acidic.

▶ An alkaline solution is basic and has a higher concentration of hydroxide ions.

The pH Concept The concentration of hydrogen ions is commonly expressed on the pH scale, which runs from 0 to 14.

▶ The mathematical expression of pH is $pH = -\log[H^+]$.

▶ A pH of less than 7 is acidic, equal to 7 is neutral, and greater than 7 is basic.

Measuring pH The pH of a solution can be measured with either a chemical acid-base indicator or with an electronic pH meter.

▶ An acid-base indicator will change color over a small range of pH.

▶ There are different indicators that change color over various pH ranges.

▶ An electronic pH meter gives a more accurate measurement of pH.

BUILD Math Skills

Calculating Logarithms Multiplication is a shortcut for addition. Logarithms are a shortcut for exponents.

To calculate the pH of a solution, you must use a logarithm. The logarithm, or log, of a number is written with a *base* number that is placed as a subscript following *log*.

If you're given a logarithmic formula in the form $\log_b (x) = y$, remember that **b** is the **base** number, **y** is the number that the base will be raised to, and b^y will equal **x**. In other words $b^y = x$.

A simple way to remember this is to think of a circle that begins at the base, $\log_b (x) = y$ flows to *y*, and ends at *x*.

For example: $\log_3 (x) = y$ has a base of 3 and would be read as "log, base 3 of *x* is equal to *y*."

Turn to the next page to learn more about calculating logarithms.

When calculating logarithms, here are a few rules to remember:

▶ If you are given b and y to find x, just take b and raise it to y. That will equal x.

▶ If you are given b and x to determine y, think of how many times b must be multiplied by itself to get x.

▶ If no base is given, then the default base number is equal to 10.

▶ $\log (cd) = \log (c) + \log (d)$

▶ $\log (c/d) = \log (c) - \log (d)$

▶ If you are given $\log_b (x^c)$, the exponent applied to x is moved to be a coefficient. For example: $\log_{10} (2^3) = 3 \cdot \log_{10} (2)$

▶ The log of 10 = 1; the log of 1 = 0; you cannot take the log of a negative number.

Sample Problem Determine x given the following equation: $\log_5 (x) = 3$.

| First, determine what you are given. | → | $b = 5$ and $y = 3$ |
| Next, take the base and raise it to the power of y to obtain x. | → | $5^3 = x = 125$
 $x = 125$ |

Sample Problem Determine y for the following equation: $\log (10^2) = y$.

| First, rewrite the equation in its simplest form using any rules that apply. Since the number designated as x has an exponent, it must be transferred to a coefficient. | → | $2 \cdot \log (10) = y$ |

Hint: Remember that since no base is specified, it is equal to 10.

| Next, determine what the log of 10 is by using your calculator. | → | $\log (10) = 1$ |
| Finally, multiply the log of 10 by the coefficient to find y. | → | $2 \cdot \log (10) = 2 \cdot 1 = 2$
 $2 = y$ |

Now it's your turn to practice calculating logarithms. Remember that it is not possible to take the log of a negative number.

1. Rewrite the following equation in log form: $2^2 = 4$.

_____

2. Determine x given $\log_3 (x) = 4$.

_____

3. Determine y for the following equation: $\log (9/8) = y$.

_____

4. Determine y for the following equation: $\log_4 (16^2) = y$.

_____

After reading Lesson 19.2, answer the following questions.

Hydrogen Ions From Water

5. What does a water molecule that loses a hydrogen ion become?

_____

6. What does a water molecule that gains a hydrogen ion become?

_____

7. The reaction in which water molecules produce ions is called the

_____ of water.

8. In water or aqueous solution, _____ are always joined to
_____ as hydronium ions (H_3O^+).

9. Is the following sentence true or false? Any aqueous solution in which $[H^+]$ and $[OH^-]$ are equal is described as a neutral solution. _____

10. What is the ion-product constant for water (K_w)? Give the definition, the expression, and the value.

_____

_____

_____

11. A(n) _____ solution is one in which $[H^+]$ is greater than $[OH^-]$. A(n)
_____ solution is one in which $[H^+]$ is less than $[OH^-]$.

12. Match the type of solution with its hydrogen-ion concentration.

_____ acidic   **a.** less than $1.0 \times 10^{-7} M$

_____ neutral   **b.** greater than $1.0 \times 10^{-7} M$

_____ basic   **c.** $1.0 \times 10^{-7} M$

The pH Concept

13. The _____ of a solution is the negative logarithm of the hydrogen-ion concentration.

14. Match the type of solution with its pH.

_____ acidic

_____ neutral

_____ basic

a. pH > 7.0

b. pH = 7.0

c. pH < 7.0

15. Look at Table 19.5. What is the approximate $[H^+]$, the $[OH^-]$, and the pH of household ammonia?

_____

16. The pOH of a solution is the negative logarithm of the _____ concentration.

17. What is the pOH of a neutral solution? _____

18. For pH calculations, in what form should you express the hydrogen-ion concentration?

_____

19. Look at the pH scale below. Label where you would find acids, bases, and neutral solutions.

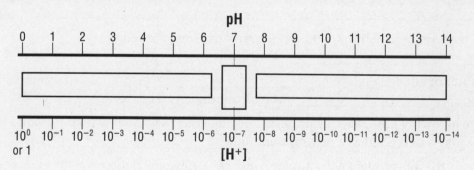

20. Is the following sentence true or false? Most pH values are whole numbers.

_____

21. If $[H^+]$ is written in scientific notation but its coefficient is not 1, what do you need to calculate pH?

_____

_____

22. Is the following sentence true or false? You can calculate the hydrogen-ion concentration of a solution if you know the pH. _____

Measuring pH

23. When do you use indicators and when do you use a pH meter to measure pH?

_____

_____

_____

24. Why is an indicator a valuable tool for measuring pH?

_____

_____

_____

25. Why do you need many different indicators to span the entire pH spectrum?

_____

_____

_____

26. Look at the figure below. Fill in the missing pH color change ranges for the indicators.

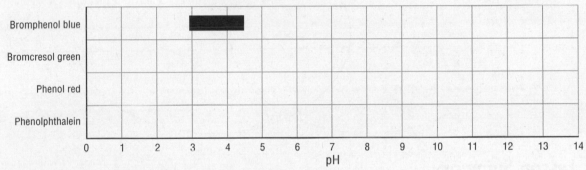

27. List three characteristics that limit the usefulness of indicators.

a. _____

b. _____

c. _____

28. What is the pH of each of the following liquids?

a. water _____

b. lemon juice _____

c. milk of magnesia _____

29. Is the following sentence true or false? Measurements of pH obtained with a pH meter are typically accurate to within 0.001 pH unit of the true pH. _____

19.3 Strengths of Acids and Bases

Essential Understanding The strength of acids and bases is determined by the degree to which they ionize in water solution.

Reading Strategy

Venn Diagram A Venn diagram is a useful tool in visually organizing related information. A Venn diagram shows which characteristics the concepts share and which characteristics are unique to each concept.

As you read Lesson 19.3, complete the Venn diagram by comparing and contrasting acids and bases.

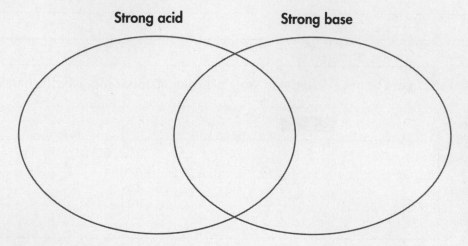

Strong acid   Strong base

Lesson Summary

Strong and Weak Acids and Bases The strength of acids and bases depends on the degree to which they ionize.

▶ Strong acids ionize completely; weak acids only ionize slightly.

▶ The acid and base dissociation constants K_a and K_b are measures of the strength of an acid or base.

After reading Lesson 19.3, answer the following questions.

Strong and Weak Acids and Bases

1. What factor is used to classify acids as strong or weak?

   _____

2. Strong acids are _____ ionized in aqueous solution; weak acids ionize _____ in aqueous solution.

3. Look at Table 19.6. Which acid is the weakest acid in the table? Which base is the weakest base?

_____

4. What do you use to write the equilibrium-constant expression?

_____

5. An acid dissociation constant (K_a) is the ratio of the concentration of the _____ form of an acid to the concentration of the _____ form.

6. What is another name for dissociation constants?

_____

7. Is the following sentence true or false? The stronger an acid is, the smaller its K_a value.

_____

8. A diprotic acid has _____ dissociation constants.

9. Look at Table 19.7. What is the second dissociation constant for the triprotic phosphoric acid? _____

10. Is the following sentence true or false? You can calculate the acid dissociation constant (K_a) of a weak acid from experimental data. _____

11. To measure the equilibrium concentrations of all substances present at equilibrium for a weak acid, what two conditions must you know?

_____

_____

_____

12. Weak bases react with water to form the hydroxide ion and the _____ of the base.

13. A base dissociation constant (K_b) is the ratio of the concentration of the _____ times the concentration of the hydroxide ion to the concentration of the _____.

14. What does the magnitude of the base dissociation constant (K_b) indicate?

_____

_____

_____

15. The words *concentrated* and *dilute* indicate how much acid or base is _____ in solution.

16. Is the following sentence true or false? The words *strong* and *weak* refer to the extent of ionization or dissociation of an acid or base. _____

19.4 Neutralization Reactions

Essential Understanding In a neutralization reaction, a strong acid and strong base produce a neutral solution.

Lesson Summary

Acid-Base Reactions Generally, an acid reacts with a base to form a salt and water.

▶ A salt is an ionic compound formed from the positive ion of the base and the negative ion of the acid.

▶ The salt formed from the neutralization of HCl and NaOH is NaCl, which is commonly called table salt.

Titration The pH of an acid or base can be determined by running a titration.

▶ An acid-base indicator is used to determine the equivalence point of the titration.

▶ By using careful measurements and calculations, the concentration of the unknown can be determined.

After reading Lesson 19.4, answer the following questions.

Acid–Base Reactions

1. Is the following sentence true or false? Acids react with compounds containing hydroxide ions to form water and a salt. _____

2. What does the reaction of an acid with a base produce?

   _____

3. In general, reactions in which an acid and a base react in an aqueous solution to produce a salt and water are called _____ reactions.

4. When is a neutralization reaction complete?

   _____

   _____

5. Salts are compounds consisting of a(n) _____ from an acid and a(n) _____ from a base.

Titration

6. How can you determine the concentration of an acid or base in a solution?

   _____

7. Complete the flow chart below showing the steps of a neutralization reaction.

A measured volume of an acid solution of _____ concentration is added to a flask.

$\downarrow$

Several drops of the _____ are added to the solution while the flask is gently swirled.

$\downarrow$

Measured volumes of a base of _____ concentration are mixed into the acid until the indicator changes _____.

8. The process of adding a known amount of solution of known concentration to determine the concentration of another solution is called _____.

9. What is the solution of known concentration called?

_____

19.5 Salts in Solution

Essential Understanding Salts in solution may be neutral, acidic, or basic depending on the acid and base from which they formed.

Lesson Summary

Salt Hydrolysis When salts dissolve in water, the ions produced react with hydrogen ions from water.

▶ If a salt donates hydrogen ions to water, it will produce an acidic solution.

▶ If a salt removes hydrogen ions from water, it will produce a basic solution.

Acidic or Basic Salt Solution?	
Acid + Base →	Salt solution
Strong acid + Strong base →	Neutral solution − neither reactant is stronger
Strong acid + Weak base →	Acidic solution − will donate more hydrogen ions
Weak base + Strong acid →	Basic solution − will remove more hydrogen ions

Buffers A buffer is a solution that can absorb small amounts of acids or bases without significant change in pH.

▶ A buffer contains a weak acid and one of its salts or a weak base and one of its salts.

▶ The weak acid can donate H^+ ions to neutralize the addition of a base, while the salt cation will neutralize an added acid by removing H^+ ions.

After reading Lesson 19.5, answer the following questions.

Salt Hydrolysis

1. What is salt hydrolysis?

_____

_____

_____

2. Complete this table of the rules for hydrolysis of a salt.

Reactants	Products
_____ acid + _____ base	Neutral solution
Strong acid + Weak base	_____ solution
_____ acid + _____ base	Basic solution

Buffers

3. What are buffers?

_____

_____

_____

4. A buffer is a solution of a _____ acid and one of its salts, or a solution of a _____ base and one of its salts.

5. Is the following sentence true or false? The buffer capacity is the amount of acid or base that can be added to a buffer solution before a significant change in pH occurs.

_____

Guided Practice Problems

Answer the following questions about Practice Problem 17b.

Calculate the pH of this solution: $[OH^-] = 8.3 \times 10^{-4}M$.

Step 1. Identify the known and unknown values.

Known	**Unknown**
$[OH^-] = \boxed{} \times 10^{-4}M$	$pH = ?$

Step 2. Calculate the $[OH^-]$ using the K_w equation.

$$K_w = [OH^-] \times [H^+]$$
$$[H^+] = \frac{K_w}{[OH^-]}$$
$$[H^+] = \frac{1 \times 10^{-14}}{8.3 \times 10^{-4}}$$
$$= 1.2 \times 10^{-11}$$

Step 3. Substitute values into the pH equation.

$$pH = -\log [H^+]$$
$$= -\log (1.2 \times \boxed{})$$

Step 4. The logarithm of a product equals the sum of the logs of its factors.

$$= - (\log \boxed{} + \log \boxed{})$$

Step 5. Evaluate log 1.2 by using a calculator. Evaluate log 10^{-11} by using the definition of logarithm.

$$= -(0.079 + \boxed{})$$

Step 6. Add and simplify. Write your answer with two significant figures to the right of the decimal point.

$$= -(-10.921) = \boxed{}$$

Answer the following questions about Practice Problem 26.

In a 0.1000M solution of methanoic acid, $[H^+] = 4.2 \times 10^{-3}M$. Calculate the K_a of methanoic acid.

Analyze

Step 1. What is known about the acid?

_____

_____

Step 2. What is the unknown? _____

Step 3. What is the expression
for the K_a of methanoic acid? $K_a =$

Calculate

Step 4. What expression can you
write to find the equilibrium
concentration of HCOOH?   _____

Step 5. Substitute values into the formula for K_a and solve.

Evaluate

Step 6. Look at Table 19.7. Explain why your answer is reasonable.

_____

_____

Extra Practice

Find the value of $[OH^-]$ for a solution with a pH of 8.00.

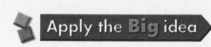

Apply the Big idea

How many moles of H_2SO_4 are needed to neutralize 1.56 moles of KOH?

19 Self-Check Activity

For Questions 1–11, complete each statement by writing the correct word or words. If you need help, you can go online.

19.1 Acid–Base Theories

1. According to Arrhenius, acids ionize to yield _____ and bases ionize to yield _____ in aqueous solution.

2. According to the Brønsted-Lowry theory, an acid is a hydrogen-ion _____, and a base is a hydrogen-ion _____.

3. According to Lewis, an acid is an electron-pair _____, and a base is an electron-pair _____.

19.2 Hydrogen Ions and Acidity

4. For an aqueous solution, the product of $[H^+]$ and $[OH^-]$ equals _____.

5. A solution with a pH less than 7.0 is _____. A solution with a pH of 7 is _____. A solution with a pH greater than 7.0 is _____.

6. Either acid-base _____ or pH meters can be used to measure pH.

19.3 Strengths of Acids and Bases

7. Acids and bases are classified as strong or weak based on the degree to which they _____ in water.

19.4 Neutralization Reactions

8. In general, acids and bases react to produce a _____ and _____.

9. Neutralization will occur when the number of moles of _____ is equal to the number of moles of _____.

19.5 Salts in Solution

10. Salts that produce _____ solutions have positive ions that release hydrogen ions to water. Salts that produce _____ solutions have negative ions that attract hydrogen ions from water.

11. A buffer is a solution of a _____ and one of its salts or a _____ and one of its salts.

If You Have Trouble With...										
Question	1	2	3	4	5	6	7	8	9	10	11
See Page	646	649	651	654	656	660	664	672	674	677	678

Review Key Equations

Read the answer and find the question that matches.

Answer

_____ 1. 0.08 M H$_2$SO$_4$

_____ 2. [H$^+$] × [OH$^-$] = 1 × 10^{-14}

_____ 3. 0.1 M NH$_4$OH

_____ 4. indicator or meter

_____ 5. 10 M CH$_3$COOH

_____ 6. $-$log[H$^+$]

_____ 7. $\dfrac{[H^+] \times [A^-]}{[HA]}$

Question

A. Which represents the ion product constant for water?

B. What is the definition of pH?

C. How do you measure pH?

D. Which represents the acid dissociation constant?

E. Which is an example of a strong acid?

F. Which is an example of a concentrated acid?

G. Which is an example of a basic salt?

Review Vocabulary

Choose a synonym from the list below for each of the four vocabulary words. Then come up with a way that will help you remember the meaning of the words. One has been done for you.

linked	split water	cushion	disconnect

Vocabulary	Synonym	How I'm going to remember the meaning
dissociation	disconnect	Dissociated ions are disconnected.
conjugate		
hydrolysis		
buffer		

20 Oxidation-Reduction Reactions

 **REACTIONS**

20.1 The Meaning of Oxidation and Reduction

Essential Understanding Oxidation and reduction are opposite chemical processes during which electrons are shifted between reactants.

Reading Strategy

Compare and Contrast Organizing information in a table helps you compare and contrast several topics at one time. Consider comparing and contrasting oxidation and reduction and how they relate to oxygen and electrons. As you read, ask yourself, "How are they similar? How are they different?"

As you read Lesson 20.1, use the compare and contrast table below. Complete the table, comparing how oxidation and reduction relate to electrons and oxygen.

Oxidation and Reduction		
	Compare	Contrast
Oxygen		
Electrons		

EXTENSION Use the information about electrons in the chart to explain why oxidation and reduction always occur together.

_____

_____

Lesson Summary

What Are Oxidation and Reduction? Oxidation and reduction are chemical processes that occur together and are called "redox" reactions.

▶ Oxidation involves losing electrons and, usually, gaining oxygen.

▶ Reduction involves gaining electrons and, usually, losing oxygen.

▶ A reducing agent loses electrons and an oxidizing agent accepts electrons.

▶ In redox reactions involving covalent compounds, electrons shift but do not completely transfer.

Corrosion Corrosion of metals is caused by a redox reaction.

▶ The presence of salts and acids can speed up corrosion.

▶ Metals that are resistant to losing electrons corrode slowly, or not at all.

▶ Some corrosion, such as rust, damages metal objects; other corrosion, such as the formation of a patina on copper, does not have negative effects on the metal.

After reading Lesson 20.1, answer the following questions.

What are Oxidation and Reduction?

1. What was the original meaning of the term *oxidation*?

_____

_____

2. Circle the letter of each sentence that is true about oxidation.

   a. Gasoline, wood, and natural gas (methane) can all burn in air, producing oxides of carbon.

   b. All oxidation processes involve burning.

   c. Bleaching is an example of oxidation.

   d. Rusting is an example of oxidation.

3. Look at Figures 20.1 and 20.2. Describe what is happening in each chemical reaction.

   a. $CH_4(g) + 2O_2(g) \rightarrow CO_2(g) + 2H_2O(g)$

   _____

   _____

   b. $4Fe(s) + 3O_2(g) \rightarrow 2Fe_2O_3(s)$

   _____

   _____

4. What is the name of the process that is the opposite of oxidation?

   _____

5. Circle the letter of each sentence that is true about oxidation and reduction.

   a. Oxidation never occurs without reduction, and reduction never occurs without oxidation.

   b. You need to add heat in order to reduce iron ore to produce metallic iron.

   c. When iron oxide is reduced to metallic iron, it gains oxygen.

   d. Oxidation-reduction reactions are also known as redox reactions.

6. What substance is heated along with iron ore in order to reduce the metal oxide to metallic iron?

   _____

7. Look at the chemical equation for the reduction of iron ore on page 693. When iron ore is reduced to metallic iron, what oxidation reaction occurs at the same time?

   _____

   _____

8. Is the following sentence true or false? The concepts of oxidation and reduction have been extended to include many reactions that do not even involve oxygen.

   _____

9. What is understood about electrons in redox reactions?

   _____

   _____

10. In the table below, fill in either "gain" or "loss" to correctly describe what happens to electrons and oxygen during oxidation and reduction.

	Oxidation	Reduction
Electrons		
Oxygen		

11. Look at Figure 20.3. Circle the letter of each sentence that is true about the reaction of magnesium and sulfur.

   a. When magnesium and sulfur are heated together, they undergo a redox reaction to form magnesium sulfide.

   b. Electrons are transferred from the metal atoms to the nonmetal atoms in this reaction.

   c. When magnesium atoms lose electrons and sulfur atoms gain electrons, the atoms become less stable.

   d. Magnesium is the oxidizing agent and sulfur is the reducing agent in this reaction.

12. Is the following sentence true or false? In any redox reaction, complete electron transfer must occur. _____

13. Is the following sentence true or false? A redox reaction might produce covalent compounds. _____

14. Draw arrows showing the shift of bonding electrons during formation of a water molecule. Then complete the table listing the characteristics of this reaction.

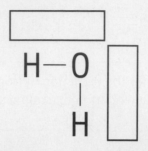

Formation of Water by Reaction of Hydrogen and Oxygen	
Chemical equation	
Shift of bonding electrons	
Reduced element	
Oxidized element	
Reducing agent	
Oxidizing agent	
Is heat released or absorbed?	

15. For each process described below, label it *O* if it is an oxidation or *R* if it is a reduction.

_____ **a.** addition of oxygen to carbon or carbon compounds

_____ **b.** removal of a metal from its ore

_____ **c.** complete gain of electrons in an ionic reaction

_____ **d.** shift of electrons away from an atom in a covalent bond

_____ **e.** gain of hydrogen by a covalent compound

Corrosion

16. Circle the letter of each sentence that is true about corrosion.

   a. Preventing and repairing damage from corrosion of metals requires billions of dollars every year.

   b. Iron corrodes by being oxidized to ions of iron by oxygen.

   c. Water in the environment slows down the rate of corrosion.

   d. The presence of salts and acids increases the rate of corrosion by producing conducting solutions that make the transfer of electrons easier.

17. Why are gold and platinum called noble metals?

_____

_____

_____

18. Look at Figure 20.5. Why is corrosion desirable in the situation shown?

_____

_____

_____

19. Look at Figure 20.6. Complete the sketch below to show how oxides form on the surface of each metal. Explain how differences between the oxides affect further corrosion of the metals.

_____

_____

_____

_____

```
┌──────────────┐          ┌──────────────┐
│              │          │              │
└──────────────┘          └──────────────┘
       │                         │
┌──────────────────┐      ┌──────────────────┐
│       Iron       │      │     Aluminum     │
└──────────────────┘      └──────────────────┘
```

20.2 Oxidation Numbers

Essential Understanding   An oxidation number is a positive or a negative number assigned to an atom to indicate how oxidized or reduced it is.

Lesson Summary

Assigning Oxidation Numbers Oxidation numbers are assigned according to established rules.

▶ If an atom is bonded to another atom, its oxidation number is the charge it would have if all the electrons in the bond were assigned to the more electronegative atom.

▶ The oxidation number of a monatomic ion is the same as its charge, in sign and magnitude.

▶ In binary ionic compounds, the oxidation number of each atom is its ionic charge.

▶ The oxidation number of an uncombined atom is 0.

▶ Some elements have only one oxidation number, but some elements have multiple oxidation numbers.

▶ The sum of the oxidation numbers of the atoms in a neutral compound is 0.

▶ The sum of the oxidation numbers in a polyatomic ion equals the ionic charge of the ion.

Oxidation-Number Changes in Chemical Reactions Oxidation numbers change any time an atom is oxidized or reduced.

▶ If the oxidation number increases, the atom or ion is oxidized.

▶ If the oxidation number decreases, the atom or ion is reduced.

After reading Lesson 20.2, answer the following questions.

Assigning Oxidation Numbers

1. Is the following sentence true or false? As a general rule, a bonded atom's oxidation number is the charge that it would have if the electrons in the bond were assigned to the more electronegative element. _____

2. For each binary ionic compound listed in the table, write the symbols for both ions, their ionic charges, and their oxidation numbers.

Compound	Ions	Ionic charges	Oxidation numbers
NaCl			
CaF_2			

3. Is the following sentence true or false? Even though water is a molecular compound, you can still obtain oxidation numbers for the bonded elements by imagining that the electrons contributed by the hydrogen atoms are completely transferred to oxygen. _____

4. Write the oxidation number, or the sum of the oxidation numbers, for the given atoms, ions, or compounds.

_____ **a.** Cu(II) ion

_____ **b.** Hydrogen in water

_____ **c.** Hydrogen in sodium hydride (NaH)

_____ **d.** Potassium sulfate (K_2SO_4)

Oxidation-Number Changes in Chemical Reactions

5. Label each change *O* if it describes oxidation or *R* if it describes reduction.

_____ **a.** Decrease in the oxidation number of an element

_____ **b.** Increase in the oxidation number of an element

20.3 Describing Redox Equations

Essential Understanding   As with all chemical reactions, redox reactions can be described by balanced chemical equations.

Lesson Summary

Identifying Redox Reactions Redox reactions are those during which an electron transfer occurs.

▶ Single-replacement, combination, decomposition, and combustion reactions are redox reactions, and double-replacement and acid-base reactions are not redox reactions.

▶ Redox reactions can be identified by a change in the oxidation number of elements during the reaction.

▶ A color change sometimes indicates a redox reaction.

Balancing Redox Equations As with other chemical equations, the chemical equations that describe redox reactions must be balanced.

▶ Redox equations can be balanced using the oxidation-number-change method or the half-reaction method.

▶ In the oxidation-number-change method, an equation is balanced by comparing the increases and decreases in oxidation number.

▶ A half-reaction is an equation showing either an oxidation or reduction that takes place in a redox reaction.

▶ In the half-reaction method, the half-reactions are balanced and then combined into a balanced redox equation.

After reading Lesson 20.3, answer the following questions.

Identifying Redox Reactions

1. Name two kinds of reactions that are not redox reactions.

   _____

   _____

2. Look at Figure 20.11b. Write the oxidation numbers of all the elements in the reactants and products. Then answer the questions about the reaction.

	Reactants		**Products**	
	Zinc	Hydrochloric acid	Zinc chloride	Hydrogen
Oxidation numbers	_____	_____	_____	_____
Chemical equation	$Zn(s)$ +	$2HCl(aq)$ →	$ZnCl_2(aq)$ +	$H_2(g)$

   a. Is this a redox reaction? _____

   b. Which element is oxidized? How do you know?

   _____

   _____

   c. Which element is reduced? How do you know?

   _____

   _____

3. When a solution changes color during a reaction, what can you conclude about that reaction?

   _____

   _____

Balancing Redox Equations

4. Answer these questions to help you balance the following equation using the oxidation-number-change method.

$$H_2(g) + O_2(g) \rightarrow H_2O(l) \text{ (unbalanced)}$$

a. What are the oxidation numbers for each atom in the equation?

b. Which element is oxidized in this reaction? Which is reduced?

_____

c. Use your answers to question 4*a* above to balance the equation. Write the coefficients needed to make the total change in oxidation number equal to 0.

$$
\begin{array}{c}
\boxed{} \times +1 \\
\overbrace{} \\
\begin{array}{ccc}
0 & 0 & +1 \; -2 \\
H_2(g) + & O_2(g) \longrightarrow & H_2O(l)
\end{array} \\
\underbrace{} \\
\boxed{} \times -2
\end{array}
$$

d. What is the final balanced equation?

_____

5. The equations for which reactions are balanced separately when using the half-reaction method?

_____

_____

6. For what kind of reaction is the half-reaction method particularly useful?

_____

7. When would you choose to use oxidation-number changes to balance an equation?

_____

_____

8. What method would you choose to balance an equation for a reaction that takes place in an acidic or alkaline solution?

_____

_____

Guided Practice Problems

Answer the following questions about Practice Problem 10.

Determine the oxidation number of each element in the following:

  a. S_2O_3 **b.** Na_2O_2 **c.** P_2O_5 **d.** NO_3^-

S_2O_3

Step 1. What is the oxidation number for oxygen? Use Rule 3. _____

Step 2. What is the oxidation number for all of the oxygen atoms? _____

Step 3. What is the oxidation number for all of the sulfur atoms? _____

Step 4. What is the oxidation number for each sulfur atom? _____

Step 5. How do you know your answers are correct?

_____

_____

Na_2O_2

Step 1. What is the oxidation number of oxygen? Use Rule 3. (Hint: This compound is a peroxide.) _____

Step 2. What is the oxidation number of sodium? _____

Step 3. How do you know your answers are correct?

The oxidation number for both oxygen atoms is _____. The sum of the oxidation numbers for all the atoms must be _____. Therefore, the oxidation number for both sodium atoms must equal _____.

P_2O_5

Step 1. What is the oxidation number for oxygen? Use Rule 3. _____

Step 2. What is the oxidation number for all of the oxygen atoms? $-2 \times 5 =$ _____

Step 3. What is the oxidation number for all of the phosphorous atoms? _____

Step 4. What is the oxidation number for each phosphorous atom? $\dfrac{+10}{2} =$ _____

Step 5. How do you know your answers are correct?

_____

_____

NO₃⁻

Step 1. What is the oxidation number for oxygen? Use Rule 3. _____

Step 2. What is the oxidation number for all of the oxygen atoms? $-2 \times 3 =$ _____

Step 3. What is the oxidation number for the nitrogen atom? _____

Step 4. How do you know your answers are correct?

_____

_____

Extra Practice

Balance this redox equation using the oxidation-number-change method.

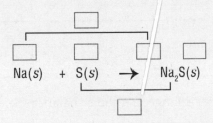

$$\text{Na}(s) + \text{S}(s) \rightarrow \text{Na}_2\text{S}(s)$$

To balance the oxidation numbers, you must multiply the oxidation number of sodium by _____. Add a coefficient of _____ in front of elemental sodium, but not in front of sodium sulfide because the sodium in sodium sulfide has a subscript of _____.

The balanced equation is _____.

Apply the Big idea

Aluminum reacts with oxygen in the air to form aluminum oxide.

a. Write the unbalanced chemical equation for this reaction.

_____

b. What is oxidized?

_____

c. What is reduced?

_____

d. What is the oxidizing agent?

_____

e. What is the reducing agent?

_____

f. Use the oxidation-number-change method to balance the equation. Show your work.

20 Self-Check Activity

For Questions 1–8, complete each statement by writing the correct word or words. If you need help, you can go online.

20.1 The Meaning of Oxidation and Reduction

1. Oxidation and _____ always occur at the same time.

2. Losing electrons is _____ and gaining electrons is _____.

3. The metal iron _____ when it reacts with oxygen to form rust.

20.2 Oxidation Numbers

4. The oxidation number of a bonded atom is the charge the atom would have if all the electrons in the bond went to the _____ element.

5. An increase in oxidation number indicates _____, and a decrease in oxidation number indicates _____.

20.3 Describing Redox Equations

6. A reaction must be a(n) _____ reaction if the oxidation number of any reactant species in the reaction changes when products form.

7. In a balanced chemical equation for a redox reaction, the total _____ in oxidation number of one reactant species must equal the total _____ in oxidation number of another reactant species.

8. When balancing a redox reaction using _____, use separate equations for the oxidation and reduction parts of the reaction.

If You Have Trouble With...							
Question	1	2	3	4	5	6	7	8
See Page	693	694	697	701	704	708	710	712

Review Vocabulary

Fill in each blank in the following paragraphs with a vocabulary term from this chapter.

When hydrogen burns, it combines with oxygen, and water forms. In this reaction, the (1) _____ of oxygen changes from 0 to −2, and that of hydrogen changes from 0 to +1. Because of this change, you know the reaction is a(n) (2) _____, also known as a(n) (3) _____. During the reaction, oxygen undergoes (4) _____ and also acts as a(n) (5) _____. At the same time, hydrogen undergoes (6) _____ and also acts as a(n) (7) _____.

A chemical equation can be written for this reaction. The equation can be balanced by using the (8) _____, in which increases and decreases in oxidation numbers are compared. It can also be balanced using the (9) _____, in which the (10) _____ for oxidation and for reduction are written and balanced separately.

21 Electrochemistry

 MATTER AND ENERGY

21.1 Electrochemical Cells

Essential Understanding Electrochemical cells produce energy in electrochemical processes and have many practical uses.

Reading Strategy

Cause and Effect A cause and effect chart is a useful tool when you want to describe how, when, or why one event causes another. It provides a pictorial display in order to recognize an effect as something that happens and a cause as the reason why it happens.

As you read Lesson 21.1, use the cause and effect chart below. Fill in the chart with a cause of the listed effect and an effect of the listed cause.

Cause	Effect
1. Atoms lose electrons.	
2.	The electrical energy needed to start a car is produced.

EXTENSION In the last two rows of the chart, write your own causes and effects from this lesson.

Lesson Summary

Electrochemical Processes During an electrochemical process, a conversion occurs between chemical energy and electrical energy.

▶ Electrochemical processes involve redox reactions because electrons are transferred.

▶ The activity series of metals helps determine the result of chemical reactions.

Voltaic Cells Voltaic cells use chemical energy from a redox reaction to produce electrical energy.

▶ A voltaic cell consists of two half-cells connected by a salt bridge.

▶ Each half-cell contains an electrode and a solution that will react with the electrode.

▶ Electrons flow from the anode, or negative electrode, to the cathode, or positive electrode.

▶ Oxidation occurs at the anode; reduction occurs at the cathode.

Using Voltaic Cells as Energy Sources Dry cells, lead-storage batteries, and fuel cells use electrochemical processes to produce energy.

▶ A common flashlight battery is a dry cell that contains a zinc anode, a graphite cathode, and a paste that acts as an electrolyte.

▶ A lead-storage battery is composed of several voltaic cells, each of which contains lead and lead(IV) oxide electrodes and concentrated sulfuric acid.

▶ Fuel cells contain renewable electrodes and a fuel that is oxidized.

After reading Lesson 21.1, answer the following questions.

Electrochemical Processes

1. What do the silver plating of tableware and the manufacture of aluminum have in common?

   _____

Look at Figure 21.1 and the related text to help you answer Questions 2–6.

2. In what form are the reactants when the reaction starts?

   _____

3. What kind of reaction occurs? Is it spontaneous?

   _____

4. Which substance is oxidized in the reaction? _____

5. Which substance is reduced? _____

6. Which atoms lose electrons and which ions gain electrons during the reaction?

   _____

7. Look at Table 21.1. What information in this table explains why the reaction in Figure 21.1 occurs spontaneously?

   _____

   _____

   _____

   _____

8. What happens when a copper strip is placed in a solution of zinc sulfate? Explain.

   _____

   _____

9. The flow of _____ from zinc to copper is an electric

   _____.

10. Circle the letter of each sentence that is true about electrochemical cells.

    a. An electrochemical cell either produces an electric current or uses an electric current to produce a chemical change.

    b. Redox reactions occur in electrochemical cells.

    c. For an electrochemical cell to be a source of useful electrical energy, the electrons must pass through an external circuit.

    d. An electrochemical cell can convert chemical energy into electrical energy, but not electrical energy into chemical energy.

Voltaic Cells

For Questions 11–15, match each description with the correct term by writing its letter in the blank.

_____ **11.** any electrochemical cell used to convert chemical energy into electrical energy

_____ **12.** one part of a voltaic cell in which either reduction or oxidation occurs

_____ **13.** the electrode at which oxidation occurs

_____ **14.** a tube containing a strong electrolyte, which allows transport of ions between the half-cells

_____ **15.** the electrode at which reduction occurs

    a. cathode

    b. salt bridge

    c. voltaic cell

    d. half-cell

    e. anode

Using Voltaic Cells as Energy Sources

16. Look at Figure 21.4. How is a common dry cell constructed?

_____

_____

_____

17. Why are alkaline cells better and longer lasting than common cells?

_____

_____

18. Which element is oxidized in a dry cell? Which element is reduced?

_____

19. What is a battery?

_____

20. How many voltaic cells are connected inside a lead storage battery typically found in a car? About how many volts are produced by each cell, and what is the total voltage of such a battery?

_____

_____

21. Look at Figure 21.5. Then, in the diagram below, label the following parts of a lead storage battery: electrolyte, anode, and cathode. Also indicate where oxidation and reduction occur while the battery is discharging.

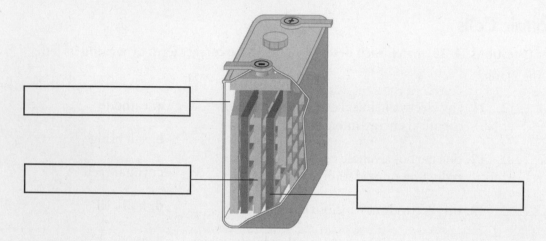

22. Are the following sentences true or false? As a lead storage battery discharges, lead sulfate builds up on the electrodes. Recharging the battery reverses this process.

_____

23. Name two advantages of fuel cells.

_____

21.2 Half-Cells and Cell Potentials

Essential Understanding The electrical potential of each half-cell determines how much electrical energy is produced by a voltaic cell.

Lesson Summary

Electrical Potential A cell's electrical potential is a measure of its ability to produce an electric current.

▶ The reduction potential of a cell describes the likelihood that its half-reaction will be a reduction reaction. The electrical potential of the entire cell is the difference in the reduction potential of its half-cells.

▶ Standard cell potential is measured at standard conditions.

▶ The standard hydrogen electrode is used with other electrodes to compare their electrical potential.

Standard Reduction Potentials
A half-cell's standard reduction potential can be found by using a standard hydrogen electrode and applying the equation for standard cell potential.

▶ The half-cell with the higher tendency to be reduced has a positive standard reduction potential.

▶ The half-cell with the lower tendency to be reduced has a negative standard reduction potential.

Calculating Standard Cell Potentials
Known standard reduction potentials can be used to predict where oxidation and reduction occur and to calculate standard cell potentials.

▶ The standard cell potential for a spontaneous redox reaction is positive; that for a nonspontaneous redox reaction is negative.

▶ Once half-cell reactions are written, the standard cell potential can be calculated by subtracting the standard cell potential for the oxidation reaction from the standard cell potential for the reduction reaction.

After reading Lesson 21.2, answer the following questions.

Electrical Potential

1. What unit is usually used to measure electrical potential?

   _____

2. What is the equation for cell potential?

   _____

3. What value have chemists assigned as the standard reduction potential of the hydrogen electrode? _____

4. Describe a standard hydrogen electrode.

   _____

   _____

   _____

Standard Reduction Potentials

5. Use of a standard hydrogen electrode allows scientists to determine the
   _____ for many half-cells.

6. Look at Figure 21.9. Which substance, zinc metal or hydrogen gas, has a greater potential to be oxidized? How can you tell?

   _____

   _____

7. In the diagram below use the value given for E^0_{cell} above the voltmeter and Table 21.2 to identify the chemical substances in the left half-cell. Use symbols to label the metal electrode and the ions in the half-cell. Also label the cathode and the anode.

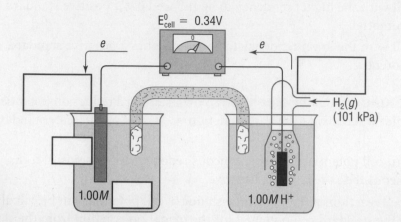

Calculating Standard Cell Potentials

8. If the cell potential for a given redox reaction is _____, then the reaction is _____. If the cell potential is _____, then the reaction is _____.

21.3 Electrolytic Cells

Essential Understanding   Electrolytic cells use the process of electrolysis to bring about chemical reactions.

Lesson Summary

Electrolytic vs. Voltaic Cells   In contrast to voltaic cells, which use a chemical reaction to produce an electric current, electrolytic cells use electrical energy to produce a chemical change.

▶ The process that uses electric energy to produce chemical change is called electrolysis and is carried out in an electrolytic cell.

▶ In a voltaic cell, electrons flow because of a spontaneous chemical reaction; in an electrolytic cell, electrons flow because of an outside power source.

Driving Nonspontaneous Processes   Nonspontaneous redox reactions sometimes occur because of electrolysis.

▶ Passing a current through a solution or a molten ionic compound can break the compound into its component elements.

▶ Electrolysis is also used in plating, purifying, and refining metals.

After reading Lesson 21.3, answer the following questions.

Electrolytic vs. Voltaic Cells

1. An electrochemical cell used to cause a chemical change through the application of electrical energy is called _____.

2. For each sentence below, fill in *V* if it is true about voltaic cells, *E* if it is true about electrolytic cells, and *B* if it is true about both voltaic and electrolytic cells.

   _____ **a.** Electrons are pushed by an outside power source.

   _____ **b.** Reduction occurs at the cathode and oxidation occurs at the anode.

   _____ **c.** The flow of electrons is the result of a spontaneous redox reaction.

   _____ **d.** Electrons flow from the anode to the cathode.

Driving Nonspontaneous Processes

3. Write the net reaction for the electrolysis of water.

   _____

4. Which three important industrial chemicals are produced through the electrolysis of brine?

   _____

   _____

5. Why are the sodium ions not reduced to sodium metal during the electrolysis of brine?

   _____

   _____

6. Deposition of a thin layer of metal on an object in an electrolytic cell is called

   _____.

7. The object to be plated is made the _____ in the cell.

Guided Practice Problems

Use this information to answer questions about Practice Problem 10.

A voltaic cell is constructed using the following half-reactions.

$$Cu^{2+}(aq) + 2e^- \rightarrow Cu(s) \qquad E^0_{Cu^{2+}} = +0.34 \text{ V}$$

$$Al^{3+}(aq) + 3e^- \rightarrow Al(s) \qquad E^0_{Al^{3+}} = -1.66 \text{ V}$$

Determine the cell reaction.

Analyze

Step 1. Which half-reaction is a reduction? An oxidation?

Reduction: _____

Oxidation: _____

Step 2. Write both half-reactions in the direction they actually occur.

_____

Calculate

Step 3. Write the cell reaction by adding the half-reactions, making certain that the number of electrons lost equals the number of electrons gained. The electrons gained and lost will cancel out.

$\square\ Cu^{2+}(aq) + 2e^- \rightarrow Cu(s)$

$\square\ Al(s) \rightarrow Al^{3+}(aq) + 3e^-$

$\boxed{\qquad\qquad\qquad\qquad\qquad}$

Evaluate

Step 4. How do you know that the cell reaction is correct?

_____

Use this information to answer questions about Practice Problem 12.

Calculate the standard cell potential of a voltaic cell constructed using the half-reactions described in Problem 10.

Analyze

Step 1. What are the known values?

_____

Step 2. What is the expression for the standard cell potential?

$E^0_{cell} = $ _____

Calculate

Step 3. Calculate the standard cell potential.

$E^0_{cell} = $ _____

Evaluate

Step 4. When a reaction is spontaneous, will the standard cell potential be positive or negative?

_____

Apply the Big idea

Zinc is sometimes used to coat iron objects to keep them from rusting. The most common way of doing this is called galvanizing. When iron items are galvanized, they are dipped in molten zinc, forming a thin coat of zinc over the iron.

a. Would a thin coat of zinc form on an iron object placed in a solution containing zinc ions? Explain your answer.

_____

_____

_____

b. Could zinc be electroplated on an iron object? Explain.

_____

_____

_____

_____

21 Self-Check Activity

For Questions 1–9, complete each statement by writing the correct word or words. If you need help, you can go online.

21.1 Electrochemical Cells

1. All electrochemical processes, such as those in a battery, use _**redox**_____ reactions.

2. In a voltaic cell, electrical energy is produced by a(n) _**spontaneous**_____ chemical reaction.

3. Dry cells, lead storage batteries, and _**fuel cells**_____ are all examples of applications that use electrochemical processes.

21.2 Half-Cells and Cell Potentials

4. The _**electrical potential**_____ of a cell is determined by the relative attraction of each half-cell for electrons.

5. The standard reduction potential of a half-cell can be determined by using a(n) _**standard hydrogen**_____ electrode and the equation for _**standard cell potential**_____.

6. A(n) _**positive**_____ cell potential for a given redox reaction means that the reaction is spontaneous.

21.3 Electrolytic Cells

7. In a(n) _**voltaic**_____ cell, electron flow comes from a spontaneous chemical reaction.

8. In a(n) _**electrolytic**_____ cell, electron flow comes from an outside power source.

9. The process of _**electrolysis**_____ is commonly used to plate, purify, and refine metals.

If You Have Trouble With...								
Question	1	2	3	4	5	6	7	8	9
See Page	728	730	732	737	738	741	746	746	746

Review Key Equations

Use the following equation and Table 21.2 to determine whether each of the listed reactions is spontaneous or not. Show your work. In each blank, write *S* if the reaction is spontaneous and *N* if the reaction is nonspontaneous.

$$E^0_{cell} = \underline{\hspace{3cm}}$$

_____ **1.** $2Cr^{3+}(aq) + 3Ni(s) \rightarrow 2Cr(s) + 3Ni^{2+}(aq)$

_____ **2.** $2K(s) + Zn^{2+}(aq) \rightarrow 2K^+(aq) + Zn(s)$

_____ **3.** $Cu^{2+}(aq) + Zn(s) \rightarrow Cu(s) + Zn^{2+}(aq)$

Review Vocabulary

For each set of vocabulary terms, write a sentence that explains how the listed terms are related.

1. electrochemical cell, voltaic cell, half-cell, salt bridge

_____

_____

2. dry cell, fuel cell, battery

_____

3. electrode, anode, cathode, voltaic cell, electrolytic cell

_____

_____

4. reduction potential, standard cell potential, cell potential

_____

_____

_____

22 Hydrocarbon Compounds

 CARBON CHEMISTRY

22.1 Hydrocarbons

Essential Understanding Hydrocarbons contain only the elements carbon and hydrogen.

 Reading Strategy

Concept Map A concept map helps you organize concepts using visual relationships and linking words. Mapping out these connections helps you think about how information fits together.

As you read Lesson 22.1, use the concept map below to organize information about hydrocarbons.

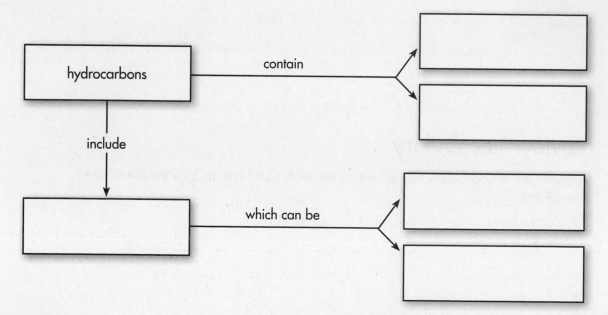

EXTENSION Draw structural formulas to show the difference between the two types of alkanes.

Lesson Summary

Organic Chemistry and Hydrocarbons Hydrocarbons are carbon-containing organic compounds that provide a source of energy.

▶ Carbon has four valence electrons, so a carbon atom always forms four covalent bonds.

▶ Hydrocarbons are nonpolar molecules.

Alkanes Alkanes are hydrocarbons that contain only single covalent bonds, either straight-chain or branched.

▶ A homologous series is a group of compounds that differ from each other by the same unit of change.

▶ A substituent is an atom or group of atoms that takes the place of a hydrogen atom on a parent hydrocarbon molecule.

After reading Lesson 22.1, complete the following questions.

Organic Chemistry and Hydrocarbons

1. What is organic chemistry?

_____

_____

2. Organic compounds that contain only carbon and hydrogen are called

_____.

3. Is the following sentence true or false? Hydrogen atoms are the only atoms that can bond to the carbon atoms in a hydrocarbon. _____

4. Circle the letter of each statement that is true about carbon's ability to form bonds.

   a. Carbon atoms have four valence electrons.

   b. Carbon atoms always form three covalent bonds.

   c. Carbon atoms can form stable bonds with other carbon atoms.

Alkanes

5. Is the following sentence true or false? Alkanes contain only single covalent bonds.

_____

6. What is the simplest alkane? _____

7. What are straight-chain alkanes?

_____

_____

8. The names of all alkanes end with the suffix _____.

Match the name of the straight-chain alkane with the number of carbon atoms it contains.

_____ **9.** nonane   **a.** 3

_____ **10.** propane   **b.** 4

_____ **11.** heptane   **c.** 7

_____ **12.** butane   **d.** 9

13. The straight-chain alkanes form a(n) _____ because there is an incremental change of a CH_2 group from one compound in the series to the next.

14. Circle the letter of each condensed structural formula for pentane.

 a. C_5H_{12} **c.** $CH_3(CH_2)_3CH_3$

 b. $CH_3CH_2CH_2CH_2CH_3$ **d.** $C-C-C-C-C$

15. The IUPAC system uses _____ to show the number of carbon atoms in a straight-chain alkane.

16. A(n) _____ is an atom or group of atoms that replaces a hydrogen in a hydrocarbon molecule.

17. Alkyl groups are named by removing the *-ane* ending of the parent hydrocarbon and adding _____.

18. What is a branched-chain alkane?

_____

_____

19. Circle the letter of the correct IUPAC name for the molecule below.

```
        CH3        CH3
         |          |
CH3 — C — CH2 — CH — CH3
         |
        CH3
```

 a. 2,2,4-triethylpentane

 b. 3-methylpentane

 c. 2,2,4-trimethylpentane

20. Draw a condensed structural formula for 2-methylhexane.

21. Why are hydrocarbon molecules, such as alkanes, nonpolar?

_____

_____

_____

22. Hydrocarbons and other nonpolar molecules are not attracted to _____

_____.

22.2 Unsaturated Hydrocarbons

 Essential Understanding An unsaturated hydrocarbon has at least one double or triple carbon-carbon bond.

Reading Strategy

Venn Diagram A Venn diagram is a useful tool in visually organizing related information. A Venn diagram shows which characteristics the concepts share and which characteristics are unique to each concept.

As you read Lesson 22.2, use the Venn diagram to compare *alkenes* and *alkynes*.

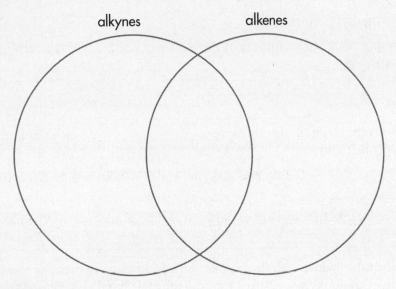

alkynes   alkenes

Lesson Summary

Alkenes An alkene is a hydrocarbon that contains at least one carbon-carbon double covalent bond.

Alkynes An alkyne is a hydrocarbon that contains at least one carbon-carbon triple covalent bond.

▶ The simplest alkyne is ethyne, which is also called acetylene.

After reading Lesson 22.2, complete the following questions.

Alkenes

1. What is an alkene?

_____

_____

2. Organic compounds that contain the maximum number of hydrogen atoms per carbon atom are called _____ compounds.

3. Which family of hydrocarbons contains only saturated compounds? _____

4. Circle the letter of the correct name for the alkene shown below.

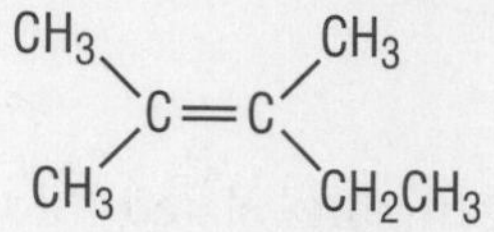

   a. 2,3-dimethyl-3-pentene

   b. 2-methyl-3-methyl-2-pentene

   c. 2,3-dimethyl-2-pentene

   d. 3-ethyl-2-methyl-2-butene

5. Is the following sentence true or false? Rotation can occur around a carbon-carbon double bond. _____

Alkynes

6. Hydrocarbons that contain one or more _____ covalent bonds between carbons are called alkynes.

7. _____ is the simplest alkyne, and is also known by the common name _____.

8. What are the major attractive forces between alkane, alkene, or alkyne molecules?

_____

9. Complete the table below with the names of the indicated alkanes, alkenes, and alkynes. For the alkenes and alkynes, assume that the multiple bond occurs between the first two carbons.

No. of carbons	Alkane	Alkene	Alkyne
C_6			
C_7			
C_8			

10. Is the following sentence true or false? The angle between the carbon atoms in a carbon–carbon triple bond is 120°. _____

22.3 Isomers

Essential Understanding   Isomers are hydrocarbons that have the same molecular formula but different molecular structures.

 Reading Strategy

Frayer Model The Frayer Model is a vocabulary development tool. The center of the diagram shows the concept being defined, while the quadrants around the concept are used for providing the details. Use this model when you want to understand a vocabulary term in more detail.

As you read Lesson 22.3, use the Frayer Model below. Place the term *isomers* in the center of the model. Read the heading in each quadrant. Write details about isomers under each heading. Use the details to improve your understanding of isomers.

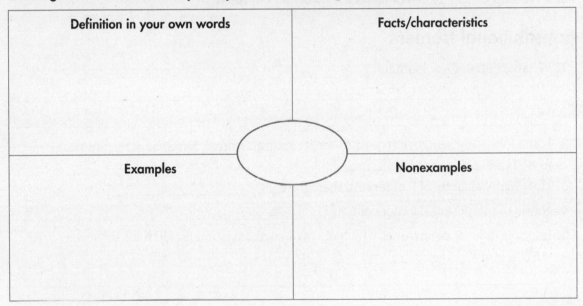

EXTENSION Draw an example of a constitutional isomer, and the *cis-* and *trans-* forms of a stereoisomer.

Lesson Summary

Constitutional Isomers Constitutional isomers, or structural isomers, have the same chemical formula, but their atoms are joined in different arrangements.

▶ Even though they have the same formula, they have different chemical and physical properties.

Stereoisomers Stereoisomers have all atoms bonded in the same order but arranged differently in space.

▶ *Cis-trans* isomers, or geometric isomers, are isomers that result from different arrangements of groups around a double bond.

▶ Enantiomers, or optical isomers, are mirror images of one another and have the same physical properties.

After reading Lesson 22.3, complete the following questions.

Constitutional Isomers

1. What are structural isomers?

_____

_____

2. Is the following sentence true or false? Structural isomers have the same physical properties. _____

3. How many structural isomers are there for C_4H_{10}? _____

4. Name the structural isomers of C_4H_{10}. _____

5. In general, what determines which of two structural isomers will have the lower boiling point?

_____

_____

Stereoisomers

6. Stereoisomers differ only in the _____ in space.

7. What two things need to be present for geometric isomers to exist?

   a. _____

   b. _____

8. What are the names of the molecules represented by the ball-and-stick models below?

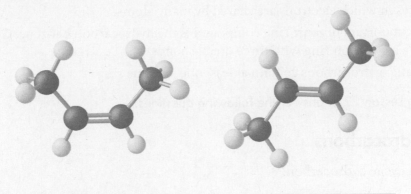

_____   _____

9. Objects that are _____ will produce a reflection that is indistinguishable from the original object.

10. Mirror images of a right hand and a left hand cannot be _____.

11. What is an asymmetric carbon?

_____

12. Is the following sentence true or false? The relationship of optical isomers is similar to that between right and left hands. _____

13. Look at Figure 22.9 on page 708. Why are these two molecules optical isomers?

_____

_____

14. Circle the two asymmetric carbons in the structure shown below.

$$CH_3 - CH_2 - CH_2 - CH - CH - CH - CH_3$$
$$| \quad | \quad |$$
$$CH_2 \quad CH_3 \quad CH_3$$
$$|$$
$$CH_3$$

22.4 Hydrocarbon Rings

Essential Understanding In some hydrocarbon compounds, the two ends of a carbon chain are attached to form a ring.

Lesson Summary

Cyclic Hydrocarbons Hydrocarbons that contain a carbon ring are called cyclic hydrocarbons.

▶ Cyclic hydrocarbons can be saturated or unsaturated.

▶ Cycloalkanes are cyclic hydrocarbons with only single bonds.

Aromatic Hydrocarbons Aromatic hydrocarbons are usually stable compounds with ring structures in which electrons are shared by many atoms.

▶ The most important organic ring compound is the hydrocarbon benzene, C_6H_6, which is drawn as a six-carbon ring with three double bonds.

▶ All aromatic hydrocarbons contain at least one benzene ring.

After reading Lesson 22.4, answer the following questions.

Cyclic Hydrocarbons

1. What is a cyclic hydrocarbon?

   _____

2. The most abundant cyclic hydrocarbons contain _____ or _____ carbons.

3. Is the following sentence true or false? Cyclic hydrocarbons that contain only single carbon-carbon bonds are called cycloalkanes. _____

4. What are the names of the cyclic hydrocarbons represented below?

   a. _____ b. _____ c. _____ d. _____

Aromatic Hydrocarbons

5. What is the origin of the name *aromatic compounds*?

   _____

6. Benzene has the chemical formula _____.

7. Is the following sentence true or false? Any substance that has carbon-carbon bonding like that of benzene is called an aromatic compound. _____

8. Another name for an aromatic compound is a(an) _____.

9. What does it mean to say that benzene exhibits resonance?

   _____

10. Molecules that exhibit resonance are more _____ than similar molecules that do not exhibit resonance.

11. The actual bonds in a benzene ring are identical _____ of single and double bonds.

12. When _____ is a substituent on an alkane, it is called a phenyl group.

13. Circle the letter of the name of the compound shown below.

    a. ethylhexene

    b. dimethylbenzene

    c. ethylbenzene

14. Derivatives of benzene that have _____ substituents are called disubstituted benzenes.

15. Why do disubstituted benzenes always have three structural isomers?

_____

Match the terms for naming a disubstituted benzene with the substituent positions they represent.

_____ **16.** *meta*   **a.** 1, 2

_____ **17.** *ortho*   **b.** 1, 3

_____ **18.** *para*   **c.** 1, 4

19. What is another name for the dimethylbenzenes? _____

22.5 Hydrocarbons From Earth's Crust

> **Essential Understanding**   Hydrocarbons in natural gas, petroleum, and coal provide much of the world's energy.

Lesson Summary

Natural Gas Natural gas contains methane, ethane, and other alkanes.

▶ When enough oxygen is present, natural gas burns with a clean, blue flame to produce carbon dioxide, water, and heat.

▶ Incomplete combustion of natural gas produces soot and carbon monoxide.

Petroleum Petroleum contains straight-chain and branched alkanes, aromatics, and other organic compounds.

▶ Petroleum refining uses boiling point to distill crude oil into fractions.

▶ One fraction is gasoline, the most commonly used petroleum product.

▶ Some fractions are cracked, or broken down, into smaller molecules to make products like paints and plastics.

Coal Over millions of years, intense heat and pressure slowly changed plant remains into coal.

▶ The types of coal include lignite, which has a high water content; bituminous, or soft coal; and anthracite, or hard coal, which is an excellent fuel source.

▶ Coals contains much more carbon than hydrogen and leaves soot when burned.

After reading Lesson 22.5, answer the following questions.

Natural Gas

1. What are fossil fuels?

_____

2. List three factors needed to produce fossil fuels from organic residue.

   a. _____

   b. _____

   c. _____

3. Petroleum and natural gas contain mostly _____ hydrocarbons.

4. What are the four main components of natural gas?

_____

5. Which noble gas is found in natural gas? _____

6. Fill in the missing reactants and products in the equation for the combustion of methane.

$CH_4(g) + 2$ _____ $(g) \rightarrow$ _____ $(g) + 2$ _____ $(g) +$ heat

7. Propane and butane are sold in _____ form to be used as _____ fuels.

8. _____ combustion of a hydrocarbon produces a blue flame; _____ combustion produces a yellow flame.

9. What toxic gas is formed during incomplete combustion of a hydrocarbon?

_____

Petroleum

10. The first oil well was drilled in _____ in the late 1850s.

11. Is the following sentence true or false? Petroleum is commercially useful without refining. _____

12. How is petroleum refined? _____

_____

13. Circle the letter of the distillation fraction that represents the highest percent of crude oil.

   a. natural gas   **c.** kerosene

   b. gasoline   **d.** lubricating oil

14. Using a catalyst and heat to break hydrocarbons down into smaller molecules is called _____.

15. Complete the table below about four fractions obtained from crude oil. Indicate where each fraction will be collected from the fractionating column shown at the right.

Fraction	Composition of carbon chains	Where in column?
Diesel fuel		
Gasoline		
Kerosene		
Lubricating oil		

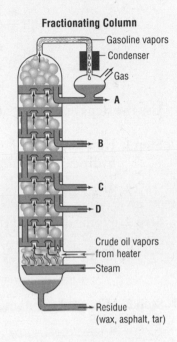

Fractionating Column

Coal

16. _____ is the intermediate material that is the first stage in coal formation.

17. Name the three types of coal and the carbon content of each.

a. _____

b. _____

c. _____

18. Is the following sentence true or false? Coal mines in North America are usually at least a kilometer below Earth's surface. _____

19. Coal consists primarily of _____ compounds of extremely high molar mass.

20. Aromatic compounds produce more _____ when burned than do _____ fuels.

21. What major air pollutants are produced by burning coal that contains sulfur?

_____

22. List four products that can be obtained by distilling coal.

a. _____   c. _____

b. _____   d. _____

23. Which of these products can be distilled further? _____

Guided Practice Problem

Answer the following questions about Practice Problem 3.

Name these compounds according to the IUPAC system.

a. CH₂ — CH₂ — CH — CH₂ — CH₃
   | |
   CH₃   CH₂
                  |
                  CH₃

b. CH₃ — CH₂ — CH — CH₃
                  |
                  CH₃

Use the steps on page 702 to name each compound.

Step 1. How long is the longest string of carbon atoms? What is the name of the parent hydrocarbon structure?

    a. _____   b. _____

Step 2. From which side will you number the carbon chain? Why?

    a. _____

    b. _____

Step 3. What are the names and positions of the substituents?

    a. _____   b. _____

Step 4. Explain why neither name will contain a prefix.

_____

Step 5. Does the name contain any commas or hyphens?

    a. _____

    b. _____

Step 6. What is the complete name of each compound?

    a. _____   b. _____

Extra Practice

Circle the symmetric carbon, if there is one, in each of these structures.

a. CH₃ — CH — CH — CH₃
        | |
        CH₃   CH₃

b. CH₃ — CH — CH₂ — CH₂
        | |
        CH₂   CH₃
        |
        CH₃

Apply the Big idea

Fill in the tables below with the structural formula and condensed structural formula for the alkenes and alkanes.

Name	Ethene	Propene
Formula	C_2H_4	C_3H_6
Complete structural formula		
Condensed structural formula		

Name	Propane	Butane	Ethane
Formula	C_3H_8	C_4H_{10}	C_2H_6
Complete structural formula			
Condensed structural formula			

22 Self-Check Activity

For Questions 1–11, complete each statement by writing the correct word or words. If you need help, you can go online.

22.1 Hydrocarbons

1. Because carbon has four valence electrons, a carbon atom always forms four _____ bonds.

2. The carbon atoms in an alkane can be arranged in a _____ chain or in a chain that has _____.

22.2 Unsaturated Hydrocarbons

3. At least one carbon-carbon bond in an _____ is a double covalent bond.

4. At least one carbon-carbon bond in an _____ is a triple covalent bond.

22.3 Isomers

5. Constitutional isomers differ in _____ properties such as boiling point and melting point. They also have different _____ reactivities.

6. Two types of stereoisomers are *cis-trans* isomers and _____.

22.4 Hydrocarbon Rings

7. In some hydrocarbon compounds, the carbon _____ forms a ring.

8. In a _____ molecule, the bonding electrons between carbon atoms are _____ evenly around the ring.

22.5 Hydrocarbons From Earth's Crust

9. Natural gas is an important source of _____ of low molar mass.

10. Petroleum refining begins with the _____ of crude oil into _____ according to boiling point.

11. Coal is classified by its _____ and _____ content.

If You Have Trouble With...										
Question	1	2	3	4	5	6	7	8	9	10	11
See Page	695	696	704	705	707	708	711	712	714	715	717

Review Key Ideas

Use the following terms to complete the concept map: *alkene, alkane, alkyne, enantiomers, constitutional isomers, aromatic compounds, cracking, cis-trans isomers, cis configuration, trans configuration, hydrocarbons, coal.*

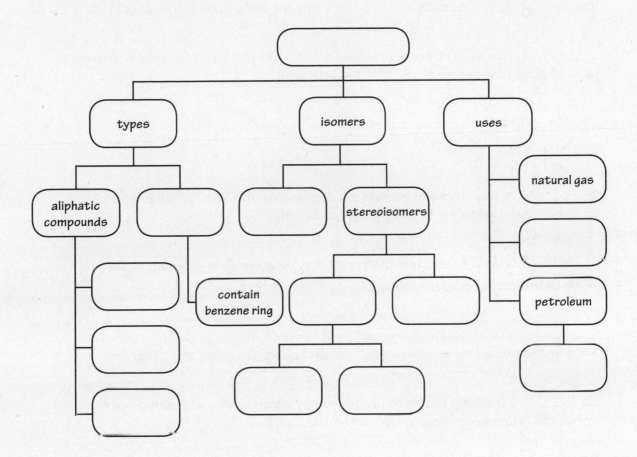

Review Key Vocabulary

Write C if the sentence is correct or I if the sentence is incorrect. For each incorrect definition, cross out the incorrect word(s) and write the word(s) that make the definition correct.

_____ 1. A group of compounds forms a **homologous series** if there is a constant increment of change in molecular structure from one compound in the series to the next.

_____ 2. An atom or group of atoms that can take the place of a carbon atom on a parent hydrocarbon molecule is called a **substituent**.

_____ 3. A hydrocarbon that contains one or more carbon-carbon double covalent bonds is called an **alkyne**.

_____ 4. **Constitutional isomers** are compounds that have the same molecular formula, but the atoms are joined together differently.

_____ 5. Pairs of molecules that are mirror images and are superimposable are called **enantiomers**, or optical isomers.

_____ 6. An **aromatic compound**, or arene, is defined as an organic compound that contains a benzene ring or other ring in which the bonding is like that of benzene.

_____ 7. **Cracking** is a controlled process by which coals are broken down or rearranged into smaller, more useful molecules.

23 Functional Groups

Big idea REACTIONS

23.1 Introduction to Functional Groups

Essential Understanding Most organic compounds contain chemically reactive components called functional groups.

Reading Strategy

Compare and Contrast Organizing information in a table helps you compare and contrast several topics at one time, such as the types of functional groups. As you read, ask yourself, "How are they similar? How are they different?"

As you read Lesson 23.1, use the compare and contrast table below to differentiate among functional groups.

Compound type	General structure	Functional group
halocarbon	R—X (X = F, Cl, Br, or I)	halogen

EXTENSION Write an example for each type of compound based on ethane (C_2H_6).

Lesson Summary

Functional Groups
A functional group is a chemically functional part of an organic compound.

▶ Substituents called functional groups are often attached to hydrocarbon chains or rings.

▶ Organic compounds can be classified according to their functional groups.

Halocarbons
A halocarbon is an organic compound that contains a halogen as its functional group.

▶ The general formula of a halocarbon is RX, where X is a halogen substituent.

▶ When a halogen is attached to an aliphatic chain, it is called an alkyl halide; when attached to an arene ring, it is an aryl halide.

▶ Common names of halocarbons begin with the name of the alkyl or aryl group and end with the name of the halogen with an -ide ending.

Substitution Reactions
A substitution reaction can be used to introduce functional groups into organic compounds.

▶ A halocarbon is produced when a halogen atom replaces a hydrogen atom on an alkane.

▶ A catalyst, such as iron, is often used in the halogenation of aromatic compounds.

▶ Halocarbons can be converted to other halocarbons, amines, or ethers by similar substitution reactions.

Type of reaction	General reaction	Specific reaction
Alkane halogenation	$R—H + X_2 \rightarrow R—X + HX$	$CH_4 + Cl_2 \rightarrow CH_3Cl + HCl$
Aromatic halogenation		
Formation of alcohol	$2R—X + 2OH^- \rightarrow 2R—OH + X^-$	$CH_3I + KOH \rightarrow CH_3OH + KI$

After reading Lesson 23.1, complete the following questions.

Functional Groups

1. Is the following sentence true or false? The saturated hydrocarbon skeletons of organic molecules are chemically reactive. _____

2. What is a functional group?

_____

_____

Use Table 23.1 to answer Questions 3 and 4.

3. Name the functional group for each general structure.

    a. R—O—R   _____

    b. R—OH   _____

    c. R—NH$_2$ _____

4. Name two compound types that have a carbonyl group as a functional group.

    a. _____   b. _____

Halocarbons

5. What are halocarbons?

_____

_____

6. Give the IUPAC and common names for the following halocarbons.

    a. CH$_3$—CH$_2$—CH$_2$—Br   _____

    b. $\begin{array}{c} H \\ H \end{array}\!\!>\!C=C<\!\!\begin{array}{c} I \\ H \end{array}$ _____

7. A halogen attached to a carbon of an aliphatic chain produces a halocarbon called a(n) _____.

8. The second part of a halocarbon common name ends with _____.

9. Highly halogenated organic compounds have higher _____ because of van der Waal interactions.

10. What uses do halogenated hydrocarbons have?

_____

_____

11. What is an aryl halide?

_____

_____

Substitution Reactions

12. Why do reactions involving organic compounds often proceed more slowly than those involving inorganic molecules and ions?

_____

_____

13. Is the following sentence true or false? The products of organic reactions are often a complex mixture of compounds. _____

14. Organic reactions that involve the replacement of one atom or group of atoms with another atom or group of atoms are called _____ reactions.

15. Label the compounds in this generalized halogenation reaction.

R—H   +   X$_2$ →   R—X   +   HX

_____   _____   _____   _____

16. Hydroxide ions can displace most halogens on carbon chains to produce a(n) _____.

23.2 Alcohols, Ethers, and Amines

Essential Understanding Three of the most important types of compounds with functional groups are alcohols, ethers, and amines.

Lesson Summary

Alcohols Organic compounds with the general formula R—OH are alcohols.

▶ Aliphatic alcohols belong to different structural groups according to the number of carbons attached to the carbon with the hydroxy group.

▶ Many alcohols are soluble in water and have high boiling points.

Naming Alcohols		
Type of compound	**Naming rules**	**Example**
1 hydroxy group attached to an alkyl group	▶ Name longest chain ▶ Drop -e, add -ol ▶ Write number at beginning to show where the OH is attached	butanol (OH at end) common name: butyl alcohol 2-hydroxy-butane
2 or 3 hydroxy groups attached to an alkyl group	▶ Use numbers ▶ Add endings -diol or -triol	1,3-propanediol 1,2,3-propanetriol
Hydroxy group attached directly to an aromatic ring	▶ Use the word phenol ▶ Place other attached groups before the word phenol	methylphenol diethylphenol

Addition Reactions New functional groups can be added to an organic molecule at the site of a double or triple bond.

▶ In an addition reaction, a substance is added at the double or triple bond of an alkene or alkyne.

▶ Water and halides can be inserted through hydration or halogenation addition reactions.

▶ A catalyst is used to enable a hydrogen to be added to a carbon-carbon double bond in a hydrogenation reaction.

Ethers An ether is an organic compound in which oxygen is bonded to two carbon groups with the general formula R—O—R.

► To form the IUPAC name for an ether, the shorter R group is written with an *-oxy* ending, followed by the larger R group name.

► To form the common name for an ether, the names of the two R groups are listed in alphabetical order, followed by the word *ether*.

► Ethers usually have lower boiling points than comparable alcohols, but higher boiling points than comparable hydrocarbons.

Amines When one or more of the hydrogen atoms in ammonia are replaced by carbon groups, the compound is classified as an amine.

► An amine can be primary, secondary, or tertiary, depending on the number of carbon groups.

► In IUPAC naming, the *-e* ending of the parent hydrocarbon is changed to *-amine*.

► The common name of an amine is made by naming the carbon group and adding *-amine*.

After reading Lesson 23.2, complete the following questions.

Alcohols

1. What are alcohols?

_____

2. The functional group in an alcohol is called a(n) _____ group.

Match each structural category of aliphatic alcohols with its description.

_____ 3. primary alcohol   **a.** three R groups attached to C—OH

_____ 4. secondary alcohol   **b.** one R group attached to C—OH

_____ 5. tertiary alcohol   **c.** two R groups attached to C—OH

6. Circle the letter of the IUPAC ending used for an alcohol with two 2 —OH substitutions.

   a. *-ol*   **b.** *-tetrol*   **c.** *-triol*   **d.** *-diol*

7. _____ is the common name for alcohols with more than one —OH substituent.

8. Write the IUPAC name and the common name for each alcohol shown.

   a. $CH_3 — CH_2 — OH$ _____

   b. $CH_3 — \overset{\displaystyle OH}{\overset{|}{CH}} — CH_3$ _____

   c. $\overset{\displaystyle}{CH_2} — \overset{\displaystyle}{CH} — \overset{\displaystyle}{CH_2}$
   $\quad\;\, |\qquad\; |\qquad\; |$
   $\quad OH\quad OH\quad OH$ _____

9. Is the following sentence true or false? Alcohols cannot form intermolecular hydrogen bonds. _____

10. What are the two parts of an alcohol molecule?

_____

11. Why are alcohols with four or more carbons not soluble in water?

_____

_____

_____

12. Name two uses for 2-propanol (or rubbing) alcohol.

a. _____

b. _____

13. Which alcohol is used in many antifreezes? _____

14. The action of yeast or bacteria on sugars to produce ethanol is called
_____.

15. How is ethanol denatured?

_____

_____

Addition Reactions

16. Adding new functional groups at the double or triple bond of an alkene or alkyne is called a(n) _____ reaction.

17. Is the following sentence true or false? Adding a hydrogen halide to an alkene results in a disubstituted halocarbon. _____

18. Look at the reaction between ethene and water:

$$\begin{array}{c} H \\ H \end{array} C = C \begin{array}{c} H \\ H \end{array} + H - OH \xrightarrow[100°C]{H^+}$$

a. Draw the structure of the product.

b. What type of compound is the product? _____

c. What is this type of addition reaction called? _____

d. What is the role of the hydrogen ions? _____

19. What type of reaction is used to manufacture solid spreads from cooking oils?
_____

20. Which hydrocarbon resists addition reactions? _____

Ethers

21. An ether is a compound in which _____ is bonded to two carbon groups.

22. How are ethers given a common name?

_____

_____

23. Circle the letter of each symmetrical ether.

    a. ethylmethyl ether

    b. diethyl ether

    c. diphenyl ether

    d. methylphenyl ether

24. Is the following sentence true or false? Ethers have higher boiling points than alcohols of comparable molar mass. _____

Amines

25. When one, two, or three of the hydrogen atoms in _____ are replaced by carbon groups, the compound is classified as an amine.

26. Circle the correct classification for a compound with the formula RNH_2.

    a. primary amine

    b. secondary amine

    c. tertiary amine

23.3 Carbonyl Compounds

Essential Understanding   The functional group with the structure C=O is a carbonyl group.

Lesson Summary

Aldehydes and Ketones Aldehydes and ketones are organic compounds with carbonyl groups attached to at least one hydrogen for aldehydes and to two carbons for ketones.

▶ There are industrial uses for such aldehydes and ketones as formaldehyde and acetone.

▶ Aldehydes and ketones cannot form intermolecular hydrogen bonds, but they can attract each other because of their polarity.

Carboxylic Acids A carboxylic acid is a carbonyl group with a hydroxy group attached.

▶ Carboxylic acids are weak acids because they ionize weakly in solution.

▶ The *-e* ending is dropped and *-oic acid* is added when naming carboxylic acids.

▶ Carboxylic acids are abundant in nature and are found in citrus fruits and fats.

To make a(n)	Begin with carbonyl group	Add	General formula	How to name
aldehyde	C=O	R and H or H and H	RCHO	▶ Drop -e and add -al
ketone	C=O	R & R	RCOR	▶ Drop -e and add -one ▶ Add number at beginning to note position of added group
carboxylic acid	C=O	OH	RCOOH	▶ Drop -e and add -oic acid

Oxidation-Reduction Reactions Aldehydes, ketones, and carboxylic acids can be converted back and forth to one another by oxidation and reduction reactions.

▶ The degree of oxidation of a compound is related to the number of oxygen atoms and hydrogen atoms attached to carbon.

▶ When an organic molecule loses hydrogen through dehydrogenation, it is an oxidation reaction.

▶ Aldehydes are easily oxidized, but ketones are relatively resistant to further oxidation.

Esters An ester is formed when the —OR group from an alcohol replaces the —OH of a carboxyl group.

▶ Esters are found in fruit and are used in perfumes because of their pleasant, fruity aromas.

▶ The general formula of an ester is RCOOR.

▶ Esters may be prepared from a carboxylic acid and an alcohol in a process called esterification.

After reading Lesson 23.3, complete the following questions.

Aldehydes and Ketones

1. A _____ consists of a carbon joined by a double bond to an oxygen atom.

2. What is the difference between an aldehyde and a ketone?

_____

_____

_____

3. What ending is used in the IUPAC system to indicate an aldehyde? A ketone?

_____

4. Circle the letter of each statement that is true about aldehydes and ketones.

   a. In an aldehyde or ketone sample, the molecules cannot form intermolecular hydrogen bonds.

   b. The molecules in an aldehyde or ketone sample do not attract each other through polar–polar interactions.

   c. Most aldehydes and ketones are gases at room temperature.

   d. Aldehydes and ketones can form weak hydrogen bonds with water.

Match the aldehyde or ketone with its use.

_____ **5.** methanal	**a.** almond flavoring
_____ **6.** propanone	**b.** preservative
_____ **7.** benzaldehyde	**c.** oil of cinnamon
_____ **8.** 3-phenyl-2-propenal	**d.** solvent

9. Aromatic aldehydes are often used as _____ agents.

Carboxylic Acids

10. What is a carboxyl group?

_____

11. Is the following sentence true or false? Carboxylic acids are weak acids.

_____

12. What ending is used under the IUPAC system to designate a carboxylic acid?

_____

13. Carboxylic acids with three or more carbons in a straight chain are also known as _____ acids.

14. Complete the table about saturated aliphatic carboxylic acids.

IUPAC name	Common name	Carbon atoms	Formula
		4	$CH_3(CH_2)_2COOH$
Octanoic acid			$CH_3(CH_2)_6COOH$
	Acetic acid	2	
Octadecanoic acid	Stearic acid		

15. What form do all aromatic carboxylic acids have at room temperature?

_____

Oxidation-Reduction Reactions

16. Are triple carbon–carbon bonds more or less oxidized than double and single carbon–carbon bonds? _____

17. What is a dehydrogenation reaction?

_____

_____

18. Circle the letter of the compound that is the final product of methane oxidation.

   a. methanol   **c.** methanal

   b. formic acid   **d.** carbon dioxide

19. Primary alcohols are oxidized to form _____, but secondary alcohols form _____ when oxidized.

20. Why are tertiary alcohols resistant to oxidation?

_____

_____

21. Is the following sentence true or false? The oxidation of organic compounds is exothermic. _____

22. What property of aldehydes do Fehling's test and Benedict's test take advantage of? What color is the precipitate that forms?

_____

Esters

23. An ester is a derivative of a _____ that has an —OR substituted for the —OH.

24. Write the general formula for an ester. _____

25. What two products are formed when an ester is hydrolyzed in the presence of a strong acid or base?

_____

23.4 Polymers

Essential Understanding   Organic compounds can bond together to form long molecular chains called polymers.

Lesson Summary

Addition Polymers An addition polymer forms when unsaturated monomers covalently bond to form a long chain.

▶ The physical properties of polymers change with the length of the carbon chain.

▶ Polymers of ethylene, propylene, styrene, and others have many industrial uses.

▶ Addition polymers are widely used as plastics, vinyl, and rubber.

Condensation Polymers When a condensation polymer is formed, water is also produced.

▶ There are two functional groups on each monomer in condensation polymerization.

▶ Polyesters and polyamides are two kinds of condensation polymers which are used to make many different kinds of products.

▶ Tough, flame resistant materials can be made from polyamides that contain aromatic rings.

After reading Lesson 23.4, answer the following questions.

Addition Polymers

1. What are polymers?

   _____

   _____

2. Is the following sentence true or false? Polymers can only contain one type of monomer.

   _____

3. Most polymerization reactions require a _____.

4. Complete the table by naming each polymer.

Polymer	Structure
	$H + CH_2 - CH_2 \overline{)_x} H$
	CH_3 $\vert$ $+ CH_2 - CH \overline{)_x}$
	Cl $\vert$ $+ CH_2 - CH \overline{)_x}$
	$+ CF_2 - CF_2 \overline{)_x}$

Match the polymer with its use.

_____ 5. polyethylene   **a.** foam coffee cups

_____ 6. polystyrene   **b.** rubber tubing

_____ 7. polytetrafluoroethene   **c.** nonstick cookware

_____ 8. polyisoprene   **d.** plastic wrap

_____ 9. polyvinyl chloride   **e.** plumbing pipes

Condensation Polymers

10. How is a polyester formed?

_____

_____

11. For condensation polymerization to occur, each monomer molecule must have _____ functional groups.

12. Name the two monomer molecules that are joined to form the polyester PET.

_____

13. Garments made from PET fibers are _____ resistant.

14. Is the following sentence true or false? The polymer produced by the condensation of a carboxylic acid and an amine is called an amide. _____

15. What common group of synthetic materials is made up by polyamides?

_____

16. _____ are an important group of naturally occurring polyamides made from monomers called _____.

Match each common polymer to its structural representation.

    a. Kevlar™   **b.** Nomex™   **c.** nylon   **d.** PET

_____ **17.**

_____ **18.**

_____ **19.**

_____ **20.**

Apply the Big idea

For each compound:

a. Name the compound.

b. Identify the type of organic compounds.

c. Identify the type of reaction that could produce the compound.

Compound	Name	Type of compound	Reaction
$BrH_2C—CH_2Br$			
$CH_3COOCH_2CH_3$			
$\left(-CH_2\left(-CH_2\right)_4 \overset{O}{\overset{\|}{C}} — \overset{O}{\overset{\|}{N}}\right)_x$			

23 Self-Check Activity

For Questions 1–13, complete each statement by writing the correct word or words. If you need help, you can go online.

23.1 Introduction to Functional Groups

1. Organic compounds can be classified according to their _____ groups.

2. The general formula of a(n) _____ is RX, where X is a halogen.

3. _____ reactions are an important method of introducing new functional groups to organic molecules.

23.2 Alcohols, Ethers, and Amines

4. The general formula of a(n) _____ is ROH.

5. _____ reactions of alkenes are an important method of introducing new functional groups to organic molecules, and are also used to convert alkenes to alkanes.

6. The general formula of a(n) _____ is ROR.

7. The general formula of a(n) _____ is RNH_2, R_2NH, or R_3N, depending on the number of R groups.

23.3 Carbonyl Compounds

8. The C=O functional group is present in _____ and ketones.

9. The general formula of a(n) _____ is RCOOH.

10. _____ is an oxidation reaction because the loss of each molecule of hydrogen involves the loss of two electrons from the organic molecule.

11. The general formula of a(n) _____ is RCOOR.

23.4 Polymers

12. An _____ polymer forms when monomers react to form a polymer.

13. Condensation polymers are formed by the joining of _____ with the loss of a small molecule such as water.

If You Have Trouble With...												
Question	1	2	3	4	5	6	7	8	9	10	11	12	13
See Page	798	800	801	804	807	810	811	812	815	816	819	822	825

Review Key Ideas

1. Write condensed structural formulas for the following compounds.

a. 1,2,2-trifluoropropane

_____

b. 1,3-butanediol

_____

c. butanoic acid

_____

d. trimethylamine

_____

e. 1-amino, 2-propanone

_____

2. What two compounds take part in the esterification reaction that produces ethyl propanoate?

_____

Review Key Vocabulary

For each of the following vocabulary words, write the letter of the correct match.

_____ **1.** aldehyde	**a.**	—Br
_____ **2.** addition reaction	**b.** ROR	
_____ **3.** carboxylic acid	**c.** RCHO	
_____ **4.** ether	**d.** ROH	
_____ **5.** substitution reaction	**e.** an atom or a group of atoms replaces another atom or group of atoms	
_____ **6.** carbonyl group	**f.** a substance is added at the double or triple bond of an alkene or alkyne	
_____ **7.** aryl halide	**g.** C=O	
_____ **8.** alcohol	**h.** RCOOH	

24 The Chemistry of Life

 CHEMISTRY AS THE CENTRAL SCIENCE

24.1 A Basis for Life

Essential Understanding Chemical reactions occur in all living organisms.

Lesson Summary

The Structure of Cells Cells are the fundamental units of life.

▶ The two major types of cells in living organisms are prokaryotic and eukaryotic cells.

▶ The rules of chemistry apply equally to both types of cells.

The Energy and Carbon Cycle Photosynthesis directly or indirectly provides all living organisms with energy.

▶ During photosynthesis, plants change the energy of sunlight into chemical energy stored in the bonds of carbohydrates.

▶ During photosynthesis, carbon dioxide and water yield a carbohydrate and oxygen gas.

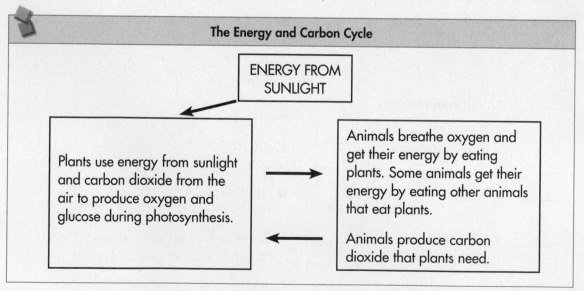

After reading Lesson 24.1, answer the following questions.

The Structure of Cells

1. What are the two major types of cell design?

a. _____   b. _____

2. Which of the two cell types are found in humans?

_____

3. Fill in the missing labels for structures in the drawing of a eukaryotic cell.

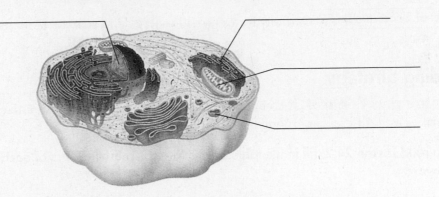

4. Is the following sentence true or false? Both cell types are surrounded by a cell membrane that acts as a selective barrier to the passage of chemicals into or out of the cell. _____

5. Only eukaryotic cells contain membrane-enclosed _____ in which specialized functions of the cell occur.

Match the organelle to its function.

_____ **6.** mitochondrion   **a.** manufacture of proteins

_____ **7.** nucleus   **b.** cell reproduction

_____ **8.** lysosome   **c.** energy production

_____ **9.** endoplasmic reticulum   **d.** digestion

The Energy and Carbon Cycle

10. What is the source of all energy for life on Earth? _____

11. Circle the letter of the process by which organisms capture solar energy and use it to make food.

a. oxidation   **b.** photosynthesis   **c.** digestion   **d.** respiration

12. How do plants use the energy they obtain from sunlight?

_____

13. Explain how animals obtain the energy they need.

_____

_____

14. What are the products of the oxidation of glucose?

_____

15. Is the following sentence true or false? The destruction of forests and pollution of the oceans has no effect on the survival of animal life. _____

24.2 Carbohydrates

Essential Understanding Carbohydrates provide energy and structural material for living things.

Reading Strategy

Compare and Contrast A compare and contrast table helps you organize the similarities and differences among concepts, objects, or processes.

As you read Lesson 24.2, fill in the table below with the characteristics of each type of carbohydrate.

Type of carbohydrate	Prefix	Meaning of prefix	Also known as	Examples
monosaccharide				
disaccharide				
polysaccharide				

EXTENSION Which two sugars are structural isomers and what makes them different?

Lesson Summary

Classifying Carbohydrates Carbohydrates contain carbon, hydrogen, and oxygen in molecules of varying size and complexity.

▶ The three major types of carbohydrates are monosaccharides, disaccharides, and polysaccharides.

After reading Lesson 24.2, answer the following questions.

Classifying Carbohydrates

1. Carbohydrates are made from aldehydes and ketones that contain many _____ groups.

2. Name the three elements present in carbohydrates.

   a. _____   b. _____   c. _____

3. What is the general formula for a carbohydrate? _____

4. What is another name for simple sugars? _____

5. Circle the letter of each simple sugar.

   a. glucose   **b.** sucrose   **c.** fructose   **d.** starch

6. Sugars formed by linking two monosaccharides are called _____.

7. What compound is lost in the reaction that links two monosaccharides?

_____

8. Is the following sentence true or false? Sucrose, or table sugar, is formed by the polymerization of two glucose molecules. _____

9. What are polysaccharides?

_____

_____

10. Complete the following table about polysaccharides.

Polysaccharide	Source	Function
starch		
		energy storage
	plants	

24.3 Amino Acids and Their Polymers

(Essential Understanding) Amino acids are the building blocks of proteins and are essential to cellular life.

Lesson Summary

Amino Acids There are 20 common amino acids that are formed and used by living organisms.

▶ Amino acids contain both an amino group ($-NH_2$) and carboxyl group ($-COOH$).

Peptides and Proteins Proteins are biological polymers made of amino acids that are linked by peptide bonds.

▶ A peptide contains two or more amino acids linked by the carboxyl group of one amino acid to the amino group of another.

▶ A peptide with more than 100 amino acids is called a protein.

▶ Proteins are fundamental components of all living cells and are necessary for the proper functioning of an organism.

Enzymes Enzymes are biological catalysts.

▶ An enzyme is a protein produced by cells and speeds up chemical reactions in living organisms.

▶ An enzyme acts as a catalyst to speed up specific chemical reactions by converting specific reactants into specific products.

After reading Lesson 24.3, answer the following questions.

Amino Acids

1. What is an amino acid? How many amino acids are found in living organisms?

   _____

   _____

   _____

2. What determines the physical and chemical properties of an amino acid?

   _____

Match the amino acid to its abbreviation.

_____ 3. Glutamine   **a.** Ile

_____ 4. Isoleucine   **b.** Trp

_____ 5. Methionine   **c.** Pro

_____ 6. Proline   **d.** Gln

_____ 7. Tryptophan   **e.** Met

Peptides and Proteins

8. What is a peptide?

   _____

   _____

9. The bond between amino acids is called a(n) _____ bond.

10. Is the following sentence true or false? The bond between amino acids always involves the side chains. _____

11. The formula for peptides is written so that the free _____ group is on the left end and the free _____ group is on the right end.

12. Is the following sentence true or false? The order of the amino acids in a peptide can be reversed and still represent the same peptide. _____

13. A(n) _____ contains more than 10 amino acids, but a(n) _____ has more than 100 amino acids.

14. The chemical and physiological properties of a protein are determined by its _____ sequence.

15. Name each type of structure that can be formed by folding long peptide chains.

_____   _____

16 What types of bonds maintain the three-dimensional shape of a folded protein?

_____

_____

17. Is the following sentence true or false? A single protein can be made from separate polypeptide chains, held together by bonds between side-chain groups.

_____

Enzymes

18. What are enzymes?

_____

19. What three properties of a catalyst do enzymes have?

a. _____

b. _____

c. _____

20. Is the following sentence true or false? Because an active site fits a specific substrate, each enzyme catalyzes only one chemical reaction. _____

21. What is the enzyme molecule joined to its substrate molecule called?

_____

Match the enzyme to its substrate.

_____ **22.** urease   **a.** carbonic acid

_____ **23.** carbonic anhydrase   **b.** hydrogen peroxide

_____ **24.** catalase   **c.** urea

25. What is a coenzyme? Give two examples.

_____

_____

_____

24.4 Lipids

Essential Understanding Lipids make cell membranes, store energy, and regulate cellular processes.

Lesson Summary

Describing Lipids Lipids are naturally occurring molecules from plants or animals that are soluble in non-polar solvents.

▶ Lipids are esters or amides of long chains of fatty acids.

▶ Phospholipids are the main constituents of cell membranes.

▶ Waxes are found in nature. The leaves of some plants have waxy coatings, which protect them from dehydration. The feathers of birds and the fur of some animals have wax coatings, which serve as a water repellent.

Types of Lipids			
	Triglycerides	**Phospholipids**	**Waxes**
Feature	natural fats and oils	hydrophilic head and hydrophobic tail form bilipid layer	low melting point
Structure	triesters of glycerol and fatty acids	contains phosphate group	esters of long-chain fatty acids and long-chain alcohols
Function	involved in long-term energy storage in the human body	control passage of material into and out of the cell	prevent water loss from plant leaves keep animals' skin, hair, and feathers pliable and waterproof

After reading Lesson 24.4, answer the following questions.

Describing Lipids

1. Fats provide an efficient means of _____ for your body.

2. What are lipids?

   _____

3. Triglycerides are triesters of one _____ molecule and three _____ molecules.

4. Complete the following table about two types of triglycerides.

Triglyceride type	State at room temperature	Primary source
fats		
		plants

5. Circle the letter of the process used to make soap.

    a. hydrogenation

    b. saponification

    c. denaturation

    d. polymerization

6. What is the molecular structure of a phospholipid?

_____

7. How does the chemical nature of a phospholipid affect its solubility?

_____

_____

8. When phospholipids are added to water, they spontaneously form a lipid
_____, with the hydrophobic tails located in the _____.

9. How does a cell membrane accomplish selective absorption?

_____

_____

_____

10. What is the molecular structure of waxes?

_____

11. Is the following sentence true or false? Waxes are liquid at room temperature.

_____

12. Name two functions of waxes in plants.

_____

24.5 Nucleic Acids

Essential Understanding Nucleic acids store and transmit genetic information.

Lesson Summary

DNA and RNA DNA is double-stranded; RNA is single-stranded.

▶ DNA consists of four long chains of nucleotides and forms a double helix.

▶ DNA stores genetic information.

▶ RNA allows cells to use information found in DNA.

The Genetic Code Almost all living organisms use the same genetic code to translate their proteins.

▶ The genetic code is a list of 64 triplet sequences in RNA and the amino acids specified by each combination.

Gene Mutations
Gene mutations are changes to the nucleotide sequence of the genetic material of an organism.

▶ Mutations range in size from a single DNA building block (DNA base) to a large segment of a chromosome.

▶ Gene mutations can be inherited from a parent or acquired during a person's lifetime.

DNA Technologies
DNA technology has revolutionized science.

▶ Recent advances in DNA technology include cloning, fingerprinting, and gene therapy.

After reading Lesson 24.5, answer the following questions.

DNA and RNA

1. What are the functions of the two types of nucleic acids?

   _____

   _____

2. The monomers that make up nucleic acids are called _____.

3. Name the three parts of a nucleotide.

   a. _____ b. _____ c. _____

4. What nitrogen bases are found in DNA? In RNA?

   _____

   _____

5. DNA molecules consist of two chains of nucleotides that are bound together into a double _____.

6. Name the complementary base pairs found in DNA.

   a. _____ b. _____

The Genetic Code

7. What is a gene?

   _____

8. How many nucleotides are needed to code for one amino acid? _____

9. The _____ is the arrangement of code words in DNA that provides the information to make specific proteins.

10. Is the following sentence true or false? Each amino acid has only one DNA code word.

    _____

11. Use Table 24.2 on page 857. Which amino acids are coded in the nucleotide sequence TACAGCCTCGACAAG?

    _____

12. Circle the letter of each code word that represents a termination signal.

    a. ATT

    b. AAC

    c. ATC

    d. AAT

Gene Mutations

13. Circle the letter of each event that could cause a gene mutation.

    a. substitution of one or more nucleotides

    b. addition of one or more nucleotides

    c. deletion of one or more nucleotides

14. What is the effect of mutations on the production of proteins?

_____

_____

_____

15. Is the following sentence true or false? Diseases resulting from gene mutations are called genetic disorders. _____

16. Name a disease that is caused by a mutation in the GALT enzyme.

_____

DNA Technologies

17. DNA base sequences differ for everyone except _____.

18. A _____ is a short segment of DNA that is repeated several times.

19. Describe the three steps in the production of recombinant DNA.

    a. _____

    b. _____

    c. _____

20. Name three medicines that are produced by recombinant DNA technology.

    a. _____

    b. _____

    c. _____

21. What is a clone?

_____

24.6 Metabolism

Essential Understanding Many thousands of chemical reactions take place in living organisms to keep them functioning properly.

Lesson Summary

ATP Adenosine triphosphate (ATP) is the universal energy-storage molecule in living cells.

▶ The hydrolysis of ATP produces ADP and releases energy.

Metabolism Reactions Metabolism refers to the biochemical processes that occur within any living organism to maintain life.

▶ Living organisms undergo catabolism and anabolism.

▶ Catabolism involves breaking down nutrients to extract energy.

▶ Anabolism involves using energy to build biological molecules.

The Nitrogen Cycle The nitrogen cycle refers to a cyclic movement of nitrogen in different chemical forms from the environment, to organisms, and then back to the environment.

▶ All living organisms require nitrogen compounds, e.g., proteins and nucleic acids.

▶ Nitrogen fixation and decay are two processes that help cycle nitrogen through the biosphere.

After reading Lesson 24.6, answer the following questions.

ATP

1. What is ATP, and what is its function?

_____

2. Energy is captured when a _____ group is added to adenosine diphosphate (ADP).

3. **a.** How much energy is stored when one mole of ATP is produced?

_____

b. How much energy is released when one mole of ATP is hydrolyzed back to ADP?

_____

4. ATP is important because it occupies an _____ position between higher-energy _____ reactions and other cellular processes.

Metabolism Reactions

5. The entire set of all chemical reactions that are carried out in a living organism is called _____.

6. What is catabolism?

_____

_____

7. Circle the letter of each product of catabolism.

    a. heat

    b. ATP

    c. complex biological molecules

    d. building blocks for new compounds

8. One of the most important catabolic processes is the complete oxidation of _____ to form _____ and water.

9. How much energy is released by the complete combustion of one mole of glucose? _____

10. How many moles of ATP are produced by the complete oxidation of one mole of glucose? _____

11. Is the following sentence true or false? All the reactions involved in the complete oxidation of glucose are shown in Figure 24.25. _____

12. Use Figure 24.25 to fill in the names of the carbon-containing molecules and ions represented.

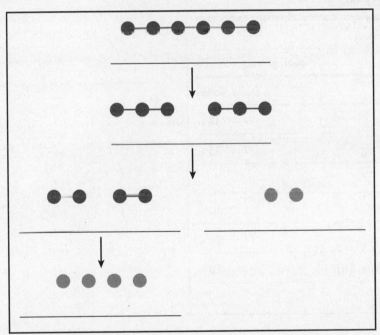

13. Anabolic reactions are _____ reactions that produce more complex biological molecules.

14. Catabolic reactions _____ energy, whereas anabolic reactions _____ energy.

15. Look at Figure 24.27. Explain why all the terms that appear in the blue ovals also appear in the red ovals.

_____

_____

_____

The Nitrogen Cycle

16. Is the following sentence true or false? Animals can use atmospheric nitrogen to produce nitrogen-containing compounds. _____

17. Certain bacteria reduce atmospheric nitrogen to ammonia in a process called

_____.

18. How do nitrogen fertilizers enter the biosphere?

_____

_____

Apply the Big idea

Nutrition Facts
Serving Size 1 cup (228g)
Servings Per Container 2

Amount Per Serving

Calories 250	Calories from Fat 110
	% Daily Value
Total Fat 12g	18%
Saturated Fat 3g	15%
Trans Fat 3g	
Cholesterol 30mg	10%
Sodium 470mg	20%
Total Carbohydrate 31g	10%
Protein 5g	

According to this label, what daily percent of lipids does this food contain? _____

Which part of the label would include sugars? _____

What amount of polypeptide chains is listed on the label? _____

24 Self-Check Activity

For Questions 1–13, complete each statement by writing the correct word or words. If you need help, you can go online.

24.1 A Basis for Life

1. Two major cell types occur in nature: prokaryotic cells and _____ cells.

2. _____ uses sunlight to reduce CO_2 to compounds with C—H bonds.

24.2 Carbohydrates

3. Most carbohydrates have the general formula _____.

24.3 Amino Acids and Their Polymers

4. An amino acid has a _____, an amino group, a hydrogen atom, and an R group bonded to a central carbon atom.

5. The sequence of amino acids determines the properties of a _____.

6. Enzymes _____ reaction rates.

23.4 Lipids

7. Lipids dissolve readily in _____ solvents.

23.5 Nucleic Acids

8. DNA stores information and governs the _____ of cells, while RNA transmits _____ stored in DNA during protein synthesis.

9. A sequence of _____ bases of DNA is required to specify an amino acid.

10. Gene mutations occur when _____ in DNA are changed.

11. Examples of _____ include DNA typing, genetically modifying foods and animals, and cloning.

23.6 Metabolism

12. In living cells, _____ is the energy carrier between reactions.

13. In _____, new compounds needed for cellular life and growth are made from the products of _____.

If You Have Trouble With...												
Question	1	2	3	4	5	6	7	8	9	10	11	12	13
See Page	838	839	841	844	845	847	850	854	856	858	859	862	864

Review Key Ideas

Each box represents a topic of one lesson in the chapter. Arrange the boxes into a graphic organizer that shows how the topics are related. Write connecting words to explain the relationships. Add boxes to show further classifications where necessary.

A Basis for Life	Amino Acids and Their Polymers	Nucleic Acids
Carbohydrates	**Lipids**	**Metabolism**

Review Key Vocabulary

Unscramble each vocabulary word from the chapter. Then write in the numbered letters to form the mystery sentence.

POSYTTINHHESSO

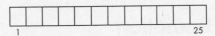

| | | | | | | | | | | | | |
|18| |11|9|17| |13| |6| | | |

DORTABCYEHAR

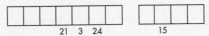

| | | | | | | | | | | |
|1| | | | | | | | |25| |

CIECUNL CIAD

| | | | | | | | | | | |
| |21|3|24| | |15| | | |

LCRAHPOCADSIYE

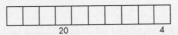

| | | | | | | | | | | | | |
| |22| |23|27|2| |8| | | | |

SEENANDOI PITESTAOPHRH

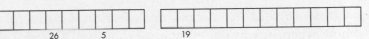

| | | | | | | | | | | | | | | | | | | |
| |26| |5| | | |19| | | | | | | | | | |

LOAMEIBTSM

| | | | | | | | | |
| |20| | | |4| | | |

RIT'NOPE

| | | | | | | |
| | |7| | | | |

DEPPETI

| | | | | | |
|16| |12|10| | |

EENG

| | | | |
|28| |14| |

Mystery sentence:

| | | | | | | | | | | | | | | | | | | | | | | | | | | | | | |
|1|2|3|4|5|6|7|8|9| |10|11| |12|13|14| |15|16|17|18|19|20|21| |22|23|24|25|26|27|28|.

25 Nuclear Chemistry

 ELECTRONS AND THE STRUCTURE OF ATOMS

25.1 Nuclear Radiation

Essential Understanding Nuclear reactions might result in the emission of three different types of nuclear radiation: alpha, beta, and gamma.

Reading Strategy

Cause and Effect A cause and effect chart is a useful tool when you want to describe how, when, or why one event causes another. A cause is the reason something happens. The effect is what happens.

As you read Lesson 25.1, use the cause and effect chart below. Complete the chart by filling in the effect of subjecting each type of radiation to a negative charge.

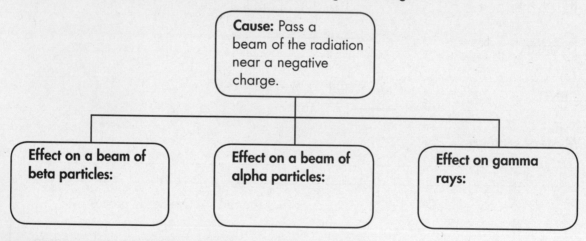

EXTENSION Draw a diagram to illustrate each of the effects.

Lesson Summary

Radioactivity Radioactivity is the spontaneous emission of particles or energy from unstable nuclei of radioisotopes.

▶ The term *radioactivity* refers to the process of emitting particles or energy from atomic nuclei.

▶ The particles or energy emitted during radioactivity is called nuclear radiation.

▶ Nuclear reactions are not affected by factors such as temperature, and their rate cannot be changed.

Types of Radiation There are three types of radiation emitted by nuclear reactions.

▶ Alpha particles are helium nuclei, each of which contains two protons and two neutrons.

▶ Beta particles are electrons formed when a neutron breaks down into a proton and a beta particle.

▶ A gamma ray is a high-energy photon that is often emitted along with an alpha particle or a beta particle.

After reading Lesson 25.1, answer the following questions.

Radioactivity

1. Which French chemist noticed that uranium salts could fog photographic plates, even without being exposed to sunlight? _____

2. What name did Marie Curie give to the process by which materials give off rays capable of fogging photographic plates? _____

3. An isotope that has an unstable nucleus is called a(n) _____.

4. Complete the table below to show basic differences between chemical and nuclear reactions.

Type of reaction	Is nucleus of atom changed?	Is reaction affected by temperature, pressure, or catalysts?
Chemical		
Nuclear		

5. Complete the flowchart below, which describes the radioactive decay process.

The presence of too many or too few _____ relative to protons leads to an unstable nucleus.

↓

At some point in time, an unstable nucleus will undergo a reaction and lose energy by emitting _____.

↓

During the process of radioactive decay, a(n) _____ radioisotope of one element is transformed eventually into a(n) _____ isotope of a different element.

Types of Radiation

6. Complete the following table showing some characteristics of the main types of radiation commonly emitted during radioactive decay.

Type			
Consists of	2 protons and 2 neutrons	electron	high-energy electromagnetic radiation
Mass (amu)			
Penetrating power (low, moderate, or high)			
Minimum shielding			

7. Look at Figure 25.2. It shows the alpha decay of uranium-238 to thorium-234.

  a. What is the change in atomic number after the alpha decay?

  _____

  b. What is the change in mass number after the alpha decay?

  _____

8. When are radioisotopes that emit alpha particles dangerous to soft tissues?

  _____

9. Look at Figure 25.3. This diagram shows the beta decay of carbon-14 to nitrogen-14.

  a. What is the change in atomic number after the beta decay?

  _____

  b. Which quantity changes in beta decay, the mass number or the charge of the nucleus?

  _____

10. Explain how gamma radiation is similar to visible light, and how it is different.

  Similar: _____

  Different: _____

11. When are gamma rays emitted?

  _____

  _____

12. Is the following sentence true or false? Gamma rays have no mass and no electrical charge. _____

13. Look at the diagram below. Below each material indicate with a checkmark which type of radiation—alpha, beta, or gamma—can be stopped by each material.

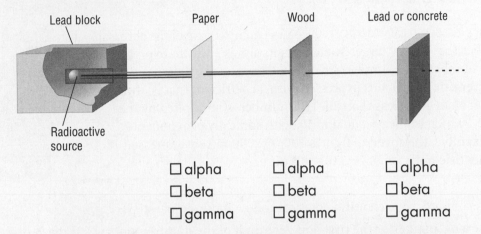

Lead block   Paper   Wood   Lead or concrete

Radioactive
source

☐ alpha   ☐ alpha   ☐ alpha
☐ beta   ☐ beta   ☐ beta
☐ gamma   ☐ gamma   ☐ gamma

25.2 Nuclear Transformations

Essential Understanding Nuclear transformations are changes in the nuclei of radioisotopes when they decay.

Lesson Summary

Nuclear Stability and Decay Most known nuclei are not stable and will decay over time.

▶ The nuclear force is a force that holds together all the particles in a nucleus.

▶ The neutron-to-proton ratio determines the stability of an isotope and the type of decay it will undergo.

▶ Unstable nuclei might undergo beta emission, electron capture, positron emission, or alpha emission.

Half-Life Half-life is a measure of how quickly an element undergoes nuclear decay.

▶ At the end of one half-life, half of a sample of radioactive atoms have decayed into a new element.

▶ Half-lives range from a second to billions of years.

▶ Radioisotopes with long half-lives are used to date objects or materials, and isotopes with short half-lives have medical uses.

Transmutation Reactions During a transmutation reaction, one element changes into another element.

▶ Transmutation can occur during radioactive decay.

▶ Transmutation also can occur when protons, neutrons, or alpha particles bombard atomic nuclei.

▶ All elements with an atomic number greater than 92 are called transuranium elements and undergo transmutation.

BUILD Math Skills

Using Scientific Notation Often in chemistry we come across a number that is very large. Scientific notation is a way to express very large numbers in a simpler, smaller notation.

Scientific notation is expressed with a coefficient that is always greater than 1 but less than 10. This number is multiplied by the "base," which is always equal to 10, with some given exponent. For example, the speed of light is 300,000,000 m/sec. Expressed in scientific notation, it is: 3.0×10^8 m/sec.

To write a number in scientific notation, follow these simple steps:

▶ Place a decimal after the first non-zero digit of the number, and cut off the zeros. (If it is a single digit such as the 3 in the speed of light above, leave one zero after the decimal.) This is the coefficient.

▶ Count the number of places from the decimal point in the original number to the decimal you added in the coefficient. This is the exponent.

The exponent does have a sign associated with it. If the number is greater than 1, the exponent is positive. If the number is less than 1, the exponent is negative.

Sample Problem Express the following number in scientific notation: 0.000000245.

First, place a decimal after the first non-zero digit of the number. In this case, the first non-zero digit is 2.	00000002.45
Next, cut off the zeros. That gives you the coefficient.	00000002.45 → ~~00000002~~.45 Coefficient = 2.45
Now count, in the original number, how many places it takes to get from the original decimal point to the decimal point in the coefficient.	It takes 7 places to get from the original decimal point to the decimal of the coefficient. Since the number is less than 1, the exponent is negative. Exponent = -7
Finally, express the number in scientific notation using the coefficient and exponent.	Scientific notation of 0.000000245 → 2.45×10^{-7}

Hint: Remember that the "base" is always equal to 10. The only things that change are the coefficient and the exponent.

Now it's your turn to practice converting numbers to and from scientific notation. Remember that if the number is less than 1, the exponent is negative; if it is greater than 1, the exponent is positive.

1. What is 678,000,000,000.0 expressed in scientific notation?

_____

2. What does the number expressed as 3.62×10^{-4} look like?

_____

3. What is 4045 expressed in scientific notation?

_____

4. How would you express 0.00005098 in scientific notation?

_____

After reading Lesson 25.2, answer the following questions.

Nuclear Stability and Decay

5. Of the more than 1500 different nuclei that are known to exist, about what portion are stable?

   a. 1 of 10   **b.** 1 of 6   **c.** 1 of 3   **d.** 1 of 2

6. For elements with low atomic numbers, stable nuclei have roughly _____ numbers of neutrons and protons.

7. Look at Figure 25.6. How does the ratio of neutrons to protons for stable nuclei change as an atomic number increases from 1 to 82?

_____

8. A positron has the mass of a(n) _____, but its charge is

_____.

9. Complete the table below showing changes in charge and number of neutrons and protons for different types of nuclear decay.

Reason nucleus is unstable	Type of decay	Change in nuclear charge	Change in number of protons and neutrons
Too many neutrons	Beta emission		
Too many protons	Electron capture		
Too many protons	Positron emission		
Too many protons and neutrons	Alpha emission		

Half-Life

10. What is half-life?

_____

_____

11. Look at Table 25.2 to help you answer the following questions.

a. What is the half-life in years of carbon-14? _____

b. How many years old is an artifact that contains 50% of its original carbon-14? An artifact that contains 25% of its original carbon-14?

_____

c. What radiation is emitted when potassium-40 decays?

_____

d. What is the half-life of potassium-40? _____

e. Which isotopes listed in Table 25.2 have a half-life similar to that of potassium-40?

_____

12. The decay reaction below shows how a radioactive form of potassium found in many minerals decays into argon (gas). Fill in the missing mass number and atomic number for the argon isotope that results from the decay of potassium-40.

$$^{40}_{19}\text{K} + {}^{0}_{-1}\text{e} \longrightarrow {}^{\square}_{\square}\text{Ar}$$

Transmutation Reactions

13. The conversion of an atom of one element to an atom of another element is called

_____.

14. What are two ways transmutation can occur?

_____

_____

15. Uranium-238 undergoes 14 transmutations before it reaches a stable isotope of

_____.

16. Is the following sentence true or false? All transuranium elements were synthesized in nuclear reactors and accelerators. _____

25.3 Fission and Fusion

Essential Understanding When a nucleus is bombarded by particles, it can split in nuclear fission or combine in nuclear fusion.

Lesson Summary

Nuclear Fission During nuclear fission, a large nucleus splits into smaller pieces, and large amounts of energy are released.

▶ Some neutrons emitted during fission cause other atoms to break apart, causing a chain reaction.

▶ The rate at which fission occurs can be controlled by neutron moderation and neutron absorption.

▶ Used fuel rods create nuclear waste, and storage of this waste over a long period of time is a problem.

Nuclear Fusion During nuclear fusion, small nuclei join to form a larger nucleus.

▶ Nuclear fusion of hydrogen atoms, forming helium atoms, is the source of energy in the sun.

▶ Fusion reactions release much more energy than fission reactions do.

▶ Currently, fusion reactions have no practical uses because of the high temperatures needed for the reactions to occur.

After reading Lesson 25.3, answer the following questions.

Nuclear Fission

1. When certain heavy isotopes are bombarded with _____, they split into smaller fragments.

2. Use the following labels to complete the diagram below: *fission, fission fragments,* and *neutrons/chain reaction.*

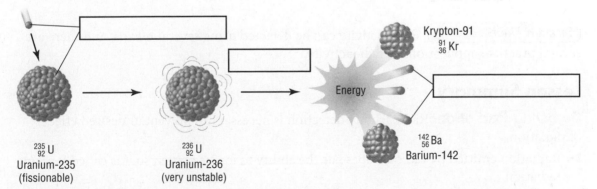

3. The uncontrolled fission of 1 kg of uranium-235 can release energy equal to _____ tons of dynamite.

4. Look at Figure 25.12. This figure shows the basic components of a nuclear power reactor.

   a. What part of the reactor contains the nuclear fuel?

   _____

   b. What are the two parts of the reactor that control the fission reaction, one by reducing the speed of neutrons, the other by absorbing neutrons?

   _____

   c. What is the role of the coolant?

   _____

   _____

5. Which parts of a nuclear reactor must be removed and replaced periodically?

   _____

6. Look at Figure 25.13. Where are spent fuel rods stored in a typical nuclear power plant?

   _____

Nuclear Fusion

7. Look at Figure 25.14. What happens to each pair of hydrogen nuclei during nuclear fusion?

   _____

   _____

8. What problem has prevented the practical use of nuclear fusion?

   _____

   _____

25.4 Radiation in Your Life

Essential Understanding Radioactivity can be detected using several means, and there are several practical applications of radioactivity.

Lesson Summary

Detecting Radiation Radioactivity detection is necessary to prevent undesired effects of radiation.

▶ Radiation emitted by radioisotopes has the ability to ionize matter, so it is called ionizing radiation.

▶ Ionizing radiation can be detected because of its effect on the materials in the detector.

▶ Instruments used to detect radiation include Geiger counters, scintillation counters, and film badges.

Using Radiation Radioisotopes have many practical uses.

▶ Radiation can be used to analyze the elements in matter, which has forensic and other applications.

▶ Radioactive tracers are used to detect the effects of pesticides and fertilizers on plants and on animals that eat the plants.

▶ Medical applications of radioisotopes include detecting and treating certain diseases and disorders.

After reading Lesson 25.4, answer the following questions.

Detecting Radiation

1. Why are beta particles called ionizing radiation?

_____

_____

2. A device that detects flashes of light after ionizing radiation strikes a specially coated phosphor surface is called a _____.

Using Radiation

3. How is neutron activation analysis used?

_____

4. Look at Figure 25.18. How is radioactive iodine-131 being used as a diagnostic tool?

_____

_____

Guided Practice Problems

Answer the following questions about Practice Problem 9.

7. Manganese-56 is a beta emitter with a half-life of 2.6 h. What is the mass of manganese-56 in a 1.0-mg sample of the isotope at the end of 10.4 h?

Analyze

Step 1. What are the known values?

_____

Step 2. How many half-lives have passed during the elapsed time?

$$\text{number of half-lives} = \frac{\text{elapsed time}}{t_{\frac{1}{2}}} = \frac{}{2.6 \text{ h/half-life}} \quad \text{half-lives}$$

Calculate

Step 3. Multiply the initial mass by $\frac{1}{2}$ for each half-life.

1.0 mg × _____ = _____ mg Mn-56

Evaluate

Step 4. How do you know your answer is correct?

_____

_____

Answer the following questions about Practice Problem 10.

8. Thorium-234 has a half-life of 24.1 days. Will all the thorium atoms in a sample decay in 48.2 days? Explain.

Step 1. How many half-lives have passed in 48.2 days?

$$\frac{48.2 \text{ days}}{\boxed{}} = \boxed{} \text{ half-lives}$$

Step 2. What fraction of the thorium will remain after 48.2 days?

_____

Step 3. Will all the thorium decay in 48.2 days? Explain.

_____

_____

Apply the Big idea

Write at least three summary sentences that explain why each particle in an atom is important in reactions, and in what type of reaction it is important. Use the following sentence format, choose the correct term and then complete the sentence. If a particle is important in both types of reactions, write a sentence for both types.

A(n) [proton, neutron, electron] is important in a [chemical, nuclear] reaction because…

_____

_____

_____

_____

_____

25 Self-Check Activity

For Questions 1–10, complete each statement by writing the correct word or words. If you need help, you can go online.

25.1 Nuclear Radiation

1. _____ reactions are not affected by external factors, such as temperature and pressure, and their rates cannot be changed.

2. The three types of nuclear radiation are _____ radiation, _____ radiation, and _____ radiation.

25.2 Nuclear Transformations

3. The type of decay that occurs in a radioisotope is determined by its _____ ratio.

4. After one _____ of a radioactive element, half of the original radioactive material remains.

5. _____ can occur by bombarding the nucleus or by radioactive decay.

25.3 Fission and Fusion

6. In a(n) _____, particles released from one nuclear reaction collide with other particles and cause more nuclear reactions.

7. In _____ reactions, small nuclei combine, producing a larger nucleus and releasing large amounts of energy.

8. In _____ reactions, large nuclei split, forming smaller nuclei.

25.4 Radiation in Your Life

9. Three instruments used to detect radiation are Geiger counters, _____ counters, and _____ badges.

10. Radioisotopes are used to both _____ and treat medical problems.

If You Have Trouble With...									
Question	1	2	3	4	5	6	7	8	9	10
See Page	876	877	880	882	885	888	891	891	894	896

Review Key Equations

Solve the problems. Use the following equation if you need to.

$$A = A_0 \times \left(\frac{1}{2}\right)^n$$

1. The half-life of carbon-14 is 5730 years. Carbon-14 can be used to date objects that are a maximum of about 58,000 years old. Approximately how many half-lives is this?

_____

2. How much carbon-14 is present in a 58,000-year-old skeleton that originally contained 456 g of carbon-14? _____

EXTENSION Iodine-131 is used in diagnosing certain medical problems because of its short half-life, which is 8.02 days. Assume a hospital lab uses 4.52 g of iodine-131 in a month. What mass of this radioisotope remains in patients after 32 days?

_____

Review Vocabulary

Use the clues to complete the puzzle. Some of the terms in the puzzle are more than one word. Then write a clue for the term in the outlined squares.

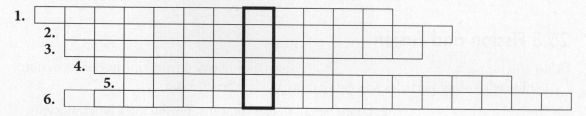

Clues

1. the strong attraction among all particles in a nucleus

2. the changing of an atom of one element to an atom of another element

3. an isotope that is unstable and, as a result, emits radiation

4. the amount of time it takes for half of the atoms in a sample of a radioisotope to transform into atoms of another element

5. the spontaneous emission of rays or particles

6. radiation, emitted by radioisotopes, that has enough energy to remove electrons from atoms it hits

Clue

_____

_____

Math Handbook

SCIENTIFIC NOTATION

Very large and very small numbers are often expressed in scientific notation (also known as exponential form). In scientific notation, a number is written as the product of two numbers: a coefficient, and 10 raised to a power. For example, the number 84,000 written in scientific notation is 8.4×10^4. The coefficient in this number is 8.4. In scientific notation, the coefficient is always a number greater than or equal to one and less than ten. The power of ten, or exponent, in this example is 4. The exponent indicates how many times the coefficient 8.4 must be multiplied by 10 to equal the number 84,000.

$$8.4 \times 10^4 = 8.4 \times 10 \times 10 \times 10 \times 10 = 84,000$$

exponential form
(scientific notation)

standard form

When writing numbers greater than ten in scientific notation, the exponent is equal to the number of places that the decimal point has been moved to the left.

$$6,300,000 = 6.3 \times 10^6 \qquad 94,700 = 9.47 \times 10^4$$

6 places

4 places

Numbers less than one have a negative exponent when written in scientific notation. For example, the number 0.000 25 written in scientific notation is 2.5×10^{-4}. The negative exponent 4 indicates that the coefficient 2.5 must be divided four times by 10 to equal the number 0.000 25, as shown below.

$$2.5 \times 10^{-4} = \frac{2.5}{10 \times 10 \times 10 \times 10} = 0.000\ 25$$

exponential form
(scientific notation)

standard form

When writing numbers less than one in scientific notation, the value of the exponent equals the number of places the decimal has been moved to the right. The sign of the exponent is negative.

$$0.000\ 008 = 8 \times 10^{-6} \qquad 0.00736 = 7.36 \times 10^{-3}$$

6 places

3 places

If your calculator has an exponent key, you can enter numbers in scientific notation when doing calculations. See the section on using a calculator (pages R62–R65) for more information on calculator operations that involve scientific notation.

Multiplication and Division

To multiply numbers written in scientific notation, multiply the coefficients and add the exponents.

$$(3 \times 10^4) \times (2 \times 10^2) = (3 \times 2) \times 10^{4+2} = 6 \times 10^6$$

$$(2.1 \times 10^3) \times (4.0 \times 10^{-7}) = (2.1 \times 4.0) \times 10^{3+(-7)} = 8.4 \times 10^{-4}$$

To divide numbers written in scientific notation, divide the coefficients and subtract the exponent in the denominator from the exponent in the numerator.

$$\frac{3.0 \times 10^5}{6.0 \times 10^2} = \left(\frac{3.0}{6.0}\right) \times 10^{5-2} = 0.5 \times 10^3 = 5.0 \times 10^2$$

Addition and Subtraction

If you want to add or subtract numbers expressed in scientific notation and you are not using a calculator, then the exponents must be the same. For example, suppose you want to calculate the sum of 5.4×10^3 and 8.0×10^2. First rewrite the second number so that the exponent is a 3.

$$8.0 \times 10^2 = 0.80 \times 10^3$$

Now add the numbers.

$$(5.4 \times 10^3) + (0.80 \times 10^3) = (5.4 + 0.80) \times 10^3 = 6.2 \times 10^3$$

Follow the same rule when you subtract numbers expressed in scientific notation without the aid of a calculator.

$$(3.42 \times 10^{-5}) - (2.5 \times 10^{-6}) = (3.42 \times 10^{-5}) - (0.25 \times 10^{-5})$$
$$= (3.42 - 0.25) \times 10^{-5} = 3.17 \times 10^{-5}$$

· ·

Sample Problem Using Scientific Notation in Arithmetic Operations

Solve each problem, and express your answer in correct scientific notation.

a. $(8.0 \times 10^{-2}) \times (7.0 \times 10^{-5})$

b. $(7.1 \times 10^{-2}) + (5 \times 10^{-3})$

Solution

Follow the rules described above for multiplying and adding numbers expressed in scientific notation.

a. $(8.0 \times 10^{-2}) \times (7.0 \times 10^{-5}) = (8.0 \times 7.0) \times 10^{-2+(-5)}$
$= 56 \times 10^{-7} = 5.6 \times 10^{-6}$

b. $(7.1 \times 10^{-2}) + (5 \times 10^{-3}) = (7.1 \times 10^{-2}) + (0.5 \times 10^{-2})$
$= (7.1 + 0.5) \times 10^{-2} = 7.6 \times 10^{-2}$

PRACTICE the Math

1. Express each number in scientific notation.

   a. 500,000   **b.** 285.2

   c. 0.000 000 042   **d.** 0.0002

   e. 0.030 06   **f.** 83,700,000

2. Write each number in standard form.

   a. 4×10^{-3} **b.** 3.4×10^5

   c. 0.045×10^4 **d.** 5.9×10^{-6}

3. Solve each problem and express your answer in scientific notation.

   a. $(2 \times 10^9) \times (4 \times 10^3)$

   b. $(6.2 \times 10^{-3}) \times (1.5 \times 10^1)$

   c. $(10^{-4}) \times (10^8) \times (10^{-2})$

   d. $(3.4 \times 10^{-3}) \times (2.5 \times 10^{-5})$

4. Solve each problem and express your answer in scientific notation.

   a. $(9.4 \times 10^{-2}) - (2.1 \times 10^{-2})$

   b. $(6.6 \times 10^{-8}) + (5.0 \times 10^{-9})$

   c. $(6.7 \times 10^{-2}) - (3.0 \times 10^{-3})$

5. Solve each problem and express your answer in scientific notation.

   a. $\dfrac{(3.8 \times 10^{-3}) \times (1.2 \times 10^6)}{8 \times 10^4}$

   b. $(1.4 \times 10^2) \times (2 \times 10^8) \times (7.5 \times 10^{-4})$

   c. $\dfrac{6.6 \times 10^6}{(8.8 \times 10^{-2}) \times (2.5 \times 10^3)}$

   d. $\dfrac{(1.2 \times 10^{-3})^2}{(10^{-2})^3 \times (2.0 \times 10^{-3})}$

6. Express each measurement in scientific notation.

   a. The length of a football field: 91.4 m.

   b. The diameter of a carbon atom: 0.000 000 000 154 m.

   c. The diameter of a human hair: 0.000 008 m.

   d. The average distance between the centers of the sun and Earth: 149,600,000,000 m.

APPLYING Scientific Notation to Chemistry

7. The following expressions are solutions to typical chemistry problems. Calculate the answer for each expression. Make sure to cancel units as you write your solutions.

   a. $5.6 \times 10^3 \text{ mm} \times \left(\dfrac{1 \text{ m}}{10^3 \text{ mm}}\right) \times \left(\dfrac{10^9 \text{ nm}}{1 \text{ m}}\right) = ?$

   b. $6.8 \times 10^4 \text{ cg H}_2\text{O} \times \left(\dfrac{1 \text{ g H}_2\text{O}}{10^2 \text{ cg H}_2\text{O}}\right) \times \left(\dfrac{1\text{mL H}_2\text{O}}{1 \text{ g H}_2\text{O}}\right) \times \left(\dfrac{1 \text{ L H}_2\text{O}}{10^3 \text{ mL H}_2\text{O}}\right) = ?$

   c. $4.0 \times 10^2 \text{ mL NaOH} \times \left(\dfrac{1 \text{ L NaOH}}{10^3 \text{ mL NaOH}}\right) \times \left(\dfrac{6.5 \times 10^{-2} \text{ mol NaOH}}{1 \text{ L NaOH}}\right) = ?$

8. A cube of aluminum measures 1.50×10^{-2} m on each edge. Use the following expression to calculate the surface area of the cube.

   $$\text{Surface area} = 6 \times (1.50 \times 10^{-2} \text{ m})^2 = ?$$

9. A small gold (Au) nugget has a mass of 3.40×10^{-3} kg. Use the following expression to calculate the number of gold atoms contained in the nugget.

   $$3.40 \times 10^{-3} \text{ kg Au} \times \left(\dfrac{10^3 \text{ g Au}}{1 \text{ kg Au}}\right) \times \left(\dfrac{1 \text{ mol Au}}{197.0 \text{ g Au}}\right) \times \left(\dfrac{6.02 \times 10^{23} \text{ atoms Au}}{1 \text{ mol Au}}\right) = ?$$

10. The volume of a sphere is given by the formula $V = \frac{4}{3}\pi r^3$, where $\pi = 3.14$ and $r =$ radius. What is the volume of a spherical drop of water with a radius of 2.40×10^{-3} m?

SIGNIFICANT FIGURES

The significant figures of a measurement are those digits known with certainty plus the rightmost digit that is estimated. Every measurement has a certain number of significant figures. For instance, if you measure the air temperature to be 218°C, this measurement has three significant figures.

Counting Significant Figures

Every nonzero digit in a measurement is significant. For example, the measurement 831 g has three significant figures. The rules for when to count zeros in measurements as significant are as follows:

▶ Zeros in the middle of a number are always significant. A length that measures 507 m has three significant figures.

▶ Zeros at the beginning of a number are not significant. The measurement 0.0056 m has two significant figures.

▶ Zeros at the end of a number are only significant if they follow a decimal point. The measurement 35.00 g has four significant figures; the measurement 2400 g has two significant figures.

Counted values (17 beakers) and the numbers in defined relationships (100 cm = 1 m) are exact numbers and are considered to have an unlimited number of significant figures. Exact numbers never affect the number of significant figures in the results of a calculation.

Each of the measurements listed below has three significant figures. The significant figures are underlined.

<u>456</u> mL   0.<u>305</u> g

<u>70.4</u> mg   0.000<u>457</u> g

<u>5.64</u> × 10³ km   <u>444</u>,000 ng

<u>1.30</u> × 10² m   0.00<u>406</u> dm

. . . .

Sample Problem Counting Significant Figures in Measurements

How many significant figures are in each measurement?

a. 3300°C   b. 110.5 kJ

c. 0.000 0176 g   d. 210,000 kcal

e. 5 notebooks   f. 0.90 lb

Solution

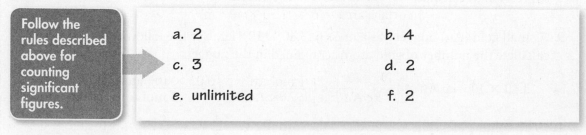

Follow the rules described above for counting significant figures.

a. 2   b. 4

c. 3   d. 2

e. unlimited   f. 2

SIGNIFICANT FIGURES IN CALCULATIONS

When measurements are used in a calculation, the answer you calculate must be rounded to the correct number of significant figures. How you round your answer depends on the mathematical operation used in the calculation.

▶ In multiplication and division, the answer can have *no more significant figures* than the least number of significant figures in any measurement in the problem.

▶ In addition and subtraction, the answer can have *no more decimal places* than the least number of decimal places in any measurement in the problem.

When a calculated answer must be rounded to the appropriate number of significant figures, use the following rules:

▶ If the first nonsignificant digit is less than 5, drop all nonsignificant digits.

▶ If the first nonsignificant digit is 5, or greater than 5, increase the last significant digit by 1 and drop all nonsignificant digits.

The Sample Problem below illustrates how to apply these rules when performing calculations involving measurements.

● ●

Sample Problem Rounding Calculated Answers

Solve each problem, and round your answer to the correct number of significant figures.

a. $(5.3 \text{ m}) \times (1.54 \text{ m})$

b. $23.5 \text{ m} + 2.1 \text{ m} + 7.26 \text{ m}$

c. $189.427 \text{ g} - 19.00 \text{ g}$

d. $\dfrac{0.497 \text{ m}^2}{1.50 \text{ m}}$

Solution

Follow the rules described above for rounding calculated answers to the appropriate number of significant figures.

a. $(5.3 \text{ m}) \times (1.54 \text{ m}) = 8.162 \text{ m}^2 = 8.2 \text{ m}^2$
   (5.3 m has two significant figures.)

b. $23.5 \text{ m} + 2.1 \text{ m} + 7.26 \text{ m} = 32.86 \text{ m} = 32.9 \text{ m}$
   (2.1 has one decimal place.)

c. $189.427 \text{ g} - 19.00 \text{ g} = 170.427 \text{ g} = 170.43 \text{ g}$
   (19.00 has two decimal places.)

d. $\dfrac{0.497 \text{ m}^2}{1.50 \text{ m}} = 0.3313333 \text{ m} = 0.331 \text{ m}$
   (0.497 and 1.50 each have three significant figures.)

PRACTICE the Math

1. How many significant figures are in each measurement?

   a. 0.723 m

   b. 14.0 g

   c. 123,000 m

   d. 6.00×10^{-2} g

   e. 0.005 12 kg

   f. 1050 cm

2. Round each of the measurements in Question 1 to two significant figures.

3. Multiply or divide the following measurements, and round your answer to the correct number of significant figures.

   a. 3.4 m $\times$ 7.8 m

   b. 7.00 cm $\times$ 9.8 cm

   c. 1.56 mm $\times$ 0.864 mm $\times$ 14.00 mm

   d. 6.88 m^2 $\div$ 2.6 m

   e. 52.98 g $\div$ 1.8 mL

   f. 0.14 kg $\div$ 0.0131 L

4. Add or subtract the following measurements, and round your answer to the correct number of significant figures.

   a. 2.34 m + 18.28 m

   b. 828.2 g − 134 g

   c. 0.278 cm + 0.0832 cm + 0.15 cm

   d. 54.2 mg − 12.66 mg

   e. 6.40 ng + 0.450 ng + 1.001 ng

   f. $(5.2 \times 10^{-2}$ dg$) + (1.82 \times 10^{-3}$ dg$)$

The next two examples show operations involving exponential numbers. For simplification, only the exponential and operator keystrokes are shown. The answer that should appear on your calculator display is written in italics.

e. Given expression: $[2.43 \times 10^{23}] \times 7.30 = 1.77 \times 10^{24}$

Using a calculator: 2.43 [**EE**] 23 [**×**] 7.30 [**=**] *1.7739*^{24}

f. Given expression: $9.93 \times 10^{15} \div 2.56 \times 10^{13} = 3.88 \times 10^{2}$

Using a calculator: 9.33 [**EE**] 15 [**÷**] 2.56 [**EE**] 13 [**=**] *3.87890625*^{02}

The answer for **e** displayed by the calculator is 1.7739×10^{24}. This number must be rounded to 1.77×10^{24}, according to the rules for significant figures in calculations.

The calculated answer for **f** must be rounded to three significant figures. Note that the final answer on the display of your calculator may be in scientific notation as *3.87890625*^{02} or in decimal form as *387.890625*, depending on your calculator settings. If you obtained the latter result, you may be able to set the calculator's display mode so that it automatically converts answers to scientific notation by using the key labeled [**SCI**] or [**MODE**].

CHAIN CALCULATIONS

Calculations that require more than one arithmetic operation are called chain calculations. Examples of chain calculations are shown below.

a. $2.58 + 7.12 + 9.30 = 19.00$

b. $6.3 + \left(\frac{7.4 \times 10^{-2}}{1.0 \times 10^{2}}\right) \times \left(\frac{2.79 \times 10^{3}}{1.9 \times 10^{-7}}\right) = 6.8 \times 10^{7}$

c. $2.98 \times \left(\frac{8.76 \times 10^{-3}}{6.22 \times 10^{-3}}\right) = 4.39$

To solve problem **a**, enter the following sequence of calculator keystrokes:

2.58 [**+**] 7.12 [**+**] 9.30 [**=**] *19.*

Note that the calculator keystrokes are exactly as they appear in reading the equation from left to right. Also notice that the calculated answer should have two decimal places, but the calculator has dropped these digits in the displayed answer because they are zeros. You must add them in reporting the correct answer, 19.00.

Problem **b** illustrates a kind of problem that comes up with startling regularity in chemistry-related dimensional analysis. The correct calculator keystrokes are as follows.

6.3 [**+**] 7.4 [**EE**][**+/−**] 2 [**÷**] 1.0 [**EE**] 2 [**×**] 2.79 [**EE**] 3 [**÷**] 1.9

[**EE**][**+/−**] 7 [**=**] *6.845778947*^{07}

Note that each operation is performed in the order it appears in the equation. The calculated answer must be rounded to two significant figures.

In problem **c**, however, performing the operations in the order they appear will *not* yield a correct answer. Instead, try completing the division operation within the parentheses first, and then add 2.98 to the result. The calculator keystrokes are as follows.

8.76 [**EE**][**+/−**] 3 [**÷**] 6.22 [**EE**][**+/−**] 3 [**+**] 2.98 [**=**] *4.388360129*

The calculated answer must be rounded to two decimal places.

Alternatively, you can use the open-parenthesis [(] and closed-parenthesis [)] keys. The [(] and [)] keys allow you to key in equation **c** as written, using the following keystrokes.

2.98 [+][(] 8.76 [EE][+/−] 3 [÷] 6.22 [EE][+/−] 3 [)][=] *4.388360129*

• •

Sample Problem Arithmetic Operations with Exponential Numbers

Use a calculator to obtain the answer shown below.

$$\frac{2.88 \times 10^7}{5.98 \times 10^{-3}} = 4.82 \times 10^9$$

Solution

Use the following keystroke sequence:

2.88 [EE] 7 [÷] 5.98 [EE][+/−] 3 [=] *4.816053512⁰⁹*

The calculated answer must be rounded to three significant figures, yielding the result 4.82×10^9.

 PRACTICE the Math

Use your calculator to solve for x in each problem. Express your answer in scientific notation and report it to the correct number of significant figures.

1. $x = 5467.4 \div 2.7$

2. $x = 26.54 + 26.8 + 58.33 + 10.00 + 87.3$

3. $x = 3.75 \times 10^{-5} + 7.00 \times 10^{-5}$

4. $x = \left(\dfrac{6.02 \times 10^{23}}{4.77 \times 10^{17}}\right)$

5. $x = 8.73 + \left(\dfrac{4.17 \times 10^{-3}}{5.27 \times 10^{-4}}\right)$

6. $x = \left(\dfrac{3.98 \times 10^5}{7.215 \times 10^{13}}\right) \times \left(\dfrac{6.21 \times 10^{14}}{5.123 \times 10^{12}}\right)$

7. $x = 2.45 \div 0.49$

8. $x = 273.0 - 42.6 + 7.0$

9. $x = \left(\dfrac{5.44 \times 10^6}{6.98 \times 10^4}\right) \times 3.89$

APPLYING Calculator Operations to Chemistry

Use your calculator and the given expression to solve each problem. Make sure to cancel units where appropriate.

10. A gold necklace found in an Egyptian pyramid has a volume of 27.5 cm³ and a mass of 530.0 g. What is the density of the gold?

$$\text{density} = \frac{\text{mass}}{\text{volume}} = \frac{530.0 \text{ g}}{27.5 \text{ cm}^3} = ?$$

11. A magnesium atom has a diameter of 3.20×10^{-10} meter. What would be the length in meters (m) of 1 mole of magnesium atoms (6.02×10^{23} atoms) laid end-to-end in a straight line?

$$\frac{3.20 \times 10^{-10} \text{ m}}{1 \text{ Mg atom}} \times \frac{6.02 \times 10^{23} \text{ Mg atom}}{1 \text{ mol Mg}} = ?$$

12. The molecular formula of the sugar glucose is $C_6H_{12}O_6$. The molar masses of the constituent elements of glucose are: carbon, 12.011 g/mol; hydrogen, 1.0079 g/mol; and oxygen, 15.999 g/mol. What is the molar mass of glucose to three decimal places?

$$(6 \times 12.011 \text{ g}) + (12 \times 1.0079 \text{ g}) + (6 \times 15.999 \text{ g}) = ?$$

13. The compound benzene, C_6H_6, has a molar mass of 78.11 g/mol, of which 72.00 g is carbon. What percent of the molar mass of benzene is carbon?

$$\frac{72.00 \text{ g C}}{78.11 \text{ g C}_6\text{H}_6} \times 100\% = ?$$

14. A gaseous compound has a density of 1.37 g/L at STP and 1 mol occupies 22.4 L at STP. What is the molar mass of the compound?

$$\frac{1.37 \text{ g}}{1 \text{ L}} \times \frac{22.4 \text{ L}}{1 \text{ mol}} = ?$$

15. How many moles of Fe_2O_3 are in 50.0 g?

$$50.0 \text{ g Fe}_2\text{O}_3 \times \frac{1.00 \text{ mol Fe}_2\text{O}_3}{159.6 \text{ g Fe}_2\text{O}_3} = ?$$

16. The formation of copper(II) sulfide (CuS) from its component elements is given below.

$$Cu(s) + S(s) \rightarrow CuS(s)$$

How many grams of CuS are produced when 2.73 mol Cu reacts with an excess of sulfur?

$$2.73 \text{ mol Cu} \times \frac{1 \text{ mol CuS}}{1 \text{ mol CuS}} \times \frac{95.6 \text{ g CuS}}{1 \text{ mol CuS}} = ?$$

17. The ideal gas constant, R, is calculated from the relationship given below. What is the value of R in units of (L·kPa)/(K·mol)?

$$R = \frac{101.3 \text{ kPa} \times 22.4 \text{ L}}{273 \text{ K} \times 1.00 \text{ mol}} = ?$$

18. A student sets up the following relationship to calculate the number of moles/liter of sodium chloride, NaCl, in 100 mL of an aqueous salt solution containing 0.50 g of NaCl. How many moles/liter of sodium chloride does the solution contain?

$$\frac{0.50 \text{ g NaCl}}{100 \text{ mL}} \times \frac{1 \text{ mol NaCl}}{58.5 \text{ g NaCl}} \times \frac{1000 \text{ mL}}{1 \text{ L}} = ?$$

CONVERSION PROBLEMS AND DIMENSIONAL ANALYSIS

Many problems in both everyday life and the sciences involve converting measurements. These problems may be simple conversions between the same kinds of measurement. For example:

a. A person is five and one-half feet tall. Express this height in inches.

b. A flask holds 0.575 L of water. How many milliliters of water is this?
In other cases, you may need to convert between different kinds of measurements.

c. How many gallons of gasoline can you buy for $15.00 if gasoline costs $1.42/gallon?

d. What is the mass of 254 cm³ of gold if the density of gold is 19.3 g/cm³?

More complex conversion problems may require conversions between measurements expressed as ratios of units. Consider the following examples.

e. A car is traveling at 65 miles/hour. What is the speed of the car expressed in feet/second?

f. The density of nitrogen gas is 1.17 g/L. What is the density of nitrogen expressed in micrograms/deciliter (μg/dL)?

Problems **a** through **f** can be solved using a method that is known by a few different names—dimensional analysis, factor label, and unit conversion. These names emphasize the fact that the dimensions, labels, or units of the measurements in a problem—the units in the given measurement(s) as well as the units desired in the answer—can help you write the solution to the problem.

Dimensional analysis makes use of ratios called conversion factors. A conversion factor is a ratio of two quantities equal to one another. For example, to work out problem **a**, you must know the relationship 1 ft = 12 in. The two conversion factors derived from this equality are shown below.

$$\frac{1 \text{ ft}}{12 \text{ in}} = 1 \text{ (unity)} = \frac{12 \text{ in}}{1 \text{ in}}$$

To solve problem **a** by dimensional analysis, you must multiply the given measurement (5.5 ft) by a conversion factor that allows the *feet* units to cancel, leaving the unit *inches*—the unit of the requested answer.

$$5.5 \text{ ft} \times \frac{12 \text{ in}}{1 \text{ ft}} = 66 \text{ in}$$

Carefully study the solutions to the remaining five example problems below. Notice that in each solution, the conversion factors are written so that the unit of the given measurement cancels, leaving the correct unit for each answer. When working conversion problems, the equalities needed to write the conversion factor may be given in the problem. This is true in examples **c** and **d**. In other problems, you need to either know or look up the necessary equalities, as in examples **b, e,** and **f.**

b. $0.575 \text{ L} \times \frac{10^3 \text{ mL}}{1 \text{ L}} = 575 \text{ mL}$ **c.** $\$15.00 \times \frac{1 \text{ gal}}{\$1.42} = 10.6 \text{ gal}$

d. $254 \text{ cm}^3 \times \frac{19.3 \text{ g}}{1 \text{ cm}^3} = 4.90 \times 10^3 \text{ g}$ **e.** $\frac{65 \text{ mi}}{1 \text{ h}} \times \frac{5280 \text{ ft}}{1 \text{ mi}} \times \frac{1 \text{ h}}{3600 \text{ s}} = 95 \text{ ft/s}$

f. $\frac{1.17 \text{ g}}{1 \text{ L}} \times \frac{10^6 \text{ } \mu\text{g}}{1 \text{ g}} \times \frac{1 \text{ L}}{10 \text{ dL}} = 1.71 \times 10^5 \text{ } \mu\text{g/dL}$

Sample Problem Applying Dimensional Analysis

A grocer is selling oranges at "3 for $1." How much would it cost to buy a dozen oranges?

Solution

The following equality is given in the problem.

$$3 \text{ oranges} = \$1$$

You can write two conversion factors based on this relationship.

$$\frac{\$1}{3 \text{ oranges}} \text{ and } \frac{3 \text{ oranges}}{\$1}$$

The given unit is oranges; the desired unit is dollars. Thus, use the conversion factor on the left to convert from oranges to dollars. One dozen equals 12, so you can start the calculation with the measurement 12 oranges.

$$12 \text{ oranges} \times \frac{\$1}{3 \text{ oranges}} = \$4$$

The given unit (oranges) cancels, leaving the desired unit (dollars) in the answer.

PRACTICE the Math

Use the following equalities for Questions 1–3.

60 s = 1 min	5.50 yd = 1 rod
12 in. = 1 ft	7 days = 1 wk
60 min = 1 h	5280 ft = 1 mi
3 ft = 1 yd	365 days = 1 yr
24 h = 1 day	

1. Write the conversion factor for each unit conversion.

  a. feet → yards **b.** years → days

  c. yards → rods **d.** days → hours

  e. feet → miles **f.** seconds → minutes

2. Solve each problem by dimensional analysis.

  a. How many feet long is the 440-yard dash?

  b. Calculate the number of minutes in two weeks.

  c. Calculate the number of days in 1800 h.

  d. How many miles is 660 ft?

  e. How many inches long is a 100-yd football field?

  f. Calculate the number of hours in one year.

  g. How many rods are in 12 miles?

  h. Calculate the number of minutes in 7 days.

3. Solve each problem by dimensional analysis.

  a. A student walks at a brisk 3.50 mi/h. Calculate the student's speed in yards/minute.

  b. Water runs through a hose at the rate of 2.5 gal/min. What is the rate of water flow in gallons/day?

  c. A clock gains 2.60 s each hour (2.6 s gained/h). What is the rate of time gained in minutes/week?

  d. A spider travels 115 inches in 1 min (speed = 115 in/min). What is the speed of the spider in miles/hour?

Name _____ Class _____ Date _____

APPLYING Dimensional Analysis to Chemistry

Use the following metric relationships to work out Questions 4 and 5.

$$10^3 \text{ m} = 1 \text{ km} \qquad\qquad 10^9 \text{ nm} = 1 \text{ m}$$
$$10 \text{ dm} = 1 \text{ m} \qquad\qquad 10^{12} \text{ pm} = 1 \text{ m}$$
$$10^2 \text{ cm} = 1 \text{ m} \qquad\qquad 10^3 \text{ cm}^3 = 1 \text{ L}$$
$$10^3 \text{ mm} = 1 \text{ m} \qquad\qquad 1 \text{ mL} = 1 \text{ cm}^3$$
$$10^6 \text{ μm} = 1 \text{ m} \qquad\qquad 1 \text{ g } H_2O = 1 \text{ mL } H_2O$$

4. Perform the following conversions.

a. 45 m to kilometers

b. 4×10^7 nm to meters

c. 8.5 dm to millimeters

d. 8.2×10^{-4} μm to centimeters

e. 0.23 km to decimeters

f. 865 cm³ to liters

g. 7.28×10^2 pm to micrometers

h. 56 g H_2O to L H_2O

5. Perform the following conversions.

a. 4.5 m/s to millimeters/minute

b. 7.9×10^{-2} km/h to decimeters/minute

c. 77 mL H_2O/s to liters H_2O/hour

d. 3.34×10^4 nm/min to centimeters/second

ALGEBRAIC EQUATIONS

Many relationships in chemistry can be expressed as simple algebraic equations. However, the equation given is not always in the form that is most useful in figuring out a particular problem. In such a case, you must first solve the equation for the unknown quantity; this is done by rearranging the equation so that the unknown is on one side of the equation, and all the known quantities are on the other side.

Solving Simple Equations

An equation is solved using the laws of equality. The laws of equality are summarized as follows: *If equals are added to, subtracted from, multiplied by, or divided by equals, the results are equal.* In other words, you can perform any of these mathematic operations on an equation and not destroy the equality, *as long as you do the same thing to both sides of the equation.* The laws of equality apply to any legitimate mathematic operation, including squaring, taking square roots, and taking the logarithm.

Consider the following equation, which states the relationship between the Kelvin and Celsius temperature scales.

$$K = °C + 273$$

Can this equation be used to find the Celsius-temperature equivalent of 400 K? Yes, it can, if the equation is first solved for the unknown quantity, °C.

In the above example, to solve for °C, subtract 273 from both sides of the equation.

$$K = °C + 273$$
$$K - 273 = °C + 273 - 273$$
$$°C = K - 273$$

Now you have solved the equation for the unknown quantity. To calculate its value, substitute the known quantity into the solved equation.

$$°C = K - 273$$
$$= 400 - 273$$
$$= 127°C$$

Another commonly used temperature scale is the Fahrenheit scale. The relationship between the Fahrenheit and Celsius temperature scales is given by the following equation.

$$°F = (1.8 × °C) + 32$$

Suppose you want to use this equation to convert 365°F into degrees Celsius. To solve for °C, you must isolate it on one side of the equation. Since the right side of the equation has 32 added to the quantity (1.8 × °C), first subtract 32 from both sides of the equation, and then divide each side by 1.8.

$$°F = (1.8 × °C) + 32$$
$$°F - 32 = (1.8 × °C) + 32 - 32$$
$$°F - 32 = (1.8 × °C)$$
$$\frac{°F - 32}{1.8} = \frac{1.8 × °C}{1.8}$$
$$\frac{(°F - 32)}{1.8} = °C$$

Now that you have solved the equation for the unknown quantity (°C), you can substitute the known quantity (365°F) into the equation and calculate the answer.

$$°C = \frac{(°F - 32)}{1.8} = \frac{(365 - 32)}{1.8} = \frac{333}{1.8} = 185°C$$

Sample Problem Solving Algebraic Equations

The heat (q) absorbed by the water in a calorimeter can be calculated using the following relationship.

$$q = m × C × \Delta T$$

In this expression, m is the mass of the water; C is the specific heat of water (4.18 J/g · °C); and ΔT is the change in temperature. If 120 g of water absorb 3500 J of heat, by how much will the temperature of the water increase?

Solution

First solve the equation for the unknown quantity, ΔT.

$$q = m × C × \Delta T$$
$$\frac{q}{m × C} = \frac{m × C × \Delta T}{m × C}$$
$$\frac{q}{m × C} = \Delta T$$

Now substitute the known values for q, m, and C.

$$\Delta T = \frac{q}{m × C}$$
$$= \frac{3500 \text{ J}}{(120 \text{ g} × 4.18 \text{ J/g· °C})} = 7.0°C$$

PRACTICE the Math

1. Solve each equation for z.

  a. $xy + z = 5$ **b.** $\dfrac{z}{a - 4} = t$

  c. $\dfrac{b}{d} = \dfrac{2a}{z}$ **d.** $\sqrt{z} = 2b$

2. Solve each equation for a. Then calculate a value for a if $b = 4$, $c = 10$, and $d = 2$.

  a. $bd = ac$ **b.** $a + b = cd$

  c. $c + b = \dfrac{a}{d}$ **d.** $\dfrac{bd}{a} = c^2$

3. Solve each equation for h. Then calculate a value for h if $g = 12$, $k = 0.4$, and $m = 1.5$.

  a. $kh = \dfrac{g}{m}$ **b.** $\dfrac{(g - m)}{h} = k$

  c. $gh - k = m$ **d.** $\dfrac{mk}{(g + h)} = 2$

 APPLYING Algebra to Chemistry

4. Solve for v in the following equation.

$$d = \frac{m}{v}$$

Let d = density, m = mass, and v = volume. What is the volume of 642 g of gold if the density of gold is 19.3 g/cm³?

5. Solve for n in the following equation.

$$P \times V = n \times R \times T$$

How many moles (n) of helium gas fill a 6.45-L (V) balloon at a pressure (P) of 105 kPa and a temperature (T) of 278 K?

$$(R = 8.31 \ (L \cdot kPa)/(K \cdot mol))$$

6. Solve for V_2 in the following equation.

$$\frac{P_1 \times V_1}{T_1} = \frac{P_2 \times V_2}{T_2}$$

A 2.50-L (V_1) sample of nitrogen gas at a temperature (T_1) of 308 K has a pressure (P_1) of 1.15 atm. What is the new volume (V_2) of the gas if the pressure (P_2) is increased to 1.80 atm and the temperature (T_2) is decreased to 286 K?

7. Solve for P_{He} in the following equation.

$$P_{total} = P_{Ar} + P_{He} + P_{Kr}$$

A mixture of gases has a total pressure (P_{total}) of 376 kPa. What is the partial pressure of helium (P_{He}), if P_{Ar} = 92 kPa and P_{Kr} = 144 kPa?

8. Solve for T_2 in the following equation.

$$\frac{V_1}{T_1} = \frac{V_2}{T_2}$$

What is the value of T_2 when V_1 = 5.0 L, V_2 = 15 L, and T_1 = 200 K?

PERCENTS

A percent is a ratio that compares a number to 100. The word *percent* (%) means "parts of 100" or "per 100 parts." Another way to think of a percent is a part of a whole expressed in hundredths. Thus, the number 0.52 ("52 hundredths") can also be expressed as 52%, or "52 per 100 parts."

You should be familiar with percents. For example, test scores are often expressed as percents. Suppose you answer 24 questions correctly on a 30 question exam. The part out of the whole, expressed as a percent, can be calculated as follows.

$$\frac{\text{Part}}{\text{Whole}} = \frac{\text{number of correctly answered questions}}{\text{number of questions asked}}$$

$$= \frac{24}{30}$$

$$= 0.80 = \frac{80}{100} = 80\%$$

Note that 0.80, 80/100, and 80% all express the same value: 80 hundredths (or "80 per 100 parts").

Another way to calculate a percent is to multiply the ratio of the part to the whole by 100%.

$$\text{Percent} = \frac{\text{part}}{\text{whole}} \times 100\%$$

Suppose a high school science club consists of 27 boys and 23 girls. What percent of the club is made up of boys?

$$\text{Percent} = \frac{\text{number of boys}}{\text{number of total members}} \times 100\%$$

$$= \frac{27}{27 + 23} \times 100\%$$

$$= \frac{27}{50} \times 100\%$$

$$= 0.54 \times 100\%$$

$$= 54\%$$

Because a percent represents a relationship between two quantities, it can be used as a conversion factor. For example, suppose a friend tells you that she got a score of 95% on a 40-question exam. How many questions did she answer correctly? A score of 95% means 95 correctly answered questions for every 100 questions asked. By expressing this relationship as a conversion factor, you can calculate the number of correctly answered questions.

$$40 \text{ questions asked} \times \left(\frac{95 \text{ correctly answered questions}}{100 \text{ questions asked}} \right)$$

$$= 38 \text{ correctly answered questions}$$

Sample Problem Using Percents as Conversion Factors

Six students are absent from their class one day. If 80% of the students in the class are present, what is the total class enrollment?

Solution

Because 80% of the class is present, the six absent students make up 20% of the class. If 20% of the students are absent, this means that 20 students are absent for every 100 students enrolled. Use dimensional analysis to calculate the total class enrollment.

$$6 \; \text{\sout{students absent}} \times \frac{100 \; \text{students enrolled}}{20 \; \text{\sout{students absent}}}$$

$$= \frac{600}{20} \; \text{students enrolled}$$

$$= 30 \; \text{students enrolled}$$

 PRACTICE the Math

1. Write each fraction as a percent.

  a. $\frac{3}{4}$ **b.** $\frac{1}{5}$ **c.** $\frac{7}{10}$ **d.** $\frac{5}{8}$

2. Write each decimal as a percent.

  a. 0.39   **b.** 0.08   **c.** 4.2   **d.** 0.5

3. Calculate a score for each exam expressed as a percent.

  a. Sixteen questions correctly answered on a 25-question exam

  b. Forty-one questions correctly answered on a 50-question exam

  c. Sixty-eight questions correctly answered on an 85-question exam

4. A quality control inspector found that 7 out of every 200 flashlights produced were defective. What percent of the flashlights were not defective?

5. A student answered 57 questions correctly on an exam and received a score of 95%. How many questions were on the exam?

6. During a flu epidemic, 28% of the students were absent. If 238 students were absent, what is this school's enrollment?

 APPLYING Percents to Chemistry

7. A mining company is abstracting silver from an ore that is 0.014% silver (by mass). How many kilograms of ore must be processed to yield 0.7 kg of silver?

8. A fertilizer is 12.0% (by mass) nitrogen and 5.5% (by mass) phosphorus. How many grams of each element are in 140 g of this fertilizer?

9. A compound is broken down into 34.5 g of element A, 18.2 g of element B, and 2.6 g of element C. What is the percent (by mass) of each element in this compound?

10. What is the percent by mass of sodium chloride (NaCl) in each of the following solutions?

  a. 44 g NaCl dissolved in 756 g of water

  b. 15 g NaCl dissolved in 485 g of water

  c. 135 g NaCl dissolved in 765 g of water

11. The antiseptic hydrogen peroxide is often sold as a 3.0% (by mass) solution, the rest being water. How many grams of hydrogen peroxide are in 250 g of this solution?

12. A nighttime cold medicine is 22% alcohol (by volume). How many mL of alcohol are in a 250-mL bottle of this medicine?

GRAPHING

The relationship between two variables in an experiment is often determined by graphing the experimental data. A graph is a "picture" of the data. Once a graph is constructed, additional information can be derived about the variables.

In constructing a graph, you must first label the axes. The manipulated variable (also known as the independent variable) is plotted on the x-axis. This is the horizontal axis. The manipulated variable is controlled by the experimenter. When the independent variable is changed, a corresponding change in the responding variable (also known as the dependent variable) is measured. The responding variable is plotted on the y-axis. This is the vertical axis. The label on each axis should include the unit of the quantity being graphed.

Before data can be plotted on a graph, each axis must be scaled. Each interval on the scale must represent the same amount. To make it easy to find numbers along the scale, the interval chosen is usually a multiple of 1, 2, 5, or 10. Although each scale can start at zero, this is not always practical.

Data are plotted by putting a point at the intersection of corresponding values of each pair of measurements. Once the data have been plotted, the points are connected by a smooth curve. A smooth curve comes as close as possible to all the plotted points. It may in fact not touch any of them.

Inverse and Direct Proportionalities

Depending on the relationship between two variables, a plotted curve may or may not be a straight line. Two common curves are shown below.

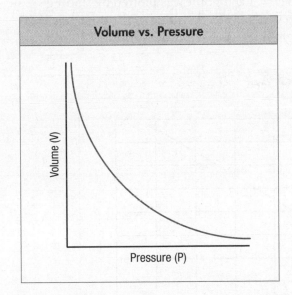

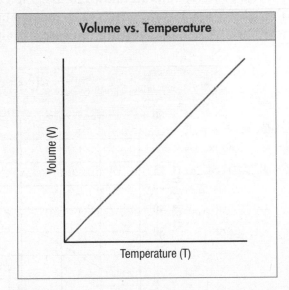

The volume vs. pressure curve is typical of an inverse proportionality. As the manipulated variable (P) increases, the responding variable (V) decreases. The product of the two variables at any point on the curve of an inverse proportionality is a constant. Thus, $V \times P =$ constant.

The straight line in the volume vs. temperature graph is typical of a direct proportionality. As the manipulated variable (T) increases, there is a corresponding increase in the responding variable (V). A straight line can be represented by the following general equation.

$$y = mx + b$$

The variables y and x are plotted on the vertical and horizontal axes, respectively. The y-intercept, b, is the value of y when x is zero. The slope, m, is the ratio of the change in y (Δy) for a corresponding change in x (Δx).

$$m = \frac{\Delta y}{\Delta x}$$

Plotting and Interpreting Graphs

Consider the following set of data about a bicyclist's trip. Assume that the bicyclist rode at a constant speed.

Distance from home (km)	15	25	35	50	75
Time (h)	1	2	3	4.5	7

Graph these data using time as the manipulated variable, and then use the graph to answer the following questions.

a. How far from home was the bicyclist at the start of the trip?

b. How long did it take for the bicyclist to get 40 km from home?

The plotted points are shown in the graph below. Each point was plotted by finding the value of time on the x-axis, then moving up vertically to the value of the other variable (distance). A smooth curve (in this case a straight line) has been drawn through the points.

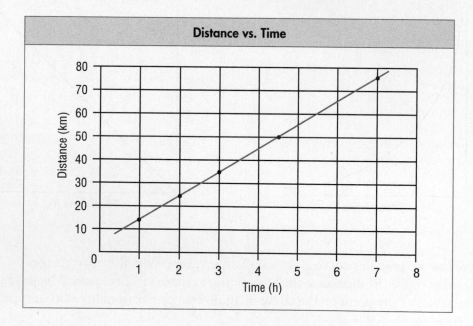

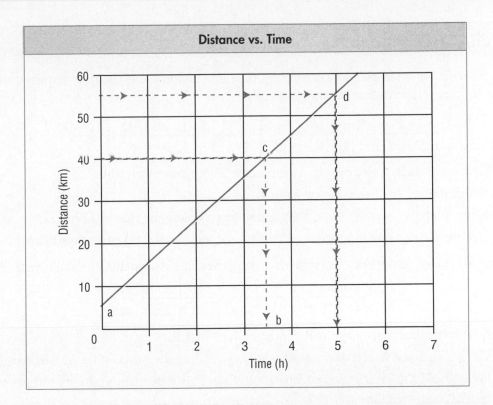

Distance vs. Time

To answer problem **a**, extend the curve so that it intersects the y-axis, as in the graph above. The graph shows that the bicyclist started the trip 5 km from home. This is the value of the vertical axis (distance) when the time elapsed is zero (point a on the graph).

For problem **b**, find the value 40 km on the y-axis of the graph. Move to the right (horizontally) in the graph until you reach the line. Drop down vertically and read the value of time at this point (point b). It takes the bicyclist 3.5 h to get 40 km from home.

Sample Problem Interpreting Graphs

Use the distance vs. time graph above to calculate the bicyclist's average speed in kilometers per hour (km/h).

Solution

Speed is distance/time. The average speed of the bicyclist is the slope of the line in the graph. Calculate the slope using the values for time and distance corresponding to points c and d.

$$m = \frac{\Delta y}{\Delta x} = \frac{55 \text{ km} - 40 \text{ km}}{5 \text{ h} - 3.5 \text{ h}} = \frac{15 \text{ km}}{1.5 \text{ h}} = 10 \text{ km/h}$$

You can now write an equation for the line.

$$y = mx + b$$
$$\text{Distance} = (10 \text{ km/h})(\text{time}) + 5 \text{ km}$$

PRACTICE the Math

1. A bicyclist wants to ride 100 kilometers. The data below show the time required to ride 100 kilometers at different average speeds.

Time (h)	4	5	8	10	15	20
Avg speed (km/h)	25	20	12.5	10	6.7	5

   a. Graph the data, using average speed as the independent variable.

   b. Is this a direct or inverse proportionality?

   c. What average speed must be maintained to complete the ride in 12 hours?

   d. If a bicyclist's average speed is 18 km/h, how long does it take to ride 100 km?

2. The data below show how the mass of a baby varies with its age during its first year of life.

Age (days)	40	110	200	270	330
Mass (kg)	4.0	5.4	7.3	8.6	9.9

   a. Graph the data, using age as the independent variable.

   b. Derive an equation in the form of $y = mx + b$. Include units on the values of y and b.

   c. Why would the values of y and b be of interest to both the baby's parents and physician?

APPLYING Graphs to Chemistry

3. Use the following data to draw a graph that shows the relationship between the Fahrenheit and Celsius temperature scales. Make °F the responding variable. Use the graph to derive an equation relating °F and °C. Then use the graph or the equation to find values for y_1, x_2, and x_3.

Temperature (°F)	50	212	356	−4	y_1	70	400
Temperature (°C)	10	100	180	−20	70	x_2	x_3

4. Different volumes of the same liquid were added to a graduated cylinder sitting on a balance. After each addition of liquid, the total volume of liquid and mass of the liquid-filled graduated cylinder was recorded in the table below.

Total volume of liquid (mL)	10	25	45	70	95
Mass of liquid and cylinder (g)	138	159	187	222	257

a. Graph the data, using volume as the manipulated variable.

b. What is the y-intercept of the line? Make sure to include the unit.

c. What does the value of the y-intercept represent?

d. Calculate the slope of the line, and make sure to include the unit.

e. What does the slope of the line represent for this liquid?

f. Write a general equation that represents the line in your graph.

5. A student collected the following data for a fixed volume of gas.

Temperature (°C)	10	20	40	70	100
Pressure (mm Hg)	726	750	800	880	960

a. Graph the data, using pressure as the responding variable.

b. Is this a direct or inverse proportionality?

c. At what temperature is the gas pressure 822 mm Hg?

d. What is the pressure of the gas at a temperature of 0°C?

e. How does the pressure of the gas change with a change in temperature?

f. Write an equation relating the pressure and temperature of the gas.

LOGARITHMS

Certain scales of measurement are based on logarithms, including the pH scale (used to measure acidity) and the decibel scale (used to measure the relative loudness of sounds). Because the pH scale is a logarithmic scale, it allows a vast range of values (from 1.0 to 10^{-14}) to be expressed simply as a number between 0 and 14.

The common logarithm (*log*) of a number is the exponent to which 10 must be raised to produce that number. If $x = 10^y$, then $\log x = y$. Thus, since $0.01 = 10^{-2}$, it follows that log $0.01 - -2$. Likewise, log $10,000 = 4$, because $10,000 = 10^4$.

Using a Calculator to Compute Logarithms

You can determine the logarithm of a number by using the [log] key on a calculator. (Do not confuse the [log] key with the [ln] key.) If you are calculating the logarithm of a measured value, then the number of decimal places in the logarithm must be rounded to equal the number of significant figures in the measurement. For example, to calculate the logarithm of 3.45, enter the keystrokes shown below.

$$\log 3.45 = [3][.][4][5] \ [\log] = 0.5378191 = 0.538$$

The number in the display (the logarithm) is *0.5378191*. This value must be rounded to three decimal places so as to equal the number of significant figures in the original number. (3.45 has three significant figures.)

Practice using the logarithm function on your calculator by working out problems **a** and **b**. For simplification, only the [log] keystrokes are indicated. Make sure to round your answers to the correct number of decimal places.

a. $\log 0.0087 = 0.0087 \ [\log] = -2.0604807 = -2.06$

(0.0087 has two significant figures, so round to two decimal places.)

b. $\log 3.11 \times 10^{-5} = 3.11 \times 10^{-5} \ [\log] = -4.5072396 = -4.507$

(3.11×10^{-5} has three significant figures, so round to three decimal places.)

• •

Sample Problem Logarithms

Use your calculator to find the logarithm of 8.10×10^3.

Solution

$\log 8.10 \times 10^3 = 8.10 \times 10^3 \ [\log] = 3.9084850 = 3.908$
antilog $(3.908) = 3.908 \ [10^x] = 8090.9590 = 8.09 \times 10^3$

 PRACTICE the Math

1. Calculate the logarithms of the following numbers.

   a. 7.56   **b.** 0.000678   **c.** 456

   d. 4.27×10 **e.** 1.485×10^{-6} **f.** 1×10^{-12}

 Applying Logarithms to Chemistry

2. The hydrogen ion concentration, $[H^+]$, of an aqueous solution can be expressed as a pH value according to the following relationship.

$$pH = -\log [H^+]$$

Determine pH values for solutions having the following $[H^+]$ values. The symbol M represents molarity, a unit of concentration.

   a. $1 \times 10^{-8} \, M$ **b.** $1 \times 10^{-1} \, M$ **c.** $4.8 \times 10^{-7} \, M$ **d.** 0.0034 M

Reference Charts

Physical Constants	
Atomic mass unit	1 amu = 1.6605×10^{-24} g
Avogadro's number	$N = 6.0221 \times 10^{23}$ particles/mol
Gas constant	$R = 8.31$ L·kPa/K·mol
Ideal gas molar volume	$V_m = 22.414$ L/mol
Masses of subatomic particles	
Electron (e⁻)	$m_e = 0.0005486$ amu $= 9.1096 \times 10^{-28}$ g
Proton (p⁺)	$m_p = 1.007277$ amu $= 1.67261 \times 10^{-24}$ g
Neutron (n⁰)	$m_n = 1.008665$ amu $= 1.67492 \times 10^{-24}$ g
Speed of light (in vacuum)	$c = 2.997925 \times 10^{8}$ m/s

SI Units and Equivalents		
Quantity	**SI unit**	**Common equivalents**
Length	meter (m)	1 meter = 1.0936 yards 1 centimeter = 0.39370 inch 1 inch = 2.54 centimeters 1 mile = 5280 feet = 1.6093 kilometers
Volume	cubic meter (m^3)	1 liter = 10^{-3} m^3 = 1.0567 quarts 1 gallon = 4 quarts = 8 pints = 3.7854 liters 1 quart = 32 fluid ounces = 0.94635 liter
Temperature	kelvin (K)	1 kelvin = 1 degree Celsius °C = $\frac{5}{9}$ (F − 32) K = °C + 273.15
Mass	kilogram (kg)	1 kilogram = 1000 grams = mass weighing 2.2046 pounds 1 amu = 1.66057×10^{-27} kilograms
Time	second (s)	1 hour = 60 minutes 1 hour = 3600 seconds
Energy	joule (J)	1 joule = 1 kg·m^2/s^2 (exact) 1 joule = 0.23901 calorie 1 calorie = 4.184 joules
Pressure	pascal (Pa)	1 atmosphere = 101.3 kilopascals = 760 mm Hg (torr) = 14.70 pounds per square inch

Periodic Table of the Elements

Representative Elements
- Alkali Metals
- Alkaline Earth Metals
- Other Metals
- Metalloids
- Nonmetals
- Noble Gases

Transition Elements
- Transition metals
- Inner transition metals

Key
- C Solid
- Br Liquid
- He Gas
- Tc Not found in nature

Atomic number — 13
Electrons in each energy level — 2 8 3
Element symbol — Al
Element name — Aluminum
Atomic mass† — 26.982

†The atomic masses in parentheses are the mass numbers of the longest-lived isotope of elements for which a standard atomic mass cannot be defined.

Group 1 (1A)

1 H Hydrogen 1.0079		
3 Li Lithium 6.941		
11 Na Sodium 22.990		
19 K Potassium 39.098		
37 Rb Rubidium 85.468		
55 Cs Cesium 132.91		
87 Fr Francium (223)		

Group 2 (2A)

- 4 Be Beryllium 9.0122
- 12 Mg Magnesium 24.305
- 20 Ca Calcium 40.08
- 38 Sr Strontium 87.62
- 56 Ba Barium 137.33
- 88 Ra Radium (226)

Group 3 (3B)
- 21 Sc Scandium 44.956
- 39 Y Yttrium 88.906
- 71 Lu Lutetium 174.97
- 103 Lr Lawrencium (262)

Group 4 (4B)
- 22 Ti Titanium 47.90
- 40 Zr Zirconium 91.22
- 72 Hf Hafnium 178.49
- 104 Rf Rutherfordium (261)

Group 5 (5B)
- 23 V Vanadium 50.941
- 41 Nb Niobium 92.906
- 73 Ta Tantalum 180.95
- 105 Db Dubnium (262)

Group 6 (6B)
- 24 Cr Chromium 51.996
- 42 Mo Molybdenum 95.94
- 74 W Tungsten 183.85
- 106 Sg Seaborgium (263)

Group 7 (7B)
- 25 Mn Manganese 54.938
- 43 Tc Technetium (98)
- 75 Re Rhenium 186.21
- 107 Bh Bohrium (264)

Group 8 (8B)
- 26 Fe Iron 55.847
- 44 Ru Ruthenium 101.07
- 76 Os Osmium 190.2
- 108 Hs Hassium (265)

Group 9 (8B)
- 27 Co Cobalt 58.933
- 45 Rh Rhodium 102.91
- 77 Ir Iridium 192.22
- 109 Mt Meitnerium (268)

Group 10 (8B)
- 28 Ni Nickel 58.71
- 46 Pd Palladium 106.4
- 78 Pt Platinum 195.09
- 110 Ds Darmstadtium (269)

Group 11 (1B)
- 29 Cu Copper 63.546
- 47 Ag Silver 107.87
- 79 Au Gold 196.97
- 111 Rg Roentgenium (272)

Group 12 (2B)
- 30 Zn Zinc 65.38
- 48 Cd Cadmium 112.41
- 80 Hg Mercury 200.59
- 112 Cn Copernicium (277)

Group 13 (3A)
- 5 B Boron 10.81
- 13 Al Aluminum 26.982
- 31 Ga Gallium 69.72
- 49 In Indium 114.82
- 81 Tl Thallium 204.37
- 113 *Uut Ununtrium (284)

Group 14 (4A)
- 6 C Carbon 12.011
- 14 Si Silicon 28.086
- 32 Ge Germanium 72.59
- 50 Sn Tin 118.69
- 82 Pb Lead 207.2
- 114 *Uuq Ununquadium (289)

Group 15 (5A)
- 7 N Nitrogen 14.007
- 15 P Phosphorus 30.974
- 33 As Arsenic 74.922
- 51 Sb Antimony 121.75
- 83 Bi Bismuth 208.98
- 115 *Uup Ununpentium (288)

Group 16 (6A)
- 8 O Oxygen 15.999
- 16 S Sulfur 32.06
- 34 Se Selenium 78.96
- 52 Te Tellurium 127.60
- 84 Po Polonium (209)
- 116 *Uuh Ununhexium (293)

Group 17 (7A)
- 9 F Fluorine 18.998
- 17 Cl Chlorine 35.453
- 35 Br Bromine 79.904
- 53 I Iodine 126.90
- 85 At Astatine (210)

Group 18 (8A)
- 2 He Helium 4.0026
- 10 Ne Neon 20.179
- 18 Ar Argon 39.948
- 36 Kr Krypton 83.80
- 54 Xe Xenon 131.30
- 86 Rn Radon (222)
- 118 *Uuo Ununoctium (299)

*Name not officially assigned

Elements 104–118 are the transactinide elements.

Lanthanide Series
- 57 La Lanthanum 138.91
- 58 Ce Cerium 140.12
- 59 Pr Praseodymium 140.91
- 60 Nd Neodymium 144.24
- 61 Pm Promethium (145)
- 62 Sm Samarium 150.4
- 63 Eu Europium 151.96
- 64 Gd Gadolinium 157.25
- 65 Tb Terbium 158.93
- 66 Dy Dysprosium 162.50
- 67 Ho Holmium 164.93
- 68 Er Erbium 167.26
- 69 Tm Thulium 168.93
- 70 Yb Ytterbium 173.04

Actinide Series
- 89 Ac Actinium (227)
- 90 Th Thorium 232.04
- 91 Pa Protactinium 231.04
- 92 U Uranium 238.03
- 93 Np Neptunium (237)
- 94 Pu Plutonium (244)
- 95 Am Americium (243)
- 96 Cm Curium (247)
- 97 Bk Berkelium (247)
- 98 Cf Californium (251)
- 99 Es Einsteinium (252)
- 100 Fm Fermium (257)
- 101 Md Mendelevium (258)
- 102 No Nobelium (259)

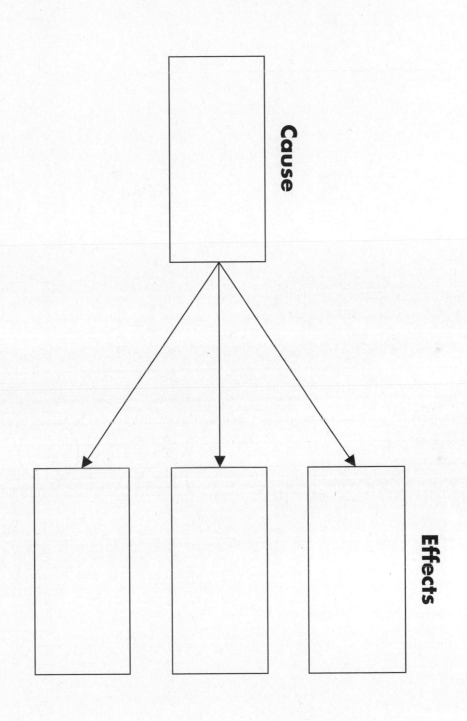

Cause

Effects

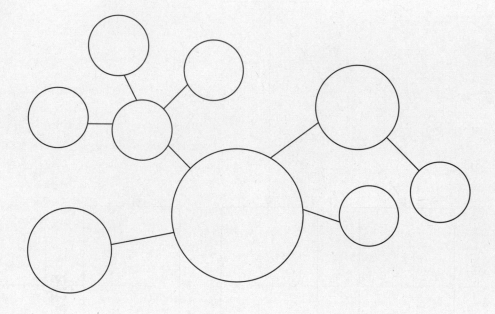

GO 3 Compare/Contrast Table

GRAPHIC
ORGANIZER

Characteristic:			
Characteristic:			
Characteristic:			
Characteristic:			

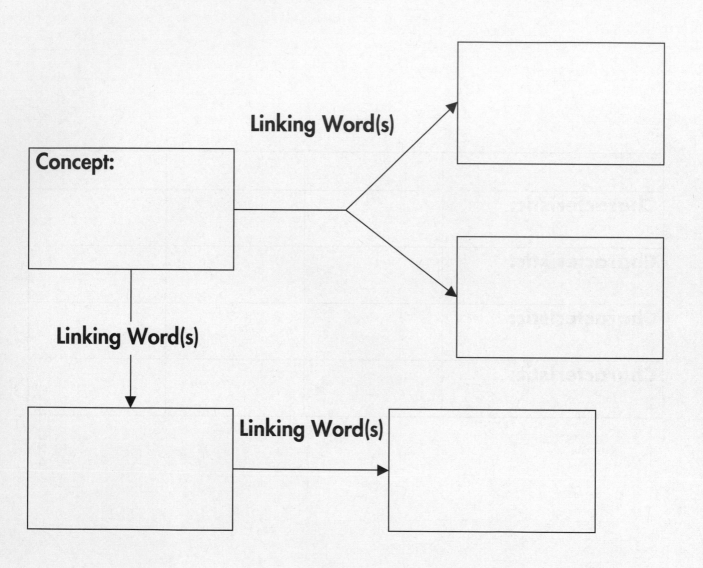

Linking Word(s)

Concept:

Linking Word(s)

Linking Word(s)

GO 5 Cornell Notes

GRAPHIC ORGANIZER

Key Words	Outline

Summary

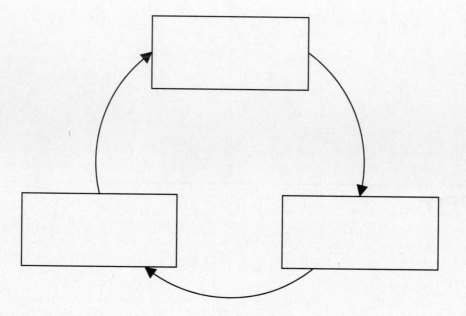

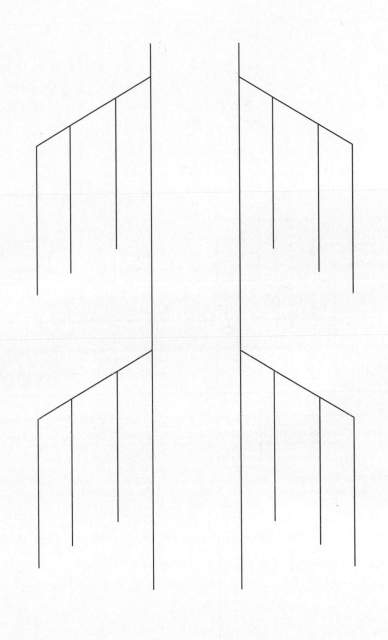

GRAPHIC
ORGANIZER

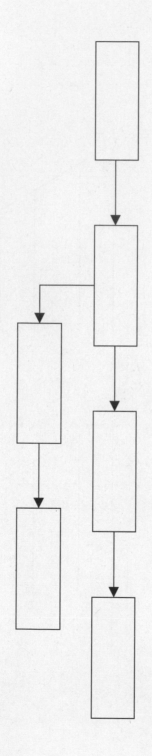

GRAPHIC
ORGANIZER

GRAPHIC
ORGANIZER

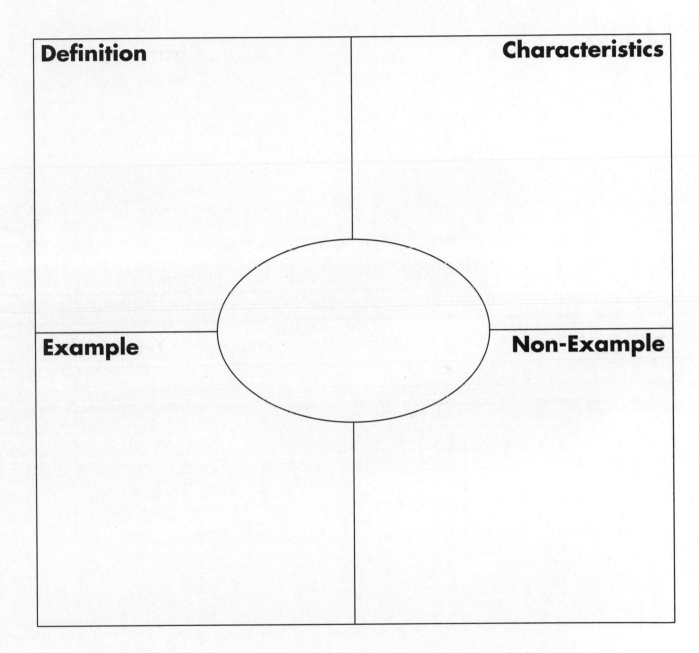

Definition

Characteristics

Example

Non-Example

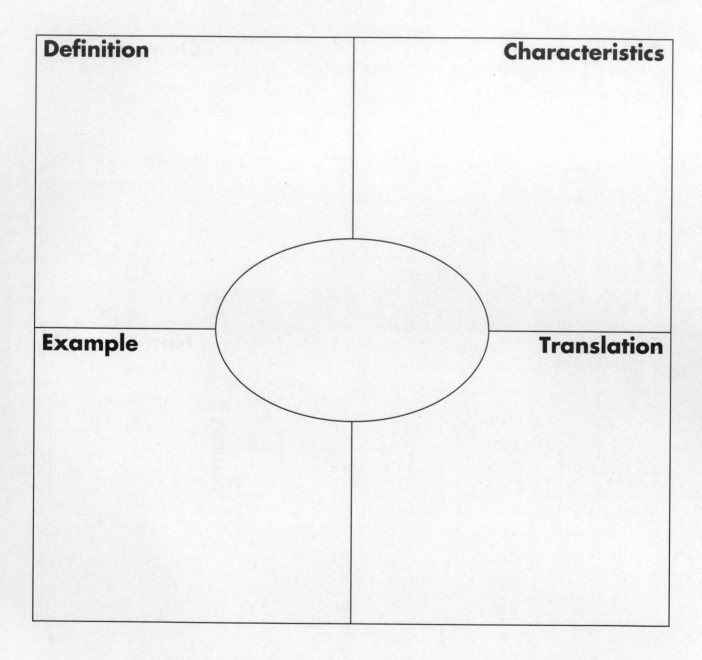

Definition

Characteristics

Example

Translation

I Know.	I Want to know.	I Learned.

GO 12 BKWL

GRAPHIC ORGANIZER

Background	I Know.	I Want to know.	I Learned.

GO 13 Main Idea and Details Chart

GRAPHIC ORGANIZER

Main Ideas	Details